Cyber-Investing

Cracking Wall Street with Your Personal Computer

David L. Brown
Kassandra Bentley

JOHN WILEY & SONS, INC.

New York • Chichester • Brisbane • Toronto • Singapore

This text is printed on acid-free paper.

REQUIREMENTS:

An IBM PC/AT 286 or higher computer or compatible computer with 640K minimum memory, 3MB hard disk space, a CGA, EGA, or VGA board, EGA or VGA color monitor, Hayes smartmodem or other compatible modem, mouse, PC DOS, MS-DOS version 2.1 or later, and a printer (optional).

This publication is designed to provide accurate and authoritative information in regard to the subject matter covered. It is sold with the understanding that the publisher is not engaged in rendering legal, accounting, or other professional services. If legal advice or other expert assistance is required, the services of a competent professional person should be sought.

Library of Congress Cataloging-in-Publication Data:

ISBN 0-471-11925-3 (cloth ed.)
ISBN 0-471-11926-1 (paper ed.)

Printed in the United States of America

10 9 8 7 6 5 4 3 2 1

To Dr. Richard C. Carlin,
founder of Telescan, who pioneered the tools
that make cyber-investing so powerful, and to all
the employees of Telescan who help bring to life
Richard's seemingly endless fountain of ideas.

PREFACE

The personal computer revolution of the past fifteen years has shattered the barrier between Wall Street and Main Street. A few short years ago, Wall Street had a lock on the kind of information needed to make a truly informed decision about trading stocks. It took a lot of manpower to research a stock and enormous computing power to manipulate that research into usable data. Few individual investors could afford to do it; they had to rely on stockbrokers at major brokerage houses who had access to large research staffs and mainframe computers. The personal computer revolution and the information explosion of the past few years has changed all that.

Today, whether you're in Sioux City, Iowa, or San Antonio, Texas, the information superhighway leads you directly to Wall Street. With cyber-investing you can retrieve—in seconds—price and volume information for any listed stock for one day or one month, for one year or twenty. You can see a company's earnings the minute they're released. You can obtain earnings estimates made by independent analysts for the next quarter, the next year, the next five years. You can read research reports written by professional analysts and inspect corporate financial statements filed with the Securities & Exchange Commission. You can consult forecasts by experts on where they think a stock is headed. You can even learn which corporate insiders are buying or selling their company's stock, how many shares they bought or sold, the price they paid, and the current size of their holdings! That's what cyber-investing is—using the tools and information available through your PC to *significantly* increase the return on your investments. Cyber-investing levels the playing field and makes it possible for individual investors to do as well in the stock market as the experts on Wall Street.

If you doubt this, listen to what Peter Lynch, the former manager of Fidelity Magellan Mutual Fund, has to say in his best-selling book, *One Up on Wall Street*:

> The amateur investor has numerous built-in advantages that, if exploited, should result in his or her outperforming the experts, and also the market in general.[1]

What might that performance be? The stock market has generated annual returns of 10 to 12 percent for the past 70 years. All growth-oriented mutual funds have averaged over 10 percent per year for the past 35 years with the top 25 averaging 18.4 percent per year over the past 15 years. Mr. Lynch himself generated annual returns of over 26 percent during his 15-year reign at Fidelity Magellan. So, when he says that an amateur investor—that's you sitting in front of your PC—should be able to beat the experts by using the "normal 3 percent of the brain," he is implying that you should be able to make more than 12 percent return per year. Anything over 15 percent should make you happy, but we think you can do even better than that. With the computerized information and tools that are now available, we think you can make more than 20 percent per year. Maybe 25 percent. Maybe even 30 percent. The purpose of this book is to help you exploit your advantages as an amateur investor in cyberspace!

How do you know that this book is for you? It is if:

- You have been toying with the idea of investing in stocks, but you don't know how to start.

- You own stocks through a company investment plan, but now want to start investing on your own.

- You are retired and are looking for ways to supplement your pension and Social Security.

- You have been using your personal computer to follow stocks and have made an occasional trade.

---

[1] Peter Lynch, with John Rothchild, *One Up on Wall Street: How to Use What You Already Know to Make Money in the Market* (New York: Penguin Books USA, 1989, p. 14).

- You regularly buy and sell stocks but are tired of relying on tips from brokers and the media.

- You're a seasoned investor, but you're unhappy with your returns.

Whatever your level of interest in the stock market, you should find something of value in this book. We will introduce you to a powerful arsenal of computerized tools that can help the beginning investor generate annualized returns of 15 to 20 percent (or more) each year. Even seasoned investors will find tools that could add 2 to 5 percent to their existing returns. Here's a sampling of the powerful tools you'll find in these pages:

- Stock search tools that can search through more than 9,000 listed stocks *in seconds* and present you with a list of stocks that best match your unique investment goals.

- Evaluation tools to help you narrow a large list of stocks to the cream of the crop.

- Fundamental tools that can reveal the underlying strength or weakness of a company.

- Technical charting tools that can draw price-and-volume stock graphs with a single keystroke and plot one of dozens of technical indicators with another keystroke.

- Technical timing tools that can detect uptrends and downtrends and indicate their likely reversal (allowing you to time your trades to minimize risk and maximize reward).

- Technical analysis tools that can reveal trading patterns which can turn an ordinary stock into a high-return investment.

- Industry group tools that can reveal which industries are gaining or losing favor with institutional investors, so you can increase your profit potential by buying stocks in the favored groups.

- Company information tools that offer a wide variety of reports on public companies.

- Portfolio management tools to update and monitor your portfolio and prepare dozens of reports, including those needed for the IRS.

- Search and analysis tools that can find mutual funds for the conservative investor and options for those with a more speculative flair.

- Creative charting tools that let you create your own technical indicators, if you are so inclined.

- Advanced trading tools that can find speculative opportunities through pending mergers and acquisitions.

This book is not a catalog of computer software but a guided tour of some of the best cyber-investing tools on the market. Some of the tools are actually *included* in this book. For a list of the software and the free online offers that are available to you only with this book, turn to page 250. This section describes the complete *Cyber-Investing Kit* that you can use to apply the techniques described in this book.

We will show the tools in action by implementing a variety of investing strategies and techniques. But this book is *not* just about our investing philosophy. We have tried to keep the material neutral by using the tools with a variety of strategies. While we favor strategies that minimize risk and maximize reward, we will demonstrate others, such as momentum investing and option trading. You may tailor them to meet your needs, if you wish, or develop completely new ones once you master the tools.

The cyber-investing process underlying any strategy is simple:

- Identify stocks that have the best price growth potential.

- Analyze them in a systematic way.

- Time each purchase to minimize risk and maximize reward.

- Manage your portfolio to stay abreast of any changes that may affect your stocks.

- Sell each stock when the time is right.

- Repeat this process again and again as you build and replenish your portfolio.

This is essentially the process of successful investing. It can help you generate annualized returns of 15 to 20 percent or more. (We have seen verified returns of more than 60 percent a year!) This is the kind of investing that can make you financially independent over time. All it takes is a willingness to learn how to use these tools, a few hours a week to build and manage your portfolio, and the discipline to stick with a system.

We decided to write this book after seeing the eagerness with which people flock to seminars to learn more about cyber-investing. One of us (David Brown) is the author of two successful market newsletters, a well-known speaker at investment seminars, and chief executive officer of Telescan, Inc., a publicly traded company that is one of the leading producers of investment products and online financial services. The other (Kassandra Bentley) is a writer who has written extensively on computer products and investment software. We have been part of the computerized investing field almost since it began. We know the market and we know the products.

As you will see, we will talk frequently about Telescan products because they are the ones we know best, but most of the strategies and techniques discussed may be adapted to other software and online products, many of which are listed in Appendix A. As part of your Cyber-Investing Kit, Telescan software has been included with this book for a free trial—including free online time. We urge you to use the free online time to follow along with the examples in this book; then experiment with the program to discover the full power of computerized investing. Later, you may choose any software you wish to implement your own strategies.

The tools and techniques presented in this book can be used in any kind of market, bull or bear, domestic or foreign. While you may never want to become a global player, it is a fact that global investing becomes more accessible every day. Many services already offer international stock quotes on markets from Canada to London, from Mexico to Tokyo. There is a lot to consider before you make the global leap, but the good news is: It doesn't matter how deep the water is if you know how to swim! This book will teach you how to swim.

DAVID L. BROWN
KASSANDRA BENTLEY

Houston, Texas
May 1995

ACKNOWLEDGMENTS

There are many who made valuable contributions to the creation of this book. We want to thank Chris Myers of Traders' Library for his enthusiasm and encouragement during its formative stages. We would like to thank Mark Draud, for his research and diligent editing of the manuscript; Luiz Alvim, for his astute comments and suggestions, especially with regard to technical analysis; Paul Alvim, Richard Ames, Tom Melton, Alex Waugh, and Marlon Wells for their careful proofreading and editing suggestions; Scott Brown, Janet Burkard, Greg Gensemer, James Castillo, Scott LaRoche, Maury Blackman, and Marcia Kennedy for their assistance in putting together the Cyber-Investing Kit; and Geri Fries, for her help in scheduling our time and keeping us on track from week to week. We also want to thank Mark W. Arnold for sharing with us his insider trading strategy which has worked so effectively for him. And we are especially grateful to Carolyn Brown who not only proofread the manuscript in various stages but offered continuous encouragement, support, and patience during the many months we spent laboring on this book.

Finally, we would like to thank Jacqueline Urinyi and Myles Thompson, our editors at John Wiley & Sons, for their enthusiasm and support, and Nancy Land for her meticulous copy-editing. Jacqueline, especially, gave us encouragement and valuable advice in the structure and organization of the book.

The stock graphs and search reports herein were supplied by Telescan, Inc., except where otherwise noted.

D.L.B.

K.B.

TRADEMARK CREDITS

AIQ TradingExpert is a registered trademark of AIQ Incorporated.

America Online is a registered service mark of America Online, Inc.

CapTool is a registered trademark of TechServe, Inc.

CompuServe is a registered trademark of CompuServe Incorporated.

Disclosure and SEC Online are registered trademarks of Disclosure, Inc.

Dow Jones News/Retrieval is a registered trademark of Dow Jones & Company.

Fidelity Online XPress is a registered service mark of Fidelity Brokerage Services, Inc.

Investex is a registered trademark of Thomson Financial Services.

MacIntosh is a registered trademark of Apple, Inc.

Macro*World is a registered trademark of MacroWorld Research Corporation.

MarketScope is a registered trademark of Standard & Poor's, a division of McGraw-Hill, Inc.

MetaStock, OptionScope, and Visual Control are registered trademarks of Equis International.

Microsoft, MS-DOS, Excel, Word, and Windows are registered trademarks of Microsoft Corporation.

Prodigy is a registered trademark of Prodigy Services Company.

Quicken is a registered trademark of Intuit, Inc.

Reuters is a registered service mark of Reuters Limited.

StreetSmart and TeleBroker are registered trademarks of Charles Schwab & Co., Inc.

SuperCharts is a registered trademark of Omega Research.

Telescan Analyzer, ProSeach, Mutual Fund Search, Options Search and Telescan Portfolio Manager are registered trademarks of Telescan, Inc.

Wealthbuilder is a registered trademark of Reality Technologies, Inc.

Windows on Wall Street is a registered trademark of MarketArts, Inc.

CONTENTS

1

INTRODUCTION

The stock market is one of the few places where an ordinary person can legitimately accumulate a great deal of money. You've probably heard of dozens of success stories, but we want to show you a few of the many companies that have had spectacular returns and then show you how those returns came about. Knowing what you're looking for is the first step toward finding it.

The average return of the 16 stocks in Exhibit 1.1 is more than 850 percent over three years. Ten thousand dollars invested in these stocks in March 1991 would have grown to $95,000 by March 1994. A $20,000 investment would have grown to $190,000. Chances are, no one would have been fortunate enough to have bought *all* these stocks in March 1991—or smart enough to have held them for three years—even with the powerful cyber-investing tools in this book. But there is nothing magic about the period March 1991 to March 1994. Exhibit 1.2 shows another list of stocks for other time periods with even more spectacular returns. If you could make these kinds of returns on just a few stocks, it wouldn't be difficult to average 20, 30, or even 40 percent per year on your entire portfolio.

We'll show you how to find stocks with this kind of potential, but you don't need spectacular performers to make spectacular returns in the stock market. We're going to show you how to generate extraordinary returns from seemingly ordinary stocks.

Exhibit 1.1   Superstars: Over three years these stocks gained an average of more than 850%—an averaged annualized return of over 107%. (Many of the stocks have since split.)

Company	March 1991	March 1994	Gain	Annualized Return
HerbaLife (HERB)	.80	21.93	2,641%	201%
EMC Corp. (EMC)	1.40	18.75	1,239	138
Cerner Corp (CERN)	3.50	46.00	1,214	136
AutoTote Corp. (TOTE)	2.00	24.25	1,113	130
American Power (APCC)	2.25	27.25	1,111	129
Best Buy Co. (BBY)	5.75	60.00	943	118
Glenayre Tech. (GEMS)	4.25	37.25	776	106
LAM Research (LRCX)	4.50	37.50	733	103
HBO & CO (HBOC)	7.00	52.25	646	96
Cheyenne Software (CYE)	5.50	40.00	627	94
Applied Materials (AMAT)	6.75	47.00	596	91
Players Int'l (PLAY)	3.50	24.00	585	90
Gentex Corp. (GNTX)	4.50	25.25	461	78
Linear Technology (LLTC)	8.50	44.50	423	74
Micron Technology (MU)	16.00	80.25	401	71
Lowe's Cos. (LOW)	14.25	65.00	356	66

FROM SUPER-BORING TO SUPERSTAR

If you could always pick stocks like those shown in Exhibits 1.1 and 1.2, you would get rich very quickly. It is impossible, of course, to pick *only* stocks that generate spectacular returns because some performance is simply too serendipitous to predict. The good news is, a stock doesn't have to be a "tenbagger" to generate high returns. (A "tenbagger" is stock that is sold for 10 times what was paid for it.) With the right tools, an average stock can often lead to spectacular returns. This is what cyber-investing can do for you.

Take Delta Airlines, for example. Delta is thought of as a solid (some would say boring) company. Its stock price has averaged a gain of 7 or 8 percent per year for the past 20 years. Had you bought Delta 20 years ago

Exhibit 1.2 More Superstars: These stocks gained from 192 percent in 7 weeks to 5,200 percent over 5 years.

Company	Buy Date/Price		Sell Date/Price		Gain	Time Period
ECI Telecom Ltd. (ECILF)	1/9/89	0.50	1/14/94	26.50	5200%	5 years
American Power Conv. (APCC)	12/27/88	0.50	12/23/93	23.50	4600	5 years
United Healthcare (UNH)	1/9/89	1.00	1/5/94	41.75	4075	5 years
LDDS Communications (LDDS)	3/17/89	1.00	3/15/94	28.25	2825	5 years
Intl. Game Technology (IGT)	10/26/90	1.50	9/29/93	40.00	2567	35 months
Informix Corp. (IFMX)	2/4/91	1.00	7/5/93	25.75	2475	29 months
Herbalife Intl. (HERB)	8/21/91	0.50	3/6/92	12.00	2300	7 months
General Datacomm. (GDC)	1/28/91	2.30	6/21/93	14.20	1637	29 months
Micron Technology (MU)	11/12/90	7.50	3/14/94	84.50	1027	28 months
Newbridge Networks (NNCXF)	9/14/92	8.50	8/26/93	74.00	770	11 months
DSC Communications (DIGI)	8/31/92	8.50	10/15/93	67.50	694	13.5 months
Advanced Micro Dev. (AMD)	11/19/90	4.25	4/26/93	30.00	606	29 months
Synoptics Comm. (SNPX)	4/29/92	7.00	5/26/93	41.00	486	13 months
Trimedyne, Inc. (TMED)	9/27/93	6.50	3/4/94	15.95	437	5 months
Software Toolworks (TWRX)	10/8/92	3.30	10/19/93	16.80	409	12 months
Integrated Device (IDTI)	11/16/92	6.50	3/14/92	30.50	369	4 months
Grumman Corp. (GQ)	11/12/90	16.75	3/14/94	65.00	288	4 months
QVC Network (QVCN)	10/22/72	21.00	6/1/93	72.00	243	7 months
Kelley Oil Corp. (KOIL)	4/12/93	9.50	6/3/93	27.70	192	7 weeks
President Riverboat (PREZ)	2/24/93	12.70	5/27/93	32.30	154	12 weeks
Mextel Communications (CALL)	11/3/92	11.75	1/4/93	27.00	130	8 weeks
Echo Bay Mines (ECO)	3/11/93	5.35	5/18/93	12.10	126	9 weeks
Protein Design Labs (PDLI)	10/2/92	6.60	12/7/92	12.60	91	8 weeks

and held on to it, you would have made a total return of 9 or 10 percent per year, including dividends. A nice average investment, but not very exciting. With computerized tools, however, you could theoretically turn Delta's 9 or 10 percent return into almost 60 percent per year.

Take a look at Delta's stock graph (Exhibit 1.3) on which we've overlaid long-term trading channels. These channels measure the range of the stock price to the high side and low side of the long-term price trend. As you can see, Delta did not make a smooth climb from $14 to $80 a share over the past 20 years. Instead, it rose and fell, advanced and retreated, on its way up. If you had bought Delta each time it neared the lower band and sold each time it neared the top band (to use an oversimplified strategy for illustration), your return on this average stock would have been about 59 percent per year. There's nothing average about that.

Making 60 percent a year on a single stock is not quite that simple or that predictable, but this strategy—buying solid, predictable, long-term performers when they are undervalued and selling them when they become overvalued—is one of the safest investing strategies you can use. And there is always an abundance of undervalued stocks. Benjamin

Exhibit 1.3   The LSQ trading channel shows the fluctuations in Delta Airlines' stock over 20 years.

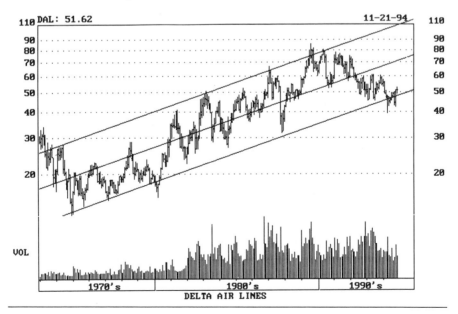

Graham, author of *The Intelligent Investor,* attributes this continuous overvaluation and undervaluation of stocks to the "miscalculation and excesses of optimism and pessimism [with which] the public has valued its shares."[1] Warren Buffett, who is called the world's most successful investor, puts it this way:

> The most common cause of low prices is pessimism—sometimes pervasive, sometimes specific to a company or industry. We want to do business in such an environment, not because we like pessimism but because we like the prices it produces. It's optimism that is the enemy of the rational buyer.[2]

Because of the human emotion that drives it, the market will overvalue and undervalue common stocks in regular fashion. This pattern can be exploited to your great advantage with modern computerized tools, as we'll show you in a later chapter.

There is another very simple way to boost your returns which is now possible with cyber-investing: Buy stocks in industries favored by institutional investors, and buy them early. This strategy is based on the concept of industry group rotation, which results from the domination of the market by institutional investors (who account for over 70 percent of all trading). Briefly stated, when an industry group moves into favor with institutional investors, the influx of large amounts of institutional money tends to create a wave of rising stock prices. Computerized tools enable you to jump on the wave as an industry group begins to move into favor, ride it to the crest, and (hopefully) jump off before the group falls out of favor and dashes you on the rocks. Tools like these can transform ordinary stocks into extraordinary returns for your portfolio.

MONKEY SEE, MONKEY DO

Many people are wary of the stock market, but consider the fact that a random selection of stocks has returned 10 to 12 percent over time. In fact, it is commonly said that anyone can make 10 percent by throwing darts at a newspaper's stock tables to make their picks. Occasionally, this is put to the test. A few years ago, a newspaper in Sweden gave five stock analysts and a chimpanzee named Ola the equivalent of $1,250 each

---

[1] Benjamin Graham, *The Intelligent Investor* (New York: Harper & Row, 1973), p. 106.
[2] Robert G. Hagstrom, *The Warren Buffett Way* (New York: John Wiley & Sons, 1994), p. 54.

to invest in the stock market. The stock experts carefully considered every selection, while Ola made selections by throwing darts at the newspaper's stock tables tacked to the wall. Guess who won? The monkey, of course! (Otherwise, it wouldn't be much of a story.) Ola increased his original investment 13 percent or $190 in one month.

A return of 13 percent in one month is fairly unusual, but making 10 percent over time with randomly selected stocks is indeed plausible. Over the past 70 years, the market has averaged about a 10 percent annual compounded return, including dividends; the average is 12 percent if you concentrate on secondary stocks (those outside the largest 1,000–2,000 companies). What this means is, you could have chosen stocks at random—even by throwing darts at stock tables—and made 10 to 12 percent over time.

Think about it. If you could make 10 to 12 percent simply by throwing darts, how much better might you do with computerized tools? Tools that allow you to identify stocks with the greatest chance of growth, to buy them at a point of minimum risk, and to sell them at a point of maximum reward? Doesn't it make sense that you can do better with computerized investing tools than a monkey can with darts?

We are not suggesting that making above-average returns is easy, but today's cyber-investing tools make it straightforward and allow you to implement a disciplined, methodical process that takes much of the risk out of the market.

MUTUAL FUNDS DO IT, TOO!

If you still aren't convinced that returns of 15 to 20 percent or more are possible, take a look at mutual funds. A mutual fund trades hundreds of thousands of shares of a single company. Money managers must patiently accumulate or sell off shares over a long period of time; otherwise, they will drive up the stock price before they can acquire a position or drive the price down before they can unload the fund's shares. Still, despite their cumbersome size and burdensome government regulations, mutual funds have done all right.

The top 25 growth-oriented funds have averaged 18.4 percent a year over the past 15 years. All growth-oriented mutual funds together—the good, the bad, and the mediocre—managed to average over 10 percent over the past 35 years. Peter Lynch, who managed the gigantic Fidelity Magellan mutual fund, averaged over 26 percent a year for 15 years. We've already mentioned the advantage which Mr. Lynch believes amateur investors have over the professionals: the ability to move quickly because of their small trades. Now, add to this agility the power of computerized tools, and you have the makings for spectacular returns.

LIFESTYLES OF THE RICH AND NOT YET FAMOUS

David Brown regularly speaks at conferences where investors gather to learn more about cyber-investing. The audiences are made up mostly of individual investors, and we have heard story upon story of ordinary people making extraordinary returns.

In the fall of 1993, Brown spoke in Orlando, Florida, at a Telescan users conference of about 150 individuals. During the course of his speech he asked for a show of hands of those who had been making more than 20 percent over a number of years. He was surprised to see over a third of the audience raise their hands. He was even more surprised to learn that many were making more than 40 percent per year. And they were at the conference to learn how to improve their performance!

Afterward, he talked with a dozen or so of the 40-percent-plus investors. Two were especially remarkable. A retired 70-year-old dentist from Connecticut had averaged an annual compounded return of 43.6 percent over the past six years. He used some of the tools described in this book and a strategy developed from the one Brown had been using in his newsletter. In a nutshell, this investor used a cyber-investing stock search tool to generate two lists. One list was based on Brown's undervalued growth strategy and the other on a popular momentum strategy (both strategies are described in this book). Then he bought the stocks that appeared on both lists. Simple, but effective.

The other investor started with an initial investment of $50,000 and built his portfolio to $1.6 million over seven years. (He had broker confirmations for every trade.) That's an annualized return of more than 60 percent per year. He declined to share his strategies, because he planned to start managing money for others. He did reveal, however, that he used the same stock search tool (which is described in Chapters 4 and 5) almost exclusively to find the stocks that generated his spectacular returns.

ANY PLAN IS BETTER THAN NO PLAN

All these successful investors have one thing in common: a disciplined, methodical approach to investing. They all use computerized search tools with different strategies and different trading rules, but each follows his own methods—whatever they are—rigorously and faithfully.

Discipline, in fact, is the one thing most successful traders have in common. Jack D. Schwager, who interviewed a number of supertraders for his book *Market Wizards,* writes:

> Each trader had found a methodology that worked for him and remained true to that approach. It is significant that discipline was the word most frequently mentioned.[3]

Discipline, no doubt, had something to do with the success stories reported by *Newsweek* magazine. In December 1991, *Newsweek* reported that a 68-year-old retired schoolteacher averaged a 37 percent annual return over four years. According to that same article, 62 percent of the investment clubs (which are made up of individual investors) surveyed by the National Association of Investors Corporation beat the S&P 500 over an average of nine years. And, they outperformed 79 percent of stock mutual funds. One of the most successful investment clubs is a group of 15 women in Beardstown, Illinois. The Beardstown Ladies, as they are called, have gained national recognition with their average annual return of 23.4 percent. According to *The New York Times,* they have done twice as well on average as the S&P 500.[4]

Yet another example of how computerized trading has generated spectacular returns is Mark W. Arnold, a vice president of a major Wall Street brokerage firm. His published return for 1993 was 38 percent and for 1994, 21.3 percent. (The latter occurred in a flat market.) His secret? The insider trading tool described in Chapter 4.

Not everyone makes spectacular returns in the market, of course. Perhaps you're thinking about friends or acquaintances who regularly tally up losses instead of gains. But ask yourself: Did they have a plan? If so, did they have the discipline to stick to it? The ones we know who lost money in the market had neither plans nor discipline. They bought on tips and sold on rumors, which means they bought high and sold low. Most of them did not diversify. They didn't rotate with industry groups. They thought they could "down-average" to break even so they bought more of a losing stock. They lacked either the dedication to develop a methodical

---

[3] Jack Schwager, *Market Wizards: Interviews with Top Traders* (New York: New York Institute of Finance, a division of Simon & Schuster, 1989), p. 439.
[4] *The New York Times,* Thursday, March 2, 1995, p. C1.

strategy or the discipline to stick to a plan, or both. It is almost certain they did not have the tools described in this book.

The experience of David Brown lends further credence to the claim that returns of 20 percent per year are possible with the computerized tools described in this book. In early 1990, Brown began publishing two newsletters. One was a long-term, very conservative stock portfolio based on a strategy called undervalued growth investing. That portfolio averaged about 18 percent per year, compounded annually, over the past four years and did not have a negative year (although there were some wide variances in performance from year to year). The second newsletter, aimed at speculators, concentrated almost exclusively in high-risk options. This portfolio also averaged nearly 20 percent per year over four years, with extremely wide variations from year to year (during two of the years, returns were in excess of 100 percent; in the other two, there were significant losses). It is important to point out that when we talk about making returns of 15 to 20 percent per year, we're talking about average compounded returns *over time*. You may make 50 percent one year and lose 10 percent the next, but your annualized compounded return over the two years would be a little over 16 percent.

Our point is this: If you can make 10 to 12 percent over time with a random selection of stocks, you should be able to do much, much better with abundant information, a disciplined approach, and powerful computerized tools. Mutual funds can do it. Dentists can do it. Retired schoolteachers can do it. We can do it. Even monkeys can do it. And so can you!

WHEN IS ONE PERCENT WORTH A MILLION BUCKS?

There is no doubt that computerized investing will take some time and effort. Depending on your level of computer literacy, it could take a couple of weekends to learn how to use the tools, then two to three hours a week to build and manage your portfolio. Is it worth this investment of time to make 15 to 20 percent or more a year? Consider this.

The difference between returns of 7.5 percent and 15 percent (on $10,000 over 20 years) is not just double, it is almost quadruple! Because of the value of compounding, $10,000 invested at 7.5 percent for 20 years becomes $42,479; at 15 percent, it grows to $163,665. Compounding is even more impressive with larger rates of return. For example, an annual return of 30 percent for 20 years transforms that $10,000 into more than $1.9 million—which makes 30 percent *eleven* times better than 15 percent!

Exhibit 1.4   This table shows the difference that one additional percentage point can make on a $10,000 investment over 20 years.

Rate	$10,000 Grows To	Difference Between
15%	$ 163,665	
16	194,608	15% and 16% = $30,943
20	383,380	
21	452,590	20% and 21% = $69,210
25	867,362	
26	1,017,211	26% and 26% = $149.849
30	1,900,500	
31	2,215,270	30% and 31% = $314,770

So you can see, compounding makes it incredibly worthwhile to aim for the higher returns.[5]

In fact, it is worth your time and effort to add even *one percentage point* to your returns. The table in Exhibit 1.4 reveals the difference that 1 percent can make on an initial investment of $10,000 for 20 years. The difference between 15 percent and 16 percent is $30,943, a year's salary for some people. The difference between 20 percent and 21 percent is worth almost $70,000, enough to put a child through college. And the difference between 30 percent and 31 percent is over $300,000, enough to buy a small yacht or a fine retirement home. Should you start with an initial investment of $30,000, that extra percentage point could be worth almost one million dollars.

ONE TOOL CAN ADD THREE PERCENT

If an additional one percentage point can be worth a million dollars, think what an additional two or three percentage points could do to your

---

[5] For those who are less mathematically inclined, there is the old "Rule of 72" which says to divide the return into 72 to get the number of years it will take to double your money. For example, at 8 percent, your money will approximately double in 9 years; at 12 percent, it will double in approximately 6 years; at 18 percent, it will double in approximately 4 years.

Exhibit 1.5   This table shows the difference that three additional percentage points can make on a $10,000 investment over 20 years.

Rate	$10,000 Grows To	Difference Between
15%	$ 163,665	
18	273,930	15% and 18% = $110,265
20	383,376	
23	628,206	20% and 23% = $244,830
25	867,362	
28	1,393,797	25% and 28% = $526,435
30	1,900,496	
33	2,999,389	30% and 33% = $1,098,893

returns. Just *one* of the tools you'll learn about in this book could make a difference of three percentage points in your returns. It did in ours!

In 1993, we backtested a technical search tool called the MACD indicator (which we will talk about later). We used the identical search that we had used in our published newsletter and tested it on 15 different 25-day periods between July 1991 and April 1993. The conclusion? This *one* computerized tool improved our annualized returns by three percentage points. What does that mean in dollars and cents? Take a look at Exhibit 1.5.

If one cyber-investing tool has the power to increase your returns as much as 3 percent, think how well could you do with a whole toolbox full? If you're 20 years old, you could conceivably be a millionaire before you're 40. If you're already 40, you might retire a millionaire. If you're at or near retirement age, remember that 70-year-old dentist who is gilding his golden years with annual returns of 43 percent. He's living proof that it is never too late to start.

FREE CYBER-INVESTING KIT

The publishers have put together a *Cyber-Investing Kit* which lets you "test-drive" many of the investing tools mentioned in these pages. The kit includes free access for 30 days to the entire Telescan system, as well as other software provided on the two diskettes in the back of this book. The software includes a research and analysis program (Telescan Analyzer™); a stock search program (ProSearch™); a technical charting and analysis program (MetaStock™); and search programs for options and mutual funds. The cyber-investing kit also contains free access for 30 days to research tools such as the Zacks Estimate Service; the Standard & Poor's MarketScope® database; more than 20 online newsletters; free or discounted admission to cyber-investing seminars held throughout the country; and a 30-day subscription to the Cyber-Investing Newsletter which uses the investing tools and techniques described in this book. See the Cyber-Investing Kit at the back of the book for more details.

HOW TO USE THIS BOOK

The best way to use this book is read Chapters 2 and 3 and then install the Telescan software and follow along with the investing process. The "Quick Start" guide in Appendix B contains information on computer requirements, installation, and using the program. We recommend that you use the free online time to practice the examples in the following chapters. This will shed much light on the points we try to make in each chapter. If you don't have a computer yet, read the book first; then reread the pertinent chapters as you begin to use the computerized tools to build your portfolio.

Here's a recap of what you'll find in the rest of the book:

Chapters 2 and 3 set the stage for the rest of the book with an in-depth discussion about what makes stocks go up—a very good thing to know—and a brief overview of the computerized investing process.

Chapters 4 through 9 describe the tools for finding and analyzing stocks. They introduce the stock search tool that is the centerpiece of the book and present several search strategies, including one based on insider buying. We show you how to test search strategies on past market periods, and we present several stock analysis tools to help you evaluate a list of stocks.

Chapters 10, 11, and 12 present technical analysis and timing tools for buying and selling stocks, and for managing your portfolio. We discuss technical buy and sell signals, targets and stops, discount brokers, electronic trading, and how to use market indexes and mutual funds to evaluate your performance.

Chapters 13, 14, and 15 describe advanced strategies and tools for the more sophisticated investor. Topics include market analysis, industry

A WORD OF CAUTION

We are very optimistic about the excellent returns that are possible from cyber-investing. Nevertheless, you must recognize that, by its very nature, there is risk in investing in common stocks. Even if you are successful in generating an average return of 15 percent or more per year, it is not highly unusual for a portfolio fall 10 or 20 percent or more in a period of months. If this should occur at a time you need the money, it could create a hardship. Furthermore, no one can assure you of returns of any level. The kind of returns we talk about in this book are based on our own experience, the experience of others, and the experience of the market in general. Nevertheless, even if these tools and techniques are applied successfully, there can be no assurance that you will generate a positive return.

Frankly, guarantees of any kind are difficult, if not impossible with any investment. Bonds, even treasury bonds, have substantial risks during periods of rising interest rates. For example, during 1994, long term investors in treasury bonds faced a net loss of near 20 percent in their portfolio. Bank certificates of deposits come the closest to guaranteed returns, but they provide no assurance that their returns will protect the purchasing power of your dollar. There have been periods when CDs suffered continual annual losses of purchasing power for significant periods.

The point is, you must take your own measure regarding the risk and reward of the stock market. History has shown that no other investment has outperformed stocks in the long run. If you choose to join the ranks of individual investors, choose your investment weapons carefully and do battle as skillfully as you can. Our job in this book is to furnish you with the weapons and help you learn the skills you need to successfully invest in the stock market. Despite our cautions, we believe that investing in stocks judiciously over time can generate handsome returns group analysis, and a brief look at options. In Chapter 15 we also show you a way to find takeover candidates for low-cost speculative opportunities.

Chapter 16 provides a glimpse into the future of cyber-investing, plus a brief assessment of global investing and what's currently available for investors on the Internet.

At the back of the book are the Cyber-Investing Kit and three appendices. The Cyber-Investing Kit contains descriptions of each offer and instructions for accessing the free online time and services. Appendix A contains a source list for a variety of computerized investing tools and services. Appendix B contains instructions for installing and using the Telescan products in the Cyber-Investing Kit, and Appendix C contains special offers for cyber-investors.

YOU MUST REMEMBER THIS . . .

As you read this book, keep in mind these things:

- Over the past 70 years, the market has averaged returns of 10 to 12 percent. Even chimps throwing darts have been able to do that well.

- Many mutual funds, despite their huge size, have averaged almost 20 percent per year. Peter Lynch, the money managers' money manager, thinks amateur investors can do better.

- Individual investors using cyber-investing tools and the strategies described in this book have enjoyed annualized returns as high as 60 percent.

- With computerized tools, ordinary stocks (like Delta) can generate extraordinary returns.

- If you can add just 1 percent to your current returns, it will be worth your time and effort to read this book and learn to use computerized investing tools.

- Aim for a goal of 20 percent per year (although we believe that returns of 30 or more are attainable).

- Even returns of 15 percent per year result can result in significant wealth over time.

If any of this sounds daunting, don't despair. The tools and techniques are presented in a simple fashion. You can use them in the same way: You may wish to start out with one or two tools, and add more as your comfort level increases. The simple search we introduce in Chapter 4 could, by itself, generate substantial returns. With a little time and effort, we believe you can master the art of cyber-investing.

Now is the time to start.

2

WHAT MAKES STOCKS GO UP?

If you were looking for a needle in a haystack, it would help to know what a needle looks like. It would be helpful to know that it is long, thin, narrow, shiny, and sharp, but the task would be a whole lot easier if you knew that the needle is made of metal and will adhere to a magnet. Similarly, when you are investing in stocks, it helps to know the qualities of a "good" stock so you'll know one when you see it. But it is even more helpful to know what makes stocks go up, because then you can use a stock search tool like a magnet to find stocks that have the best chance of price growth. So before we introduce the computerized tools and techniques, we want to talk about what makes stocks go up.

There are two *predictable* reasons why stock prices appreciate: Either the company's earnings[1] actually increase or the price-to-earnings (P/E) ratio goes up, or both. It should be fairly obvious why the stock price goes up when earnings increase. When we buy stocks, we're basically paying companies to earn money for us, as shareholders. The more money they

---

[1] Throughout this book, when we talk about earnings we are talking about earnings per share (EPS)—a company's after-tax earnings divided by the number of outstanding shares. Earnings should not be confused with dividends, which are sometimes paid to shareholders out of a company's profits.

earn, the more the market will pay for their stock. It is less obvious why P/E ratio goes up and how it affects the stock price.

P/E ratio is the price of the stock divided by its current earnings per share, but it is more than that. It is the price the market pays for earnings, and it is more influenced by earnings *potential* than by current earnings. Thus, a stock's P/E ratio can increase because of the market's *perception* of the company's future earnings potential. The market becomes aware of this increased earnings potential through earnings estimates published by Wall Street analysts who follow the company or from institutional investors who employ specialists to do the same. Either way, when the market reacts to news of increased earnings potential, money begins to flow into the stock and the stock price starts to rise. The importance of this will become clear.

As you may have noticed, P/E ratios vary greatly among companies, and it doesn't seem to have much to do with current earnings. One company with respectable current earnings may have a P/E of 5 while another with near negligible earnings may have a P/E over 100. In this chapter, we will illustrate why this happens. Nothing is more important in investing than understanding how P/E ratios change, and what happens when they do. It has everything to do with whether or not you make money in the stock market.

COMPARING PRICE-TO-EARNINGS RATIOS

Let's look at the P/E ratios of Paine Webber and America Online (Exhibit 2.1). In June 1994, Paine Webber was selling at $15½ based on fiscal 1993 earnings of $3.10 and thereby had a P/E ratio of 5. America Online was selling at $71, based on fiscal 1993 earnings of $0.61, which gave it a P/E ratio of 116. (This was before America Online's 2-for-1 split in November 1994.)

Exhibit 2.1   A comparison of P/E ratios for America Online and Paine Webber.

	June 1994 Stock Price	1993 Fiscal Earnings	June 1994 P/E
America Online	$71	$0.61	116
Paine Webber	15½	3.10	5

Exhibit 2.2   A consensus of analysts' earnings estimates for America Online and Paine Webber as of June 1994.

	Year End	Estimated Average Earnings Per Share
America Online	1993	$0.61 actual
	1994	0.76 actual
	1995	1.40
	Projected 5-Year Growth Rate	50%
Paine Webber	1993	$3.10 actual
	1994	2.50
	1995	2.36
	Projected 5-Year Growth Rate	8.5%

Source: Courtesy of Zacks Investment Research through Telescan, Inc., in June 1994.

Paine Webber's 1993 earnings were almost five times higher than America Online's. Why, then, would anyone pay $71 for America Online and only $15 for Paine Webber? The reason is *expectation* of future earnings.

Exhibit 2.2 shows the consensus of Wall Street analysts' future earnings estimates for America Online and Paine Webber (available through many online services).[2] Look at the 1995 estimates. The analysts think that America Online's earnings are going to grow 130 percent by 1995 (from $0.61 in 1993 to $1.40 in 1995). But they don't have such high expectations for Paine Webber: They are projecting a *decrease* of 23.9 percent in 1995 (from 1993's $3.10 to $2.36). But that's still more than the $1.40 which America Online is projected to make in 1995. So what's going on?

The fact is, investors (particularly, institutional investors) look further into the future than just one or two years. They normally seek to acquire a position in a stock of up to several hundred thousand shares or more, and it may take them many months to accumulate (or sell) a position

---

[2] All earnings estimates in this book have been obtained from Zacks Investment Research through Telescan. Zacks reports are also available directly (see listing in Appendix A) and through Internet (see Chapter 16).

without unduly affecting the stock price. Thus, professional investors often look as far as five years down the road. And, when we look at Paine Webber and America Online in five years, there is an even greater disparity between their projected earnings growth rate: 8.5 percent for Paine Webber versus 50 percent for America Online.

If these earnings growth rates are achieved, the gap between the two companies will continue to widen (Exhibit 2.3). By the year 2000, America Online's earnings will almost triple Paine Webber's, and just one year later—by 2001—America Online will earn *six times* more than Paine Webber. Does that justify paying nearly five times more for America Online *now* than for Paine Webber? Maybe not, but many institutional investors may believe that America Online's future earnings increases will be even greater than 50 percent.

In reality, America Online may not be able to sustain a 50 percent growth five or six years in the future. And Paine Webber might turn around and start to grow at more than 8.5 percent. Only time will tell where these two companies will be by the year 2001. But are you beginning to see the logic to the process? The great gap between the P/E ratios of the two companies is mirrored by the great gap that the market sees between their expected earnings far into the future.

Expected earnings that boost P/E's are not the only reason for rising stock prices. Changes in ownership, for example, can cause a big jump in stock price: a merger, a takeover, a new investor who takes a major position in the stock. We've all heard of these, but it is much harder to profit from them. These anomalous events are almost impossible for nonprofessionals to predict and difficult to discover in time to gain much profit (although we'll talk about some possible clues in Chapter 15). On the other

Exhibit 2.3   Projected earnings for America Online and Paine Webber, based on the analysts' estimated 5-year growth rates.

	5-Year Growth Rate	1995	1996	1997	1998	1999	2000
America Online	50.0%	$1.40	$2.10	$3.15	$4.73	$7.09	$10.68
Paine Webber	8.5	2.36	2.56	2.78	3.01	3.27	3.55

Source: 5-year growth rate obtained from Zacks Investment Research through Telescan, Inc., in June 1994.

hand, rising P/E's (based on increased expectations of earnings) are relatively easy to predict and find, and they are one of the best ways to make money systematically in the market. Stocks will not always live up to expectations, of course, which brings us to the risk of high P/E's.

HIGH P/E'S: RISKY BUSINESS

You might conclude, based on the discussion so far, that you should look for companies like America Online, with high P/E's and projected growth rates of 50 percent. After all, you would be assured of 50 percent return per year, if the P/E doesn't change. And therein lies the rub. There is a significant risk in stocks with high P/E's, because P/E's do change. They fall, too.

Historically, the average P/E for stocks has been about 14. If a stock's P/E is over 100, there's not a lot of room for it to rise, but it does have a long, long way to fall. Why would it fall? Because it is often difficult to live up to high expectations. It is exceedingly difficult for a company to continue to grow at 50 percent or more, year after year. Too many things can happen to make the company stumble: Competition could put a squeeze on its profit margins; some unforeseen event could adversely affect the whole industry and take the company down with it. Remember, just as P/E's can rise on optimistic *expectations* of future earnings, they can fall on pessimistic expectations about those earnings. Rumors and fears about an industry can get out of hand, and when that happens, a company's P/E ratio may fall even while earnings continue to increase. If this happens, the stock price may fall precipitously before you can get out of the stock. Nothing is more frustrating than to see a company's stock price in a freefall even though the company's earnings continue to rise.

U.S. SURGICAL: GOING BOTH WAYS

U.S. Surgical Corporation is a good example of both a rising P/E based on high expectations and a falling P/E based on fear (Exhibit 2.4). The company began as a manufacturer of surgical staplers and entered a period of extraordinary growth in the early 1990s with its laparoscopic products. Earnings went from $0.38 in 1988 to $2.32 in 1992, a growth rate well in excess of 50 percent per year. They had earnings surprise after earnings surprise after earnings surprise. As analysts began raising their earnings

Exhibit 2.4   U.S. Surgical moved sharply on expectations and fell even more sharply on fear.

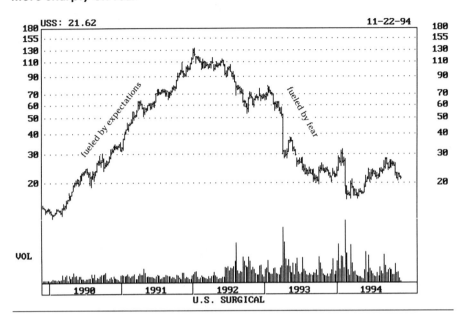

U.S. SURGICAL

projections from 20 percent to 30, 40, and 50 percent, the P/E rose from 12 to 67, causing the stock price to climb from $7 a share to $126 a share.

In this euphoric atmosphere, U.S. Surgical introduced its first line of synthetic sutures in 1991 and promptly captured an impressive market share. By the end of 1992, its new suture products represented about half of the company's revenues. The future looked bright. But during the first half of 1992, U.S. Surgical's stock price leveled and took a steep dive (losing almost 40 percent) in the second half of 1992—even though 1992 earnings were 47 percent higher than 1991's. Why? Because of competitive pressures and fears about the industry.

The main cause, no doubt, was the specter of health care reform that was spooking all medical stocks, even before Clinton was elected. In addition, Johnson & Johnson entered the synthetic sutures market. The head-on competition from Johnson & Johnson brought U.S. Surgical back to reality, forcing it to cut prices and creating margin pressure. Seeing the reduced profit margins, Wall Street began to doubt that U.S. Surgical could continue to grow at 50 percent a year, and analysts revised their earnings estimates downward. U.S. Surgical's stock price began to fall. By the first quarter of 1993, it had lost 57 percent from its 1991 high (from $126 to $54), and its P/E dropped from 67 to 23. Then the earnings did fall apart in 1993 (with a loss of $2.48), and the stock dropped all the way to $17.

That's the danger of high P/E's. If the P/E drops by more than the earnings growth rate, it can wipe out an entire year's gain (and more) in the stock price. Incidentally, there was a clue that 1992 earnings weren't going to do well: Insiders were dumping the stock in unprecedented amounts! (We'll talk more later about the importance of insiders.)

RISING P/E'S: TAKING CARE OF BUSINESS

It should be clear by now that the greatest rewards lie in buying stocks with relatively low P/E's which are expected to increase. Where do we find these rising P/E's? We look for companies that have been out of favor with investors for some reason but are expected to turn around. Let's return to Paine Webber and consider what might happen *if* the company should revitalize its earnings growth.

What do you think would happen if Paine Webber should develop some exciting new products, begin a great new advertising campaign, and hire the top salespeople away from its competitors? For one thing, Wall Street might become more optimistic about its earning potential. Analysts might begin to project a 5-year growth rate of 15 to 20 percent, instead of the current 8.5 percent. A 20-percent growth rate would elevate Paine Webber's earnings estimates to $5.18 by 1998 (Exhibit 2.5). The market would take notice of the enhanced earnings growth, and as

Exhibit 2.5 This table compares Paine Webber's earnings based on analysts' estimates to an imaginary growth rate of 20 percent.

5-Year Growth Rate	1994	1995	1996	1997	1998	1999	2000	2001
8.5%	$2.50*	$2.36*	$2.56	$2.78	$3.01	$3.27	$3.55	$3.85
20.0	2.50	3.00	3.60	4.32	5.18	6.22	7.46	8.95

Source: The 8.5% growth rate and the 1994 and 1995 estimates (*) are from Zacks Investment Research; other figures are the authors' projections.

awareness set in, investors might be willing to pay 10 to 20 times earnings for Paine Webber's stock, instead of the current 5 times earnings.

Exhibit 2.6 shows what could happen to Paine Webber's stock price if this imaginary scenario took place. If the company were to begin an accelerated earnings growth rate of 20 percent and if the P/E ratio were to rise even to 10 by the end of 1994, based on this imaginary event, the stock price would jump to $25. Anyone who had the foresight to buy Paine Webber at $15 in the summer of 1994 would have made almost 60 percent by the end of the year. Let us emphasize that this is a fictitious situation. But if this kind of growth were to take place, things could be much better than we've described. If the market were truly to believe in an earnings growth rate of 20 percent, it would more likely drive the P/E to 20, not 10. Should that happen in our imaginary scenario, the stock price would go to $50, and the smart investor who bought the stock at $15 would make over 200 percent!

Too theoretical? What do you think caused the meteoric growth of stocks like those shown in Chapter 1? Rising P/E's. What fueled U.S. Surgical's initial climb? Rising P/E's. So why not rush right out and buy stocks with low P/E's, like Paine Webber? Because you need to see solid evidence that earnings growth is going to materialize. Some of the clues (which we'll talk about later) are insider buying, upward revision of earnings estimates, increased volume, and industry group momentum. These events often precede rising P/E's.

Exhibit 2.6   This table shows what Paine Webber's stock price could be if its P/E ratio went to 10 or 20, based on the imaginary 20 percent earnings growth rate.

	1994	1995	1996	1997	1998	1999	2000	2001
Earnings (20% EPS Growth Rate)	$2.50	$3.00	$3.60	$4.32	$5.18	$6.22	$7.46	$8.95
Stock Price with P/E of 10	25	30	36	43	52	62	75	90
Stock Price with P/E of 20	50	60	72	86	104	124	149	179

A rising P/E ratio was responsible for one of the best examples of profit that we made on a single stock: Computer Associates. But we waited for evidence of improved earnings growth before we plunged in.

Computer Associates: The Case of the Rising P/E

Computer Associates used to design software primarily for mainframe computers. For several years, the company went through a period of sluggish earnings due to the stagnancy of the mainframe computer market (well known to any holder of IBM stock). In late 1991, the stock was selling at $7½ with earnings of $0.89 and a P/E ratio of 8 (Exhibit 2.7). Then in 1992, the company announced, among other things, aggressive plans to enter the PC software market. Earnings began to materialize almost immediately, climbing to $1.95 in fiscal 1993. The stock price rose to $43, and the P/E ratio went to 22. Thus, while the earnings more than doubled,

Exhibit 2.7 Computer Associates' earnings doubled between 1991 and 1993, but the stock price increased by about 500 percent.

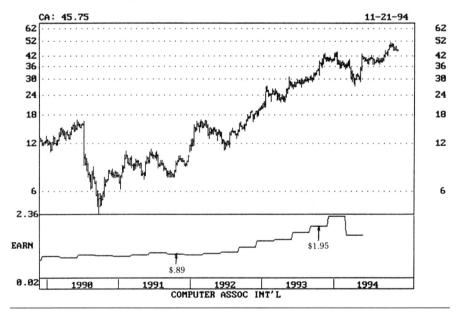

the P/E almost tripled—boosting the stock price almost 500 percent over a two-year period.

The important point is this: Rising earnings and rising P/E's create geometric increases in stock prices—and that can mean spectacular returns for you.

Rising P/E's Soften the Fall

The key word is *rising* P/E's. High P/E ratios, as we mentioned before, carry significant risk. Buying a stock with a high P/E is like standing at the open door of an airplane at 30,000 feet without a parachute. If the stock takes a dive—if the earnings don't materialize or if the stock gets caught in a firestorm of industry fears and rumors—it has a long way to fall. On the other hand, buying a stock with a low but rising P/E is like standing on the roof of a two-story building in a windstorm. If worse comes to worst, it's not that far to the ground; chances are, you could survive the fall.

Let's look at an example. Say you buy a stock with a P/E ratio of 10, expecting earnings to grow 20 percent per year and the P/E to rise. If you're wrong about the P/E and right about the earnings, you wouldn't lose any money; you would still make 20 percent due to the increase in earnings. Even if the P/E should fall, you would still be cushioned by the earnings. In fact, the P/E could fall 20 percent, and if the earnings growth held steady at 20 percent, you wouldn't lose a nickel.

Of course, you could be wrong about the earnings growth as well. Even with sophisticated computerized tools, you will sometimes be wrong. But buying stocks with P/E's on the low side will protect you from a deep decline, simply because there is a much shorter distance for the P/E to fall.

The Risk of Low P/E's

Before we leave the subject, we want to provide a word of caution. Very low P/E ratios often reflect the market's serious concerns about a company's continued viability, as opposed simply to expectations of lowered earnings. Hence, under normal market conditions, a P/E ratio below 5 should be viewed as red flag against the stock in question. There are some very keen minds analyzing such things, so you would be wise to follow their lead and steer clear of extremely low P/E's.

UP P/E, DOWN P/E: THE EFFECT OF INTEREST RATES ON MARKET P/E

The market is subject to the vagaries of the economy, and particularly to the rise and fall of interest rates. The following table shows the approximate effect of interest rates on P/E ratio for various earnings growth rates of a company. Other interest levels would, of course, dictate lower or higher P/E's.

Market Interest Rate	Long-Term Earnings Growth Rates	Rational P/E
6%	10%	18
6	15	24
6	20	33
6	30	58
6	40	78
8	10	15
8	15	20
8	20	27
8	30	48
8	40	82
10	10	12
10	15	17
10	20	23
10	30	40
10	40	68
12	10	10
12	15	14
12	20	19
12	30	33
12	40	57

The reasoning behind this seesaw of interest rates and P/E ratio is the competition for investment dollars. Generally, the market requires about four percent more from equity investments, such as stocks with their earnings risks, than for risk-free government securities. So as interest rates rise, money flows out of stocks into less risky bonds and CDs causing P/E ratios to fall in general, regardless of the earnings growth rates of companies. Conversely, falling interest rates provide a strong impetus to buy stocks and can cause P/E's in general to rise, irrespective of earnings growth.

Obviously, individual investors can't do anything about market interest rates. The key here is to be aware of how current P/E's relate to historical P/E's so that you can judge for yourself the risk in the market. Chapter 13 discusses tools and techniques for analyzing market risk.

YOU MUST REMEMBER THIS . . .

As we go forward to the rest of the book, we hope you will take these points with you:

- P/E ratios are extremely important.
- P/E's vary enormously from stock to stock.
- Buying stocks with high P/E's is dangerous; the risk/reward ratio is very poor since they have much farther to fall than to rise.
- Stocks with extremely low P/E's can signal a weak company with poor prospects for growth.
- The smart move is to buy stocks with rising P/E's: companies with a good chance of earnings growth but selling at a relatively low P/E ratio.

Now we're going to tell you how to find them.

3

THE CYBER-INVESTING PROCESS

You now know what makes stocks go up, if you didn't know before. And obviously, the information is out there. Your mission, then, is to use the tools and techniques in this book to generate long-term annual returns of 15 to 20 percent or more by investing in carefully chosen stocks. But venturing into cyberspace without a plan is like trying to get from New York to California without a roadmap. You might enjoy the scenery, but until you find the right highway and get on it, you'll never reach your destination.

Similarly, you can wander all over the information superhighway and have a perfectly grand time trying out all the tools, but unless you have a plan and a procedure for implementing it, you will never accomplish your mission. We're going to give you a plan—a five-step computerized investing process that you may use in its entirety or adapt to your own needs and investing style (see Exhibit 3.1). The procedures for implementing the plan are described in the next nine chapters. The following is a brief overview.

Exhibit 3.1   The Cyber-Investing Process.

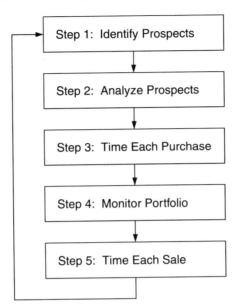

THE PLAN: A FIVE STEP CYBER-INVESTING PROCESS

Step 1: Identify Prospects

The first step is to identify prospects for possible purchase. We will use a powerful stock search tool to demonstrate three different investing strategies: One based on insider buying; one on value investing (under-valued growth stocks with increasing earnings and rising P/E ratios); and one on momentum investing. Once you understand how these searches are created, you should be able to build dozens more that reflect your unique goals and investing style.

Step 2: Analyze Prospects

The second step in the investing process is a two-stage evaluation of the prospects found by a search. We will show you how to analyze stocks using a variety of technical charting tools and how to obtain company information from online services including earnings estimates, news articles, and research reports.

Step 3: Time Each Purchase

Step 3 shows you how to maximize potential profits by timing your stock purchases with technical buy signals. Those who are fundamentally inclined may look on this as some sort of technical voodoo, but the tools are available. Why not use them? We are about three-quarters fundamentalist ourselves, but our experience and our own testing of technical signals against historical markets have proven to our satisfaction that technical timing can add from one to three percent annually to our returns. If you remember from Chapter 1 how much three percent can be worth, you won't want to bypass this step.

Step 4: Manage Your Portfolio

The fourth step begins with the purchase of your first stock and continues as long as you own a stock. Portfolio management includes managing diversification, monitoring holdings, and reviewing your performance. It also includes staying aware of market conditions which might dictate a review of how you allocate your assets. This could lead to "taking a few chips off the table" at market highs or investing more aggressively at market lows. As you will see, however, we believe that the computerized tools we use in this five-step investing process will make you much more independent of market conditions than most other investing programs.

Step 5: Time Each Sale

Step 5 has to do with the sale of a stock and how to time it to your best advantage. There are positive and negative reasons to sell a stock, both of which have to do with the stock's risk/reward relationship. Just as with buying stocks, you can enhance your returns by using technical indicators to find the most propitious time to sell. This also helps you avoid most disasters.

YOU MUST REMEMBER THIS . . .

This five-step process is a map, so to speak, for your first venture into cyber-investing. With this process, you can:

- Find a list of stocks that most closely match your major investment goals.

- Narrow the list of stocks to a few "top" stocks.

- Maximize your profit potential with technical buy signals.

- Implement good management procedures.

- Reduce risk and enhance profits by paying attention to a stock's risk/reward relationship.

Once you've learned how to use this process, you can adapt it to fit your own goals and investing style.

Now let's look at the cyber-investing process and tools in action.

4

A HIGH-TECH DIVINING ROD

In movies of the Old West there was often a grizzled prospector waving a three-pronged stick over the ground expecting it to vibrate whenever it sensed the presence of gold. This so-called "divining rod" never really worked, but the old guys kept using it anyhow and every now and then someone would strike gold. Well, if they could see us now . . .

Today's gold mines are on Wall Street, and the modern prospector can sit in front of a computer screen with a high-tech divining rod that would have made celluloid prospectors weep for joy—because this one does, in fact, find the gold! The modern divining rod is a computerized search tool that can sort through some 9,000 stocks in seconds to find the handful that best match your specific investment goals. All you need is a personal computer connected to an online database. If you don't know what an online database is, you haven't yet ventured onto America's information highways. An online database is a reservoir of data maintained at a central location and connected to users through a modem in their PCs. (A modem uses an ordinary telephone line to transmit data.) *Online* is the key word. Ideally, it means that the data is maintained and updated continually so that the information is timely. (Imagine making an investment decision with week-old or month-old stock prices.) Nothing is more critical than timeliness when you're prospecting for stocks.

Computerized search products have been around for a decade, but they've come a long way in the past few years. In the beginning, they were very simplistic; their primary purpose was to eliminate companies that didn't meet a specific requirement. You could, for example, eliminate companies with P/E ratios lower than 5 and higher than 50 and end up with a list of stocks, in no particular order, that had P/E's between 5 and 50. Such a list had limited use. Search products have improved steadily over the years, but the most modern one has taken a giant leap forward.

A COMPUTERIZED DIVINING ROD

The search product we will focus on is ProSearch™, which is produced by Telescan, Inc. We are going to talk about it exclusively for several reasons. First, it is the search tool we know best. Second, it has been hailed by *Business Week* and *Forbes* magazines as the best on the market, possibly because it has features not found in other search products.[1] Also, as part of the Cyber-Investing Kit contained in this book, you can use ProSearch free for a trial period in order to practice and apply the strategies described. What better way to understand these tools? Many of the search strategies we'll be talking about, however, can be adapted to other programs.

We call ProSearch a "search tool," but it is more like a computerized toolbox. It contains more than 200 separate indicators that can be combined in a myriad of different ways to create thousands of different search strategies. Each indicator is, in effect, a separate search tool with which to screen Telescan's online database of over 9,000 stocks. Like its predecessors, ProSearch lets you eliminate companies that do not meet your basic requirements, but it does much, much more. It will score and rank the stocks that meet your basic requirements so that the very best (according to your specifications) rise like cream to the top of the list. If you ask for stocks with the highest historical earnings, the first stock on your list will have *the* highest earnings of all 9,000 stocks. If you ask for stocks with the highest estimated earnings over the next five years, the stocks on your list will be ranked from highest to lowest according to estimated 5-year earnings growth rate. If you ask for stocks that had the biggest price gain today,

---

[1] *Business Week,* October 25, 1993, pp. 142–143; *Forbes,* June 20, 1994, pp. 162–66.

INSTALLING PROSEARCH

ProSearch is part of the Telescan 3.0 System, which is included in your Cyber-Investing Kit. Installation is as simple as inserting the Telescan program disk (in the back of this book) into Drive A or B and typing "install." This also installs ProSearch. As a book purchaser, you will have 30 days of free online time and free searches. To activate ProSearch, you must log on to the database and then select ProSearch from the Program Menu, or press Ctrl-S. See the Cyber-Investing Kit for computer requirements, log-on information, and instructions on using the program.

the biggest gainer would be listed first, with the rest of the stocks in descending order. A single indicator is rarely used alone in a search: many different objectives (up to 40) may be combined into a complex search strategy. ProSearch would then find the stocks that best meet the *combined* goals.

In this chapter, we are going to create a search step by step. *If you have not already done so, we suggest you install the Telescan program, which includes ProSearch, and use part of your free online time to duplicate the searches as we go along.* Searches can be constructed offline, but you must go online to submit the search.

We could start with a search for stocks that have low but rising P/E's, like the ones we talked about in Chapter 2. But that particular search is much too complicated to start with. You might end up with some great stocks, but you would not understand how to build a search for yourself. (It would be a little like catching the fish for you instead of teaching you how to fish.)

It just so happens that there is a very simple way to find companies that have excellent chances for rising earnings and rising P/E ratios: Follow the lead of the people who know the company the best—the corporate insiders and the Wall Street analysts who study the company. We will start with this simple but effective search, and add to it one piece at a time. In the next chapter, then, we will expand this insider buying search and develop two additional searches which are more complex: one that searches for the low P/E, high-growth stocks described in Chapter 2 and one based on high momentum stocks for the more technically inclined.

THE INSIDE SCOOP

Michael Milkin and Ivan Boesky were right: Inside information pays off. Insiders know better than anyone else whether a company's earnings are likely to increase.[2] The chairman, the president, the vice presidents, the directors—they're the ones at the controls, the ones who direct the meetings that plan the events that we read about in the newspaper. They know the topics of the yet-to-be-released news, the contents of the currently unpublished annual report, the figures on the not-yet-public bottom line. They know what's going to happen before it happens, and when they see a rosy future they often start buying their company's stock.

Take Neutrogena Corporation. Exhibit 4.1 shows the heavy insider buying that was going on during mid-1994. Notice that early in the year the

Exhibit 4.1   This graph shows the insider activity in Neutrogena stock in 1994.

---

[2] Corporate insiders are defined by the Securities and Exchange Commission (SEC) as the officers, directors and major shareholders (those with over 10 percent) of a company. Insiders are required by the SEC to file reports on all trades made in their company's stock within the first 10 days of the month following the trade.

insiders were selling as the stock fell from $22 to $16. But as the stock bottomed out near $16, they started buying. They bought steadily through the spring and summer months, and in August, the world found out why. The company was acquired by Johnson & Johnson, and the stock rose to nearly $26 a share. (Keep in mind that the insiders may not have known anything about the merger and simply thought their stock was undervalued.)

If we had the space, we could show you dozens and dozens of graphs that prove insiders frequently buy when their stock is about to take off. But we can do better than that. We can show you how to profit *legally* from insider activity, with an "insider buying" search.

One of the strongest advocates of the insider buying search is Mark W. Arnold, vice president of a major Wall Street brokerage firm, whom we mentioned earlier. "No one," he says, "has shown me an approach which generates consistently better results than following the lead of corporate insiders." In *Trading on Tomorrow's Headlines,* he reveals his 1993 study of stock performance based on insider buying activity. As a group, these stocks outperformed the market by 31 percentage points: a return of 38.7 percent versus 7.1 percent for the S&P 500.[3]

Mr. Arnold is not the only one who believes in following the lead of insiders. Former Fidelity Magellan guru Peter Lynch wrote: "There's no better tip-off to the probable success of a stock than that people in the company are putting their own money into it.[4] In his book *Winning on Wall Street,* market wizard Martin Zweig quotes his 1974–1976 study on stocks with insider buying.[5] He found that stocks with heavy insider buying outperformed the S&P 500 by almost 200 percent (45.8 percent compared with 15.8 percent). Dr. Zweig also documents four other academic studies that confirm his findings. We also can substantiate the value of insider trading with our own research. Over a 12-month period (4/1/92 through 3/31/93), our insider buying search had a higher return (40.4 percent) than all other searches tested during that period.[6]

Because it is so valuable to know which companies have the most insiders buying company stock, we have chosen to introduce you to the search tool with a simple search based on high insider buying. When we flesh out the search strategy in the next chapter, it will become a formidable tool indeed.

---

[3] Mark W. Arnold, *Trading on Tomorrow's Headlines* (Houston: Telescan, Inc., 1995).
[4] Lynch, *One Up on Wall Street,* p. 134.
[5] Martin Zweig, *Winning on Wall Street* (New York: Warner Books, 1986).
[6] David Brown and Mark Draud, *ProSearch Strategy Handbook* (Houston: Telescan, 1993).

Creating the Search Request

Creating a search with ProSearch takes four general steps: (1) Select the indicators that you want to use to find and rank stocks; (2) specify the number of stocks you want to see on the search report; (3) determine the universe of stocks that you want to consider; and (4) submit the search to the online database and wait a few seconds for the results. If you are following along on ProSearch, all except the fourth step may be done offline.

First, we will select "insider trading" from a list of over 200 indicators and tell the computer to search for the *highest* net insider buying.[7]

Next, we'll ask the computer to return 10 stocks on our search report. ProSearch will return 10 to 200 stocks; in the interest of space, we chose 10.

Then, we will designate the entire database of 9,000-plus listed stocks ("All Stocks") as our universe. We could, if we wished, specify just optionable stocks or some other portion of the database.

Finally, we'll log on to the database and submit the search by pressing the "submit search" key. (Be sure to save your search first.) Within seconds, we will be presented with a search report that ranks the companies according to the number of insiders buying the stock: The more insiders that are buying, the higher the company will be ranked.

It's as simple as that. And there are just two differences between this simplest of searches and the most complicated search you can create: You can select more indicators (up to 40), and you can specify two other ways for the computer to use the indicators, which we will address shortly.

Search Results: They Must Know Something We Don't

Let's take a look at the results of our simple insider buying search (Exhibit 4.2). We asked for the top 10 stocks that had the highest net insider buying. The search program totaled the net insider buying for all 9,000 stocks, ranked them from highest to lowest, and returned a list of the 10 top-ranked stocks. Keep in mind these were the companies with the most insider buying on the date of the report. Tomorrow the list may be different. Next week it certainly will.

---

[7] To arrive at net insider buying, Telescan subtracts the number of insiders selling stock from the number of insiders buying stock and totals it over a three-month period. A figure of 3, for example, means that there are three more insiders buying than there are insiders selling during the three-month period.

Exhibit 4.2   A very simple insider buying search showing the top 10 stocks with the highest insider buying on August 2, 1994.

ProSearch Report
8/2/94

Indicator	Action
Insider Buying	The higher, the better

Stocks	Percentile Rank	Industry Group Symbol
1> NABC—NAB ASSET CORP COM		
Insiders Buying = 28	99%	.TFB
2> WLC—WELLCO ENTERPRISES		
Insiders Buying = 24	99	.TSX
3> SCK—SC BANCORP		
Insiders Buying = 22	99	.TBW
4> APGG—APOGEE INC		
Insiders Buying = 21	99	*
5> THDO—3DO COMPANY		
Insiders Buying = 20	99	.TSO
6> AEPI—AEP INDUSTRIES		
Insiders Buying = 19	99	.TPL
7> INHL—INHALE THERAPEUTIC SYS		
Insiders Buying = 18	99	*
8> MEGF—MEGAFOODS STORES		
Insiders Buying = 18	99	.TSU
9> REDF—REDFED BANK		
Insiders Buying = 17	99	*
10> CGP—COASTAL CORP		
Insiders Buying = 17	99	.TOP

*Company had not been assigned to an industry group at the time of this search.

Note: The initials stand for the stock symbol. The indicator and score appear on the second line of each item.

The number 1 stock on our report is NAB Asset Corp with a net of 28 insiders buying the stock; the number 10 company, Coastal Corporation, had a net of 17 insiders buying the stock. As part of its scoring and ranking process, ProSearch places each stock in a percentile rank from zero to 99 for the selected indicator. In other words, it divides up the 9,000 stocks and places approximately 90 of them in each of 100 percentiles. We will put this feature to good use later.

Who's Buying and How Much?

In cyberspace, information is nothing if not abundant. Not only can we find out the numbers of insiders buying their company's stock, we can also learn the names of the insiders, the number of shares they bought, the price they paid, and the total number of shares they now own. All this information can be obtained (with a couple of keystrokes) from Telescan and other online services. A sample "insider text report" is shown in Exhibit 4.3.

INSIDERS + WALL STREET EXPERTS: TWO THUMBS UP

At this point we have done something exceedingly simple, but powerful. We have interrogated the host database and asked it rank all 9,000 stocks in order of net insider buying; and it has returned to us a list of the top 10 companies with the heaviest insider buying, ranked from 1 to 10. These are interesting stocks but, by themselves, not yet interesting enough to rush out and buy. We need more evidence that something potentially profitable (to us!) is going on in these companies.

Earlier, we said we wanted stocks that had votes of confidence from both corporate insiders and Wall Street analysts. So we will add an indicator that looks into the hearts of the analysts to see what they think about the companies that have high insider buying.

When the Analysts Speak . . .

Analysts are men or women employed by brokerage firms (usually) to research individual companies and write reports of their findings. They become experts on each company, learning the business, studying the industry, reading trade publications, visiting the company, talking with

Exhibit 4.3 List of insiders buying and selling stock in NAB Asset Corporation as of August 2, 1994.

NABC Insider Trading—8/02/94

SEC	Name	Position	Trade	Shares	Type	Price	Holdings	Ownership
07/94	STEYER THOMAS F	Director	940601	23000	P	5.06	613280	I
07/94	RUTTENBERG ERIC M	B. Owner	940601	23000	P	5.06	472744	I
07/94	MOORE MERIDEE A	B. Owner	940601	23000	P	5.06	472744	I
07/94	MELLIN WILLIAM F	B. Owner	940601	23000	P	5.06	472744	I
07/94	FISH JASON M	B. Owner	940601	23000	P	5.06	472744	I
07/94	FAIRMAN FLEUR E	B. Owner	940601	23000	P	5.06	613280	I
07/94	DOWNES JOSEPH F	B. Owner	940601	23000	P	5.06	472744	I
07/94	COHEN DAVID I	B. Owner	940601	23000	P	5.06	472744	D
07/94	FARALLON CAP INSTL	B. Owner	940601	23000	P	5.06	178313	I
06/94	MOORE MERIDEE A	B. Owner	940505–0516	8700	P	5.00–5.00	449744	I
06/94	MELLIN WILLIAM F	B. Owner	940505–0516	8700	P	5.00–5.00	449744	I
06/94	FARALLON CAPITAL PA	B. Owner	940516	5600	P	5.00	221211	D
06/94	FARALLON CAP INSTL	B. Owner	940505	3100	P	5.00	149713	D
06/94	COHEN DAVID I	B. Owner	940505–0516	8700	P	5.00–5.00	449744	I
06/94	STEYER THOMAS F	Director	940505–0517	21700	P	5.00–5.00	590280	I
06/94	RUTTENBERG ERIC M	B. Owner	940505–0516	8700	P	5.00–5.00	449744	I
06/94	FISH JASON M	B. Owner	940505–0516	8700	P	5.00–5.00	449744	I
06/94	FARALLON CAPITAL MA	B. Owner	940517	13000	P	5.00	140536	D
06/94	FAIRMAN FLEUR E	B. Owner	940505–0517	21700	P	5.00–5.00	590280	I
05/94	STEYER THOMAS F	B. Owner	940405–0425	15800	P	5.06–5.06	806653	I
05/94	RUTTENBERG ERIC M	Officer	940405–0425	15800	P	5.06–5.06	586931	I
05/94	MOORE MERIDEE A	Officer	940405–0425	15800	P	5.06–5.06	586931	I
05/94	MELLIN WILLIAM F	Officer	940405–0425	15800	P	5.06–5.06	441043	I
05/94	FISH JASON M	Officer	940405–0425	15800	P	5.06–5.06	586931	I
05/94	COHEN DAVID I	Officer	940405–0425	15800	P	5.06–5.06	586931	I

SEC = SEC release date
Type = P: open market purchase   S: open market sale   X: exercise options
Ownership = D: direct   I: indirect

corporate officials, analyzing the conditions inside and outside the company—in short, taking the company's temperature on a regular basis. Then they make projections about the company's earnings on a quarterly and annual basis. In most cases, they also make a projection of the company's annualized 5-year growth rate of earnings per share (sometimes called a "secular forecast"). A large company may have a following of 30 or more analysts; a small company, one or two. Collectively, they are referred to as "Wall Street analysts," "research analysts," or "industry analysts." And, when the analysts speak, the market listens.

At no time does the market listen harder than when analysts change their minds and raise or lower their projections. These revisions are measured by a ProSearch indicator called the "one-month change in consensus

---

IS TIMELINESS AN ISSUE?

Research analysts first publish their earnings projections in-house, which means that the customers of those firms have first crack at the stocks. Does that mean that the impact of any upward revision is lost before individual investors can learn about it? Apparently not, according to our historical testing of the "one-month change in consensus analysts' estimates" indicator. At the time we ran our tests, the information about upward revisions would have been available to the public for an average of three weeks, but our tests on six market periods (including bear, bull, and sideways markets) showed that the one-month change indicator is the single best indicator for predicting stock price increases.

It would appear that the positive impact from upward revisions of earnings estimates continues for many weeks after the announcement. That's long enough for the information to be published on on-line databases. (Currently, there is a lag of one to seven days from release of estimates to inclusion in the Telescan database.) The reason this is true might be that most users of this data have been institutional investors who typically take many weeks, even months, to acquire a position in a stock. So after the information is released, it needs to be digested and then acted upon over a considerable length of time. For those who have to see it to believe it, we'll show you later how to use ProSearch to do your own "backtesting."

---

analysts' estimates." That's a mouthful, but the indicator is really very simple: It measures the average increase (or decrease) in earnings estimates for the current fiscal year. Usually, estimates that are revised *upward* signal that something positive is happening in the company: It may be gaining more market share; it may have a new product that is taking the market by storm; it may be doing an exceptional job of cutting costs. Any of these (or other) events could point to increased growth for the company. When such an event is acknowledged by an upward revision in analysts' estimates, it can give a big boost to the company's stock price. A downward revision would obviously have the reverse impact.

Our own research has shown that, over a large number and different types of market periods, an upward revision in earnings estimates is the single best indicator for predicting stock price increases. Combining this indicator with the insider buying indicator can only increase the power of a search. The results of such a search should include those companies that have received thumbs up from the two groups that know them best. What better list could you have?

We'll re-select the insider buying indicator and add the one-month change indicator, and ask for the highest combined scores on both.

Search Results: Combo Mombo

A look at the search report (Exhibit 4.4) shows considerably different results from the previous search. The number one stock is Coda Energy with only five insiders buying but a whopping 40 percent change in earnings estimates. Chesapeake Energy with 13 insiders buying, didn't make the previous report, but it is number 2 here, with a 13 percent upward revision in earnings estimates. 3DO Company was number 5 on the previous report with 20 insiders buying; here it is number 10, brought down by its relatively low revision of earnings estimates.

As you can see, this search has given us a list of companies ranked by the best *combined* scores on insider buying and upward Wall Street revisions. That's why the company with the most insider buying (NAB Asset Corp. with 28) is not even listed; it does not have an upward revision by analysts. That's why the company with the highest upward revision by Wall Street analysts (Asarco, Inc. with 314 percent) is not listed; it does not have any insider buying. (We ran a separate search to find out who had the highest upward revision by analysts.) It is the *combination* of the two indicators that is important in this simple search. Although every company on the list has a strong vote of confidence by two critical groups, this search gives us the best of two worlds, not necessarily the best of each.

Exhibit 4.4   A search report ranked by insider buying and upward revisions in earnings estimates: The top 10 stocks on August 2, 1994.

ProSearch Report
8/2/94

Indicator	Action
Insider Buying	The higher, the better
1-Month Change in Earnings Estimates	The higher, the better

Stocks	Percentile Rank	Industry Group Symbol
1> CODA—CODA ENERGY INC		
Insiders Buying = 5.0	98%	.TEX
Upward Revision = 40	99	
2> CSPK—CHESAPEAKE ENERGY		
Insiders Buying = 13	99	.TEX
Upward Revision = 13	97	
3> SWFT—SWIFT TRANSPORTATION		
Insiders Buying = 6.0	98	.TTR
Upward Revision = 12	97	
4> ALB—ALBEMARLE CORP		
Insiders Buying = 9.0	99	*
Upward Revision = 7.3	96	
5> QLGC—QLOGIC CORP		
Insiders Buying = 3.0	96	*
Upward Revision = 40	99	
6> LQ—LAURENTIAN CAPITAL		
Insiders Buying = 5.0	98	.TIL
Upward Revision = 10	97	
7> CELS—COMMNET CELLULAR		
Insiders Buying = 16	99	.TTC
Upward Revision = 5.6	95	
8> RIGS—RIGGS NATL CORP		
Insiders Buying = 6.0	98	.TBS
Upward Revision = 8.0	96	
9> NWIB—NORTHWEST ILL BANCORP INC		
Insiders Buying = 4.0	97	.TBM
Upward Revision = 10	97	
10> THDO—3DO COMPANY		
Insiders Buying = 20	99	.TSO
Upward Revision = 4.5	94	

*Company had not been assigned to an industry group at the time of this search.

Note: The initials stand for the stock symbol. The indicators and scores appear on the lines following each item.

NARROWING THE UNIVERSE

Despite the votes of confidence from insiders and analysts, we wouldn't rush out to buy the stocks from the previous search because, so far, our search is still very simple. We haven't done any further screening with the search tool, nor have we done any analysis to determine the merits of the stocks. What we have is a working list of 10 candidates that seem ideal based on two indicators. Normally, we would expand our search by adding a number of other indicators to score and rank the stocks, but we're still in the get-acquainted stage with the search tool and we want to keep things simple. For now, we will just narrow the universe of the search a little.

Eliminate the Undesirable

Our next screening technique harks back to the earliest computerized search programs. These primitive tools could only screen out the undesirable: Enter a minimum goal, they eliminated all stocks below it; enter a maximum goal, they got rid of all stocks above it. This was a relatively crude technique, but it was useful then and it's still useful now. In fact, most programs still work on this simple screening principle. ProSearch offers it as one of its operating modes because it is very useful for separating the wheat from the chaff.

Let's apply the elimination method to our insider buying/upward revision search. Let's assume that, regardless of how many insiders are buying or how optimistic the analysts are, we don't want any stocks priced below $5 or above $100. Very low-priced stocks are saddled with a higher commission percentage-wise, and they may not be marginable. Very high-priced stocks require either a larger dollar investment or a smaller incremental purchase; those who like to buy in 100-share increments may not want to put $10,000 or more in one position. Whatever the reasons, we're eliminating off the top what we consider ineligible stocks. To do this, we will add the "stock price indicator" to the preceding search and tell the computer to eliminate all stocks below $5 and above $100. In other words, we're narrowing our universe of stocks to those that meet our minimum goal which, in this case, is a stock priced between $5 and $100. When we rerun the search, the program will not have to consider the lower-priced or higher-priced stocks. It will simply score the stocks in our designated universe for high insider buying and high upward revisions in Wall Street estimates.

Exhibit 4.5   A search report ranked by insider buying and upward revisions in earnings estimates but with restricted stock price: The top 10 stocks on August 2, 1994.

ProSearch Report
8/2/94

Indicator	Action
Insider Buying	The higher, the better
1-Month Change in Earnings Estimates	The higher, the better
Stock Price	Eliminate below $5 and above $100

Stocks	Percentile Rank	Industry Group Symbol
1> CODA—CODA ENERGY INC		
Insiders Buying = 5.0	98%	.TEX
Upward Revision = 40	99	
Stock Price = 6.5	25	
2> CSPK—CHESAPEAKE ENERGY		
Insiders Buying = 13	99	.TEX
Upward Revision = 13	97	
Stock Price = 12	55	
3> SWFT—SWIFT TRANSPORTATION		
Insiders Buying = 6.0	98	.TTR
Upward Revision = 12	97	
Stock Price = 38	90	
4> ALB—ALBEMARLE CORP		
Insiders Buying = 9.0	99	*
Upward Revision = 7.3	96	
Stock Price = 17	71	
5> LQ—LAURENTIAN CAPITAL		
Insiders Buying = 5.0	98	.TIL
Upward Revision = 10	97	
Stock Price = 11	51	
6> CELS—COMMNET CELLULAR		
Insiders Buying = 16	99	.TTC
Upward Revision = 5.6	95	
Stock Price = 21	77	
7> RIGS—RIGGS NATL CORP		
Insiders Buying = 6.0	98	.TBS
Upward Revision = 8.0	96	
Stock Price = 10	43	
8> NWIB—NORTHWEST ILL BANCORP INC		
Insiders Buying = 4.0	97	.TBM
Upward Revision = 10	97	
Stock Price = 17	71	
9> THDO—3DO COMPANY		
Insiders Buying = 20	99	.TSO
Upward Revision = 4.5	94	
Stock Price = 15	65	
10> HAUL—ALLIED HOLDINGS		
Insiders Buying = 6.0	98	.TTR
Upward Revision = 5.6	95	
Stock Price = 16	68	

*Company had not been assigned to an industry group at the time of this search.
Note: The initials stand for the stock symbol. The indicators and scores appear on the lines following each item.

The results of this expanded search are shown in Exhibit 4.5. Notice that the stock price is now listed for each stock. Notice too that the number 5 stock from the previous report, QLOGIC Corp, is missing from the new report. That's because it was priced at $4.40. The elimination of this stock allowed the lower ranked stocks to move up and a new stock, Allied Holdings, to edge into the number 10 position.

Don't Set Impossible Standards

Eliminating stocks that do not meet your minimum requirements is an important step in the search process. But you can be overly zealous in this regard. If you use too many indicators to eliminate stocks from the search universe, you may end up like the lover who is searching for the perfect mate: All possible candidates are eliminated because the standards are too high. Be careful not to put in too many restrictions. We recommend that you use a few indicators to eliminate stocks that do not meet your minimum requirements; then use the most important indicators—most important to *your* investment goals—to score and rank the remaining stocks.

MAKING LISTS, SAVING TIME

So far we've shown you how to use the search tool to score and rank stocks and to eliminate stocks. There's yet another way to use it. You may simply list information about a stock on the search report. Some of the information may be used later to evaluate the stocks and narrow the list of candidates; other data may be needed when you're ready to place an order with your broker. Either way, listing information during the search saves you from having to look it up later.

We've already emphasized the importance of P/E ratio, so we'll use this indicator to demonstrate the list-only feature. We are assuming, for the sake of illustration, that we don't want to eliminate stocks even if they have very high P/E's and that we don't want to rank stocks by their P/E's. All we want to do in this search is simply list the P/E ratio so we don't have to look it up when we make our purchase decision. So we'll add the "P/E ratio indicator" to our previous search and tell the computer to list the information.

The results from this search are shown in Exhibit 4.6. Notice that the list is exactly the same as the previous search, except P/E ratio is now listed. That's because P/E ratio was not used to eliminate or rank the

Exhibit 4.6   A search report ranked by insider buying and upward revisions in earnings estimates but with restricted stock price and listing of P/E ratio: The top 10 stocks on August 2, 1994.

ProSearch Report
8/2/94

Indicator	Action
Insider Buying	The higher, the better
1-Month Change in Earnings Estimates	The higher, the better
Stock Price	Eliminate below $5 and above $100
P/E Ratio	List only

Stocks	Percentile Rank	Industry Group Symbol
1> CODA—CODA ENERGY INC		
Insiders Buying = 5.0	98%	.TEX
Upward Revision = 40	99	
Stock Price = 6.5	25	
P/E Ratio = 130	98	
2> CSPK—CHESAPEAKE ENERGY		
Insiders Buying = 13	99	.TEX
Upward Revision = 13	97	
Stock Price = 12	55	
P/E Ratio = 309	98	
3> SWFT—SWIFT TRANSPORTATION		
Insiders Buying = 6.0	98	.TTR
Upward Revision = 12	97	
Stock Price = 38	90	
P/E Ratio = 28	79	
4> ALB—ALBEMARLE CORP		
Insiders Buying = 9.0	99	*
Upward Revision = 7.3	96	
Stock Price = 17	71	
P/E Ratio = 38.6	85	
5> LQ—LAURENTIAN CAPITAL		
Insiders Buying = 5.0	98	.TIL
Upward Revision = 10	97	
Stock Price = 11	51	
P/E Ratio = 10	21	
6> CELS—COMMNET CELLULAR		
Insiders Buying = 16	99	.TTC
Upward Revision = 5.6	95	
Stock Price = 21	77	
P/E Ratio = N/A		

Exhibit 4.6   (continued)

Stocks	Percentile Rank	Industry Group Symbol
7> RIGS—RIGGS NATL CORP		
Insiders Buying = 6.0	98	.TBS
Upward Revision = 8.0	96	
Stock Price = 10	43	
P/E Ratio = 17	57	
8> NWIB—NORTHWEST ILL BANCORP INC		
Insiders Buying = 4.0	97	.TBM
Upward Revision = 10	97	
Stock Price = 17	71	
P/E Ratio = 10	20	
9> THDO—3DO COMPANY		
Insiders Buying = 20	99	.TSO
Upward Revision = 4.5	94	
Stock Price = 15	65	
P/E Ratio = N/A		
10> HAUL—ALLIED HOLDINGS		
Insiders Buying = 6.0	98	.TTR
Upward Revision = 5.6	95	
Stock Price = 16	68	
P/E Ratio = 7.6	8	

* Company had not been assigned to an industry group at the time of this search.

Note: The initials stand for the stock symbol. The indicators and scores appear on the lines following each item. An "N/A" means the data wasn't available or pieces of the data that make up the calculation, such as negative numbers, cause it to be invalid. The most likely reason for a P/E ratio of "N/A" is that the company had no earnings or had negative earnings at the time of the search.

stocks. The computer simply retrieved the P/E ratio for each stock and listed it on the report.

BACK TO THE FUTURE

These searches, as simple as they are, clearly illustrate the premise of this book: There is an enormous amount of information available and now you have the tools to use it to your advantage.

Ten years ago the individual investor had great difficulty finding insider trading data. Only in recent years have insiders been required to disclose their activity as early as one month after the trade. Even more recently has that data been published in a timely fashion. And only now can it be obtained cheaply and quickly from an online service as soon as it is published by the SEC. Although there are services that publish printed reports on a monthly basis, a great deal of immediacy is lost.

Moreover, Wall Street earnings projections have become available as a computerized search tool only in the past couple of years. Before that, it was a tedious and time-consuming process to track down the estimates, calculate the revisions, and make comparisons with other stocks to see which were the highest. Needless to say, the only ones who could afford to do that were professional money managers.

Today, all this information and more is at your fingertips. You can access it with speed, ease, and economy. And, in cyberspace, you can do it from Main Street, U.S.A., as easily as you can from Wall Street.

YOU MUST REMEMBER THIS . . .

We have demonstrated with very simple searches the tremendous power of computerized search tools. Even these simple searches can narrow the playing field of 9,000 stocks down to a small list of stocks that meet the stated goals. As we go on to more complex searches, keep these points in mind:

- So far we've used only a total of four indicators in a search, but you may use as many as 40 in ProSearch.

- It is a good idea to use just a few indicators to narrow the search universe to stocks that meet your minimum requirements.

- The indicators that are most important to your investment goals should be used to score and rank the selected stocks from best to worst.

- Less important indicators may be used to list information needed to make a final decision.

- We strongly recommend that you not buy the stocks from a search until you look at their stock graphs and put them through the kind of analysis described in Chapters 7 and 8.

In the next chapter, we'll expand our insider trading search and develop two completely different searches to show you the wide range of possibilities. Then you can judge for yourself how best to develop your own working list of stocks. Again, we'll be focusing on Telescan's ProSearch, mainly because the scoring and ranking method isn't available in other search products, nor are some of the indicators that we've found to be the most powerful. Nevertheless, many of the strategies that we use can be adapted to other search products.

5

PROSPECTING FOR STOCKS

A computerized search tool streamlines the process of finding stocks that have a high probability of price increase. No longer are you dependent on stock tips from the media or your broker or from a well-meaning friend. Now you can sit at your computer and search the entire universe of listed stocks to find the top 10 or top 200 prospects that best match the standards that you impose. And, you can do it in seconds.

In the previous chapter we used a few simple searches to introduce you to the best prospecting tool we know. Now we're going to create, step-by-step, three relatively complex searches to show you the range and the subtlety of this search tool. By the time you finish this chapter, you will be able to prospect on your own, designing searches to match *your* specific investment goals.

First, we'll expand the insider trading search from the previous chapter, and then we'll develop two entirely different searches, one based on value investing and the other on momentum investing. These are searches that we actually use in real life, but they represent only a small fraction of what you can do with a computerized search tool. Our goal is not to sell you on the investing philosophies underlying the searches, but to give you practice in creating searches. Again, it would be a good idea to actually create the searches on ProSearch as we go along.

SEARCH 1: FOLLOW THE INSIDERS

The insider trading search created in the previous chapter contained four indicators:

1. Insider buying (the higher, the better).
2. One-month change in earnings estimates (the higher, the better).
3. Stock price (eliminate stocks below $5 and above $100).
4. P/E ratio (list only).

We will now expand this search to accomplish four objectives: (1) ensure some minimum level of insider buying and upward revisions of earnings estimates; (2) confirm the low P/E ratio; (3) eliminate stocks with bearish technical patterns; and (4) list certain additional information for reference purposes.

Setting Standards

When we add more indicators to our original insider trading search, it is possible to end up with a list of stocks that have high insider buying but no upward revision of earnings estimates. Or stocks with high upward revisions and no insider buying. That's because ProSearch uses *combined* scores to rank the stocks. Thus, high scores from other indicators can force less desirable stocks to the top of the list.

If we want to ensure some minimum level of insider buying *and* upward revision of earnings estimates, we will need to use our two most important indicators *twice:* once to eliminate stocks that don't meet certain minimum levels and once to score and rank the stocks. We'll select the "insider trading indicator" and require a minimum of two insiders buying the stock and also specify the higher the better. (If you are using Pro-Search, you will see that these two steps can be done at one time on the same screen.) Then we will select the "one-month change in analysts' estimates indicator" and require a minimum upward revision of 0.1 percent, as well as asking for the higher, the better. This will assure us that every stock selected will have at least two insiders buying and at least some upward revision of earnings.

It's All Relative

In Chapter 2 we established the importance of low P/E ratios that have a good chance of rising. Even though our current search is not built around low P/E's, we're still interested in them. To make sure our stocks have relatively low P/E ratios, we'll use an indicator called "relative P/E ratio" which measures a stock's current P/E versus its own history and tells us where it currently lies between its all-time high and all-time low P/E. Possible scores are 0 to 100 percent. Zero means the stock is currently selling at its all-time low P/E ratio; 100 means it is selling at its all-time high P/E. The numbers between zero and 100 are percentages of the all-time high P/E.

Obviously, the farther the current P/E ratio is from its all-time high, the more room it has to increase. This is not to say a high P/E can't rise to a new all-time high. It can, but common sense tells us that it is less likely than if it is somewhere in the middle of its historical range. So we will use the relative P/E ratio indicator *twice:* we'll ask the computer to eliminate all stocks with scores above 60 percent—that is, the P/E ratio must be less than 60 percent of the difference between the lowest and highest historical P/E for that stock; then we'll ask for the *lowest* relative P/E scores on the remaining stocks, the lower the better.

Throw Out the Bears!

ProSearch has a very wide range of technical indicators that analyze patterns of price movement in a stock. One of the simplest and most popular is the "200-day moving average indicator" (see Chapter 9 for a discussion of moving averages). Stocks generally are considered to be in a bullish pattern and more likely to increase when they're selling above their 200-day moving average; they're considered to be in a bearish pattern and more likely to decline when they are selling below their 200-day moving average.

In ProSearch, the 200-day moving average indicator represents the stock price as a percentage of its 200-day moving average. In other words, a score of 100 would indicate that a stock is at its 200-day moving average; 105 would mean it is 5 percent above the 200-day moving average; 95 would mean it is 5 percent below.

To eliminate what we consider bearish stocks, we'll use the 200-day moving average indicator and require that stocks be at least within 90 percent of their 200-day moving average (i.e., no further than 10 percent below it). In some searches, we would require that the stocks be at or above their 200-day moving average, but we want to give a little more leeway to a search based on insider buying. Frequently, when insiders believe their company's stock is undervalued, it has already fallen below its 200-day moving average. So, with this kind of search, it may be too restrictive to insist that a stock be above its 200-day moving average before we buy it. If it is within 10 percent, we think it has probably recovered sufficiently from its lows.

Here is the insider buying search as it now stands. We have established *five* minimum requirements that a stock must meet even to be considered:

1. The stock price must be between $5 and $100.
2. There must be at least two insiders buying.
3. It must have at least a 0.1 percent upward revision in earnings estimates.
4. The relative P/E ratio must be 60 percent or lower.
5. The stock must be no further than 10 percent below its 200-day moving average.

Then we have asked the computer to score and rank the stocks within that universe on three criteria:

1. Insider buying—the higher, the better.
2. Upward revision of earnings estimates—the higher, the better.
3. Relative P/E ratio—the lower, the better.

Weighty Matters

The above score-and-rank indicators are not all equally important, but they will be treated equally by the search unless we do something about it. Fortunately, ProSearch allows you to "weight" the indicators that it uses for ranking stocks, and thereby emphasize their relative importance to your overall goals (see "The Weighting Issue" sidebar in this chapter). We selected weights of 100 percent for insider trading, 60 percent for

THE WEIGHTING ISSUE

ProSearch allows you to "weight" the score-and-rank indicators so that your more important objectives receive greater emphasis. It provides five percentages that can be assigned to an indicator (100%, 80%, 60%, 40%, and 20%). These percentages tell the program how much of the indicator's score to use in the combined score for ranking the stocks. For example, if you have a search that includes high projected earnings, high historical earnings and low P/E ratio, you might weight the indicators 100%, 80%, and 40%, respectively. The program would then add the scores of the three indicators as follows:

High projected earnings	100% of the score
High historical earnings	80% of the score
Low P/E ratio	40% of the score

The total combined score would then be used to rank the stocks. (This is a simplified explanation of the algorithm used in the program.)

Changing the weighting of even one indicator in a search will change the results of the search. Thus, weighting allows you to tailor a search precisely to your goals.

---

analysts' estimates, and 20 percent for relative P/E ratio. Changing these percentages will change the results of the search.

Information, Please

We have already mentioned that information can be listed during a search without affecting the search. Let's use that feature now to list two additional pieces of information: the number of analysts that follow the company and market capitalization.

Among its other objectives, this search is going to find stocks with the greatest upward revisions in earnings estimates. A strong upward revision can occur if several analysts raise their estimates or if one analyst raises his or her estimate by a large percentage. All things considered, it is probably better to have several analysts raising their estimates 5 or 6 percent than to have an optimistic Lone Ranger upping his estimate 20 percent. Hence, it is a good idea to find out how many analysts follow the company. If there are several and if the upward revision is substantial, the clear implication is that many analysts are revising their estimates upward. With that in mind, we'll include an indicator called "number of analysts projecting earnings for the current fiscal year," and ask the computer to list the information.

Finally, we'll ask the computer to list the total market capitalization of each company. Market capitalization is simply the total number of outstanding shares times the current stock price. If a company has 10 million shares outstanding and the stock is selling for $20, it has a $200 million market capitalization. Publicly held companies range from a market capitalization of a few million dollars to more than $30 billion. When a stock has less than $100 to $200 million in capitalization, it is generally said to be a "small cap" stock. Stocks with large capitalization ("large cap stocks") are those over $1 billion. Of course, many stocks fall in between these two extremes.

Why do we want to know the market capitalization? Personally, we like to know it because we have a slight preference for small cap stocks although we're willing to buy either small or large cap issues. Some investors shy away from small cap stocks; others, particularly institutions, insist on large cap stocks. If you have a strong bias either way, you may prefer to use the market capitalization indicator in your search to restrict a search to small cap or large cap stocks. You may also restrict a search to Nasdaq stocks or stocks listed on the New York Stock Exchange or American Stock Exchange.

It's a Wrap

Our insider buying search request (Exhibit 5.1) now includes 11 indicators (abbreviations in parentheses identify the indicators in the search report). Five indicators will be used to *eliminate* stocks with certain characteristics; three will be used to *score and rank* the stocks in the search universe (the combined score will be used to rank the stocks); and three will be used to *list* information that we need to make our final decision.

Search Results: Insiders' Choice

We can now submit the search just as we did as before. The top 10 stocks from this expanded insider trading search are shown in Exhibit 5.2. The number 1 stock, Riggs National Corporation, looks promising although the highest ranked stock may not be the one you'll buy, once you evaluate the list. Riggs has six insiders buying, a 14 percent upward revision

Exhibit 5.1   Search request #1: Stocks with high insider buying.

Indicators	Action: Narrow the Universe
Stock Price (Price)	Eliminate below $5 and above $100
Insider Buying (Insdr)	Eliminate stocks with fewer than 1 insiders buying
1-Month Change in Earnings Estimates (1mEGC)	Eliminate stocks with less than .1% upward revision
Relative P/E Ratio (RelPE)	Eliminate scores above 60%
200-Day Moving Average (200MA)	Eliminate stocks more than 10% below their 200-day moving average

Indicators	Action: Score and Rank Stocks
Insider Buying (Insdr)	The higher, the better 100%
1-Month Change in Earnings Estimates (1mEGC)	The higher, the better 60%
Relative P/E Ratio (RelPE)	The lower, the better 20%

Indicators	Action: List Information
P/E Ratio (P/E)	List only
Number of Analysts Following Company (#AnCF)	List only
Market Capitalization (Capzn)	List only

Note: The abbreviation shown in parentheses after the indicator name identifies the indicator on the search report.

Exhibit 5.2   Results of Search 1: The top 10 stocks on August 10, 1994, with the highest insider buying, the greatest upward revision of earnings estimates, and the lowest relative P/E.

ProSearch 4.0 Top Stock Report

All Stocks

8/10/94

```
 1> RIGS    - RIGGS NATL CORP              .TBS
    P/E  = 17      ( 58)   Price= 10     ( 41)   Insdr= 6.0    ( 98)
    #AnCF= 4.0     ( 59)   1mEGC= 14     ( 97)   Insdr= 6.0    ( 98)
    200MA= 109     ( 90)   RelPE= 19     ( 33)   Capzn= 30     ( 70)
    RelPE= 19      ( 33)   1mEGC= 14     ( 97)

 2> CWM     - CWM MORTGAGE HLDGS           .TRM
    P/E  = 19      ( 64)   Price= 8.9    ( 31)   Insdr= 4.0    ( 97)
    #AnCF= 4.0     ( 59)   1mEGC= 4.5    ( 93)   Insdr= 4.0    ( 97)
    200MA= 95      ( 37)   RelPE= 9.7    ( 19)   Capzn= 28     ( 69)
    RelPE= 9.7     ( 19)   1mEGC= 4.5    ( 93)

 3> GET     - GAYLORD ENTERTAINMENT 'A'    .TLS
    P/E  = 26      ( 77)   Price= 24     ( 80)   Insdr= 2.0    ( 95)
    #AnCF= 10      ( 82)   1mEGC= 4.5    ( 93)   Insdr= 2.0    ( 95)
    200MA= 92      ( 26)   RelPE= 2.1    (  3)   Capzn= 209    ( 91)
    RelPE= 2.1     (  3)   1mEGC= 4.5    ( 93)

 4> MOT     - MOTOROLA, INC                .TSM
    P/E  = 25      ( 76)   Price= 53     ( 92)   Insdr= 4.0    ( 97)
    #AnCF= 33      ( 99)   1mEGC= 3.4    ( 92)   Insdr= 4.0    ( 97)
    200MA= 110     ( 90)   RelPE= 11     ( 22)   Capzn= 3027   ( 99)
    RelPE= 11      ( 22)   1mEGC= 3.4    ( 92)

 5> HRH     - HILB,ROGAL & HAMILTON        .TIK
    P/E  = 16      ( 52)   Price= 12     ( 52)   Insdr= 3.0    ( 96)
    #AnCF= 8.0     ( 77)   1mEGC= 2.5    ( 90)   Insdr= 3.0    ( 96)
    200MA= 97      ( 58)   RelPE= 1.6    (  2)   Capzn= 17     ( 60)
    RelPE= 1.6     (  2)   1mEGC= 2.5    ( 90)

 6> HUM     - HUMANA INC                   .THM
    P/E  = 22      ( 71)   Price= 19     ( 73)   Insdr= 11     ( 99)
    #AnCF= 20      ( 95)   1mEGC= 2.2    ( 89)   Insdr= 11     ( 99)
    200MA= 102     ( 79)   RelPE= 11     ( 22)   Capzn= 307    ( 93)
    RelPE= 11      ( 22)   1mEGC= 2.2    ( 89)

 7> ALW     - ALLWASTE INC                 .TPO
    P/E  = 22      ( 71)   Price= 6.9    ( 23)   Insdr= 4.0    ( 97)
    #AnCF= 8.0     ( 77)   1mEGC= 3.1    ( 91)   Insdr= 4.0    ( 97)
    200MA= 132     ( 98)   RelPE= 12     ( 23)   Capzn= 25     ( 68)
    RelPE= 12      ( 23)   1mEGC= 3.1    ( 91)

 8> SHEL    - SHELDAHL, INC                .TEC
    P/E  = 25      ( 76)   Price= 11     ( 48)   Insdr= 2.0    ( 95)
    #AnCF= 2.0     ( 38)   1mEGC= 6.3    ( 95)   Insdr= 2.0    ( 95)
    200MA= 97      ( 53)   RelPE= 13     ( 25)   Capzn= 7.1    ( 43)
    RelPE= 13      ( 25)   1mEGC= 6.3    ( 95)

 9> DSL     - DOWNEY S & L ASSN            .TSL
    P/E  = 13      ( 35)   Price= 19     ( 73)   Insdr= 1.0    ( 92)
    #AnCF= 3.0     ( 50)   1mEGC= 6.8    ( 95)   Insdr= 1.0    ( 92)
    200MA= 98      ( 64)   RelPE= 6.1    ( 12)   Capzn= 31     ( 71)
    RelPE= 6.1     ( 12)   1mEGC= 6.8    ( 95)

10> PL      - PROTECTIVE LIFE CORP         .TIL
    P/E  = 8.8     ( 12)   Price= 41     ( 90)   Insdr= 7.0    ( 98)
    #AnCF= 6.0     ( 70)   1mEGC= 1.3    ( 85)   Insdr= 7.0    ( 98)
    200MA= 94      ( 32)   RelPE= 3.3    (  6)   Capzn= 56     ( 79)
    RelPE= 3.3     (  6)   1mEGC= 1.3    ( 85)
```

in earnings estimates, and a relative P/E ratio of only 19 percent. In glancing at the list, you may wonder why Humana, Inc., with 11 insiders buying and a relative P/E of 11 percent, or Protective Life Corporation, with 7 insiders and a 3.3 percent relative P/E, were not ranked higher. It is because their upward revisions in earnings estimates are low (2.2 percent and 1.3 percent, respectively). Remember, we're looking for the best *combination* of the three indicators, not for best individual scores. The 14 percent upward revision of earnings estimates helped push Riggs to the top of the list.

A closer analysis would likely reveal other characteristics that might enhance or eliminate some of the stocks. At this point, we know nothing about the recent price movement of the stock or the latest quarterly earnings or the industry group, all of which would be important considerations. We could use indicators in the search to list this information, to require some minimum level of performance in these areas, or to score and rank the stocks on these criteria. But we wanted to keep the search relatively concise at this point. When you're creating your own searches, by all means include as many indicators as the search allows. Meanwhile, if you use this search as is, be sure to use the analysis tools described in Chapters 7 and 8 to evaluate the stocks from the search.

SEARCH 2: THE BARGAIN HUNTERS

We will now return to our goal of finding stocks with the best potential for rising P/E ratios. This is called "value investing." Value investors look for fundamentally sound stocks that are selling for less than their intrinsic value. These investors believe that, if their analysis is accurate, such stocks should move back up for fundamental reasons. Our second search then will be based on what we call "undervalued growth stocks," a classic value investing strategy.

What is an undervalued growth stock? Let's break it down. We all know what a growth stock is: one whose earnings and price have been steadily growing over a long time. This could be 3, 5, or 10 years, depending on your individual time horizon. A growth stock is also expected to continue to grow for a long time.

We also know what undervalued means: something that is selling for less than it is worth. An undervalued growth strategy then would be designed to identify stocks with high historical growth and high projected growth but which, for some reason, are selling at less than what appears to be their real value.

As with any search, we need to do three things: Eliminate stocks that don't meet our standards; rank the remaining stocks in order of best to worst, according to other conditions that we impose; and list information to aid us in our final selection. In this search, we will not discuss the list-only indicators because they will be addressed in Chapter 7 as tools to evaluate the results of this undervalued growth search.

The Basic Search

Our basic undervalued growth search has three requirements:

1. The stock must be priced low compared with its long-term price trend (the lower, the better).

2. The long-term price trend must be high (the higher, the better).

3. Projected earnings for the next five years must be high (the higher, the better) and comparable to the past growth rate.

To accomplish these basic objectives, we will use three indicators, and one of them we'll use twice.

Bargains Only.   We hope to find stocks that are selling for less than they're worth, bargain stocks, stocks that are temporarily "undervalued." The first thing we have to do is define our terms in order to quantify them. An undervalued stock is one that is selling at a low price with respect to its long-term price range but still has a five-year outlook comparable to its history. We can determine undervaluation with a search tool based on a trendline called a least squares (LSQ) line.

Don't be put off by the term "least squares." It refers to a mathematical formula used to plot a line on a stock graph through the stock's historical prices so that roughly half the price activity is above the line and half below the line. The current price is then established with relation to this line. Basically, the LSQ line tells you where the midpoint of all the data is. You don't have to know the mathematical formula; the computer does all the work. The LSQ line is the middle line in Exhibits 5.7 and 5.8 (see Chapter 8 for further discussion of this concept).

ProSearch provides a very useful tool based on LSQ lines called the "LSQ Deviation indicator." While this may sound even more ominous than an LSQ line, it is quite a simple concept. Basically, the indicator tells us how far below or above the LSQ line the current stock price is—how far it has deviated from the LSQ line. So if we're trying to find stocks that are well below their LSQ line—that is, stocks that are possibly undervalued—we will require them to have deviations of a certain percentage below the LSQ line. In this search, we'll use the 10-year LSQ deviation indicator *twice:*

1. We'll use it to *eliminate* stocks that aren't deviated at least 10 percent below their long-term LSQ line.

2. We'll use it again to *rank and score* stocks according to where they fall below the LSQ line. The lower they are, the higher the ranking.

Track Records Count.   High growth stocks, by definition, have high historical growth rates. One way to evaluate historical growth is to measure the increase in stock price over time. To this end, we'll use the "10-year price growth rate indicator" and ask for the highest scores. This will tell us how much the stock price has increased over the past 10 years; the higher the increase, the better the score.

The Future of Earnings.   When Wall Street analysts project high earnings growth for a company, it's a positive sign for the continued growth of the stock—especially if they're willing to stick their necks out and peer five years into the future. If you'll recall, this is what makes P/E's rise rapidly! The "5-year projected EPS growth rate indicator" scores each stock by how much its earnings are projected to grow each year over the next five years. We'll use this tool and ask for the highest scores; the higher the growth rate, the better the score.

To summarize our basic search, we will eliminate all stocks that are not undervalued according to their long-term price trend (at least 10 percent below their LSQ line); then, within that universe, we will ask the computer to return stocks that are the most undervalued, with the best price growth rates and the best five-year projected earnings growth rates.

Only Movers and Shakers Allowed

One of the options in a computerized search program is to eliminate unacceptable stocks before we even begin the search. We've already used one indicator to narrow our search universe to only those stocks that meet our requirements for undervaluation; now we'll use three more indicators to restrict the universe to stocks that are on an uptrend and have positive momentum. If we did not eliminate downtrending stocks or those with low momentum at this point, we would have to do it later in the analysis stage.

Wanted: Stocks with Positive Attitude.   It doesn't do much good to get a bargain-priced stock that's headed south. To make sure every stock in our search universe is technically positioned to head in the right direction, we can use a technical indicator that measures overbought and oversold conditions—the "moving average convergence/divergence (MACD) indicator." We'll discuss the MACD concept in a later chapter, but basically, it answers these questions: How strongly does the market feel about a stock? How likely will the current trend continue? You don't have to understand the concept behind a technical indicator to use it; you just need to know what to ask the computer to do with it.

The MACD indicator comes in daily and weekly versions; we'll use the longer-term weekly indicator and require it to have at least turned positive. That will tell us that the stock has turned up, not down.

Wanted: Stocks on the Move.   With the MACD indicator, we've made sure that the stocks in our search universe are technically positioned to go up, not down. But stocks that are selling at low levels with respect to their history frequently linger there for a while. We don't want be the first skater on the pond. If we can see that the stock has had a positive move over the past three weeks, we'll know that the ice has been tested. Therefore, we'll use a "3-week relative performance indicator" which measures the amount of movement in the stock price over the past three weeks, and tell the computer to eliminate stocks that haven't had an upward movement.

Wanted: Stocks from Good Families.   A stock needs the momentum of its industry group behind it to make any kind of big move in P/E ratio. Since rising P/E's are our ultimate goal, we should make sure the industry groups also have upward momentum. We'll use the "group rank indicator" and tell the computer to eliminate all stocks whose industry groups are not in the top half of all industry groups, with regard to momentum.

Our search universe is now restricted to stocks that are undervalued according to their long-term trend; that are in a positive technical position; that have had a recent upward price movement; and that have industry group momentum behind them.

Seasoning the Search

This is a good search as far as it goes. The tools we've selected will eliminate undesirable stocks and will then rank the remaining ones according to our basic objectives. But there are still things we need to know about the stocks. We know they are undervalued compared with their long-term price trend, but what about the short term? We know the stocks are on their way up, but how much momentum do they really have? And what has the industry group done lately? Is it surging forward or running out of steam?

What we need is a little seasoning for our search. Something to bring out the flavor of the stocks and make the best ones even better. The seasoning won't change the nature of the search—if we started out with chicken soup, we'll end up with chicken soup—but it will coax to the top of the list those stocks that most closely match our requirements.

A Dash of Short-Term LSQ.   We can be pretty sure that every stock on our list is a "bargain" compared with its long-term history. Why? Because we eliminated all stocks except those that are more than 10 percent below their 10-year trendline. Then we ranked the remaining stocks by how far they are below that trendline. But what about short-term? We need to add a dash of *short-term* LSQ to intensify the undervalued flavor. We'll ask for a low 3-year LSQ deviation score, which means the computer will rank the stocks according to how far they are deviated below their 3-year LSQ line. Stocks that have had significant gains or losses over a 10-year pattern frequently have a 3-year pattern that looks much different. While we think the long-term pattern is much more important, it is wise to pay attention to the shorter term as well.

A Pinch of Earnings Momentum.   We've asked for stocks with a recent price move, but we would like reassurance that the stock is indeed on its way up. A pinch or two of earnings momentum would be nice. ProSearch has several tools that compare earnings for each of the last four quarters with the same quarter a year ago. What we're looking for are stocks with the highest *rate of change* in quarter-over-quarter earnings growth, not necessarily the highest quarterly earnings. We'll use two quarterly indicators—one for the most recent quarter and one for the second most recent quarter—and ask for the highest scores.

A Bit of Price Momentum.   Another way to confirm that a stock is on its way up is to measure the rate of the change in stock price over time. Pro-Search has an indicator that ranks stocks by stock price, plus several related indicators that measure the change in the price rank. We'll use two of the latter—for 3 weeks and 6 weeks—and ask for the highest scores.

A Touch of Industry Group Momentum.   We have already eliminated all below-average industry groups with the group rank indicator. But that doesn't tell us whether a group is on its way up or on its way down. An industry group ranked in the 75th percentile that used to be in the 90th percentile is going the wrong way. A touch of industry group momentum is needed to increase the chances that the industry group is headed in the right direction. We'll use the "3-week group rank change indicator" and ask for the highest scores.

It's a Wrap, Too!

Our search request for undervalued growth stocks (Exhibit 5.3) now includes 13 indicators. Four indicators are used to create the basic search (one being used twice); three are used to further narrow the universe; and six are used for "seasoning"—they will also score and rank the stocks to help bring the most desirable ones to the top of the list. The weighting percentages assigned to the score-and-rank indicators are shown in the completed search request.

Search Results: Bargain Stocks with Room to Grow

Exhibit 5.4 shows the top 10 stocks from our undervalued growth search. The number one stock is Telephone & Data Systems. Its stock price has been growing at 29 percent over the past 10 years; earnings gains have been outstanding in the last two quarters at 44 percent and 28 percent, respectively, and are projected to grow at an outstanding 31 percent per year over the next five years; and the stock is selling at 42 percent below its 10-year LSQ line and 11 percent below its 3-year LSQ. This would appear to be an investment with great potential, but let's look at the rest of the list.

Wal-Mart showed up as the fifth most undervalued growth stock. Its growth has indeed been exceptional over the past 10 years at 29 percent. So why is it now undervalued and selling 37 percent below its LSQ line? Probably because earnings are projected to grow at only 19 percent over

Exhibit 5.3   Search request #2: Undervalued growth stocks.

Indicators	Action: The Basic Search
10-Yr LSQ Deviation (10LDv)	Eliminate stocks that aren't at least 10% below their LSQ line
10-Yr LSQ Deviation (10LDV)	The lower, the better 100%
10-Yr Price Growth Rate (10$Gr)	The higher, the better 80%
5-Yr Projected EPS Growth Rate (5yPEG)	The higher, the better 100%

Indicators	Action: Narrow the Universe
8/17/9 Weekly MACD (Mc8wC)	Eliminate stocks that aren't techncally positive
3-Week Relative Performance (3-Wk)	Eliminate stocks that have not had a positive move within the past 3 weeks.
Group Rank (GrpRk)	Eliminate stocks below 50% ranking

Indicators	Action: Seasoning
3-Yr LSQ Deviation (3LDv)	The lower, the better 60%
Quarter-over-Quarter Earnings—Most Recent Quarter (%cELt)	The higher, the better 80%
Quarter-over-Quarter Earnings—Second Most Recent Quarter (%cE-2)	The higher, the better 60%
3-Wk Price Rank Change (c$-3)	The higher, the better 80%
6-Wk Price Rank Change (c$-6)	The higher, the better 40%
3-Wk Group Rank Change (cGRP3)	The higher, the better 20%

Note: The abbreviation shown in parentheses after the indicator name identifies the indicator on the search report.

Exhibit 5.4 Results of Search 2: The top 10 undervalued growth stocks on August 2, 1994.

ProSearch 4.0 Top Stock Report
All Stocks
8/02/94

```
 1> TDS     - TELEPHONE & DATA SYS              .TTE
    %cELt= 44      ( 91)   10LDv= -42   (  6)   10LDv= -42    (  6)
    %cE-2= 28      ( 86)   3LDv = -11   ( 32)   Mc8wC= 98     ( 96)
    c$-3 = 5.4     ( 88)   5yPEG= 31    ( 93)   3-Wk = 115    ( 92)
    c$-6 = 3.8     ( 81)   10$Gr= 29    ( 95)   GrpRk= 101    ( 76)
    cGRP3= -0.3    ( 26)
 2> GGTI    - GTI CORP                          .TEZ
    %cELt= -60     ( 62)   10LDv= -29   ( 13)   10LDv= -29    ( 13)
    %cE-2= -57     ( 63)   3LDv = -54   (  1)   Mc8wC= 132    ( 98)
    c$-3 = 7.2     ( 91)   5yPEG= 20    ( 74)   3-Wk = 117    ( 93)
    c$-6 = 8.8     ( 91)   10$Gr= 24    ( 92)   GrpRk= 98     ( 55)
    cGRP3= 2.8     ( 84)
 3> CML     - CML GROUP                         .TLP
    %cELt= 13      ( 81)   10LDv= -53   (  3)   10LDv= -53    (  3)
    %cE-2= 14      ( 80)   3LDv = -60   (  0)   Mc8wC= 7.0    ( 19)
    c$-3 = 5.2     ( 88)   5yPEG= 19    ( 68)   3-Wk = 104    ( 74)
    c$-6 = 1.4     ( 68)   10$Gr= 31    ( 95)   GrpRk= 100    ( 67)
    cGRP3= -1.8    ( 14)
 4> WSAU    - WAUSAU PAPER MILLS                .TPA
    %cELt= 9.3     ( 79)   10LDv= -39   (  8)   10LDv= -39    (  8)
    %cE-2= 6.2     ( 77)   3LDv = -16   ( 22)   Mc8wC= 39     ( 83)
    c$-3 = 2.6     ( 78)   5yPEG= 16    ( 59)   3-Wk = 104    ( 74)
    c$-6 = 1.4     ( 68)   10$Gr= 39    ( 97)   GrpRk= 104    ( 87)
    cGRP3= 5.3     ( 96)
 5> WMT     - WAL-MART STORES                   .TDP
    %cELt= 10      ( 79)   10LDv= -37   (  8)   10LDv= -37    (  8)
    %cE-2= 15      ( 81)   3LDv = -5.2  ( 57)   Mc8wC= 54     ( 90)
    c$-3 = 2.5     ( 77)   5yPEG= 19    ( 67)   3-Wk = 104    ( 76)
    c$-6 = 1.5     ( 69)   10$Gr= 29    ( 95)   GrpRk= 98     ( 52)
    cGRP3= 1.7     ( 63)
 6> SCA     - SURGICAL CARE AFFIL               .THC
    %cELt= 10      ( 79)   10LDv= -62   (  1)   10LDv= -62    (  1)
    %cE-2= 5.0     ( 76)   3LDv = 21    ( 92)   Mc8wC= 73     ( 94)
    c$-3 = 13      ( 97)   5yPEG= 18    ( 67)   3-Wk = 113    ( 91)
    c$-6 = 15      ( 96)   10$Gr= 50    ( 97)   GrpRk= 100    ( 71)
    cGRP3= 2.6     ( 81)
 7> CCON    - CIRCON CORP                       .TMI
    %cELt= 450     ( 99)   10LDv= -44   (  5)   10LDv= -44    (  5)
    %cE-2= -45     ( 63)   3LDv = 0.0   ( 74)   Mc8wC= 27     ( 76)
    c$-3 = 6.3     ( 90)   5yPEG= 18    ( 67)   3-Wk = 108    ( 85)
    c$-6 = 4.0     ( 81)   10$Gr= 14    ( 78)   GrpRk= 99     ( 61)
    cGRP3= 2.0     ( 72)
 8> CEFT    - CONCORD EFS                       .TFB
    %cELt= 10      ( 79)   10LDv= -45   (  5)   10LDv= -45    (  5)
    %cE-2= -3.6    ( 71)   3LDv = 4.1   ( 80)   Mc8wC= 38     ( 82)
    c$-3 = 8.0     ( 92)   5yPEG= 22    ( 80)   3-Wk = 113    ( 90)
    c$-6 = 2.9     ( 77)   10$Gr= 52    ( 97)   GrpRk= 98     ( 55)
    cGRP3= -0.5    ( 24)
 9> GPI     - GUARDSMAN PRODUCTS                .TPN
    %cELt= 43      ( 91)   10LDv= -27   ( 15)   10LDv= -27    ( 15)
    %cE-2= 25      ( 85)   3LDv = -20   ( 17)   Mc8wC= 22     ( 69)
    c$-3 = 3.0     ( 80)   5yPEG= 27    ( 88)   3-Wk = 106    ( 80)
    c$-6 = -2.2    ( 20)   10$Gr= 8.6   ( 56)   GrpRk= 99     ( 58)
    cGRP3= 1.8     ( 68)
10> TSS     - TOTAL SYSTEMS SVCS                .TBU
    %cELt= 13      ( 81)   10LDv= -14   ( 28)   10LDv= -14    ( 28)
    %cE-2= 16      ( 81)   3LDv = -22   ( 14)   Mc8wC= 26     ( 75)
    c$-3 = 7.8     ( 92)   5yPEG= 17    ( 63)   3-Wk = 112    ( 89)
    c$-6 = -1.5    ( 24)   10$Gr= 17    ( 85)   GrpRk= 98     ( 55)
    cGRP3= 1.7     ( 63)
```

the next five years. Not a bad growth rate, but the market may have been expecting much more. It is not good to disappoint the market.

Take a look at Surgical Care (SCA), ranked sixth. At 62 percent below . its LSQ line, SCA would have to nearly triple in price to get back to its long-term trendline. Yet it has grown at 50 percent per year over the past 10 years. If you'll take a closer look, however, you'll see one reason why it may be selling so far below its long-term trend. It is projected to grow only at 18 percent per year for the next five years. That's not bad, but it's a long way from 50 percent. You can even see the growth starting to slow. In the last two quarters, it has only grown at 10 and 5 percent, respectively.

When you look closely at the figures, it becomes apparent why each stock is on the list. All match the conditions set forth in our search criteria: They have all had impressive 10-year growth rates; they're all expected to have five more years of good earnings; and they're all currently undervalued as measured by their long-term LSQ lines. The problem becomes one of choosing among stocks with good potential (the subject of Chapters 7 and 8).

Keep in mind that this is still a fairly simple search. There is still much information that we should study before we make a purchase decision. Much of it can be obtained with list-only indicators at the same time you run the search, as we'll show you later. Nevertheless, even without further analysis, the stocks from this search—if you bought them all—would most likely outperform the market over a reasonable length of time. We will put this to the test in the next chapter.

SEARCH 3: STOCKS ON THE FAST TRACK

Now we're going to wipe the slate clean and pretend we're a whole different breed of investor. Let's imagine that we're no longer excited about insider buying or value investing; instead, we will become advocates of momentum investing, one of today's more popular investing concepts.

Momentum investors are more technically oriented than value investors. They are concerned primarily with a stock's price pattern; they're less concerned with high P/E ratios, earnings, or insider selling. Specifically, they look for price patterns that indicate upward momentum. If they find a fast-moving stock, they'll hop on and ride it until it shows signs of slowing or until they see one moving faster.

In a momentum search, we're looking for companies that have the greatest possible price momentum, the greatest possible industry group momentum, and the greatest possible earnings momentum. We'll find them just as we did in the other searches: We'll use certain indicators to eliminate stocks, other indicators to score and rank the remaining stocks, and still others to list relevant information.

No Tortoises Allowed

The first thing we'll do is eliminate all those steadily plodding stocks that may be acceptable to a long-term investor but are anathema to momentum investors. As momentum investors, we want the quick burst of energy from fast-moving stocks; we want momentum and we want it now.

Computerized search programs like ProSearch offer several indicators that rank stocks according to their momentum in price, earnings, and industry group. We'll use three of them to separate the hares from the tortoises—"price rank," "EPS rank," and "group rank"—and we will tell the computer to eliminate all stocks that are ranked below 70 percent in each area. That means we will have a search universe limited to high-momentum stocks: stocks whose prices are increasing faster than 70 percent of all stocks, whose earnings are growing faster than 70 percent of all stocks, and whose industry groups are moving faster than 70 percent of all industry groups.

Go with the Mo

As a result of the preceding restrictions, every stock found by this search will be in the top 30 percent of *all* stocks with regard to price, earnings, and industry group momentum. It is possible, however, that one of these stocks could be moving down in rank, rather than moving up, and still be in the top 30 percent. To make sure that momentum is increasing and not decreasing, we need to coax to the top of the list those stocks with the largest increase in price rank, earnings rank, and industry group rank. In effect, we want to maximize the momentum of the stocks at the top of the list. To accomplish this, we'll use several indicators in the ProSearch tool kit that measure the *change* in price rank, earnings rank, and industry group rank.

- We want the stock price moving up as fast as it can, gaining momentum at the expense of other stocks. So we'll use the three indicators that measure the change in price rank and ask the computer for the highest scores over one week, three weeks, and six weeks.

- Earnings should be moving up strongly, as well. We'll use three indicators that measure the change in earnings rank and ask for the highest scores over the last three quarters (13 weeks, 26 weeks, and 39 weeks).

- Unlike salmon, stocks don't swim well against the current. If the industry group is going south while the stock is pushing northward, chances are the stock won't get very far. It needs to have the momentum of the industry group behind it. To make sure it gets it, we'll use the 3-week group rank change indicator and ask for the higher, the better.

Follow the Money

There's one more factor to add to our momentum search: the "accumulation/distribution indicator." This is an interesting tool based on a concept that seeks to determine the direction of money flow in a stock by measuring the volume on "up days" and "down days." If, over a specified period, volume is higher on days when the stock price is rising ("up days") than on days when the stock price is falling ("down days"), money is said to be flowing into the stock. This could indicate that there are simply more buyers than sellers, or it could mean that institutional investors (who more heavily influence the market) are moving into the stock. Either way, the stock is said to be "under accumulation," which could be interpreted as "the institutional investors are moving in." The reverse signals that the stock is "under distribution": Money is flowing out of the stock, which could mean that institutions are selling. Obviously, accumulation enhances a stock's momentum, and it should drive up the P/E ratio. So if we want to "follow the money" (and we do), we will pay attention to the accumulation/distribution indicator.

ProSearch scores the accumulation/distribution indicator a little differently from other indicators. Stocks under accumulation are scored from 60 to 100; the higher the score, the more consistently the money is flowing into the stock. Stocks under distribution are scored from 40 to zero; the lower the score, the more consistently the money is flowing out of the stock. Scores between 40 and 60 are essentially neutral.

To make sure the institutional money is working for us, rather than against us, we'll use the accumulation/distribution indicator twice: once to eliminate all stocks with scores below 60, and then to rank the remaining stocks by the highest scores.

Info Check

When we look at the high-momentum stocks found by this search, we would like to see the relationship between their current P/E and relative P/E ratios (although true momentum advocates would ignore P/E ratios). But even with a technically oriented search, the fundamentalist in us insists that we at least look at the P/E. Therefore, we will select the P/E ratio indicator and relative P/E ratio indicator and tell the computer to list the information. We will also list the stock price, which we list in every search just for convenience.

Wrap It Up, Again

Our momentum search request (Exhibit 5.5) now includes 15 indicators. Four indicators will be used to eliminate stocks; eight will be used to score and rank the remaining stocks (using the weighting percentages shown in the search request); and three will be used to list information. This may sound like a lot of indicators, but you could use up to 25 more, if you wish. In many searches, we use the maximum of 40 indicators, although the majority are used just to list information that will be used to evaluate the stocks.

Search Results: Stocks with Big-Mo

The results of the momentum search are shown in Exhibit 5.6. These are the 15 highest momentum stocks out of 9,000 on the day of the search; the higher they are on the list, the greater the combined momentum of price, earnings, and industry group. With stocks on the fast track, we would prefer to select those that have not yet peaked. That's where a comparison of the P/E ratio and relative P/E ratio comes in handy. We would also take a hard look at the accumulation/distribution ranking; the higher ranking would get our attention.

At first glance, we would reject the top three stocks on the report. Plasma Therm (No. 1) has an extremely high current P/E ratio (70); Worthen Banking Corp. (No. 2) and Union Carbide (No. 3) are both near their all-time high P/E's (with relative P/E's of 96 percent and 93 percent, respectively). This is not unusual for a momentum stock, however. CCB Financial (No. 4) appears to be an attractive candidate, with a current P/E of 11, a relative P/E of only 62 percent, and an accumulation/distribution score of 74. So does Technitrol, Inc. (No. 12), which has a slightly

Exhibit 5.5   Search request #3: Momentum stocks.

Indicators	Action: Narrow the Universe
Price Rank ($Rank)	Eliminate stocks below 70% ranking
EPS Rank (EPSRk)	Eliminate stocks below 70% ranking
Group Rank (GrpRk)	Eliminate stocks below 70% ranking
Accumulation/Distribution (AcDst)	Eliminate stocks below 60% ranking

Indicators	Action: Score and Rank Stocks
1-Wk Price Rank Change (c$-1)	The higher, the better 100%
3-Wk Price Rank Change (c$-3)	The higher, the better 80%
6-Wk Price Rank Change (c$-6)	The higher, the better 40%
13-Wk EPS Rank Change (cEA13)	The higher, the better 100%
26-Wk EPS Rank Change (cEA26)	The higher, the better 80%
39-Wk EPS Rank Change (cEA39)	The higher, the better 40%
3-Wk Group Rank Change (cGRP3)	The higher, the better 60%
Accumulation/Distribution (AcDst)	The higher, the better 20%

Indicators	Action: List Information
P/E Ratio (P/E)	List only
Relative P/E Ratio (RelPE)	List only
Stock Price (Price)	List only

Note: The abbreviation shown in parentheses after the indicator name identifies the indicator on the search report.

Exhibit 5.6   Results of Search 3: The top 15 stocks with greatest momentum on August 10, 1994.

ProSearch 4.0 Top Stock Report

All Stocks

8/10/94

```
 1> PTIS   - PLASMA THERM INC                    .TSM
    GrpRk= 103     ( 82)   EPSRk= 89      ( 80)   $Rank= 200    ( 99)
    GrpCh3Wk=1.3   ( 75)   EPSCh13Wk=24   ( 94)   $Ch1Wk= 5.8   ( 95)
    AcDst= 71      ( 75)   EPSCh26Wk=41   ( 96)   $Ch3Wk= 9.0   ( 96)
    EPSCh39Wk-72   ( 99)   $Ch6Wk= 43     ( 99)   AccDst= 71    ( 75)
    P/E  = 70      ( 94)   RelPE= 36      ( 53)   Price= 5.6    ( 19)
 2> WOR    - WORTHEN BANKING CORP                .TBS
    GrpRk= 106     ( 93)   EPSRk= 92      ( 86)   $Rank= 115    ( 92)
    GrpCh3Wk= 2.6  ( 92)   EPSCh13Wk=18   ( 89)   c$-1 = 4.6    ( 93)
    AcDst= 68      ( 70)   cEA26= 23      ( 84)   c$-3 = 3.2    ( 87)
    cEA39= 30      ( 87)   c$-6 = 3.0     ( 76)   AcDst= 68     ( 70)
    P/E  = 12      ( 33)   RelPE= 96      ( 96)   Price= 30     ( 86)
 3> UK     - UNION CARBIDE                        .TCD
    GrpRk= 106     ( 94)   EPSRk= 94      ( 89)   $Rank= 118    ( 95)
    GrpCh3Wk= 0.6  ( 65)   EPSCh13Wk=18   ( 89)   c$-1 = 4.0    ( 92)
    AcDst= 69      ( 71)   cEA26= 28      ( 89)   c$-3 = 8.4    ( 95)
    cEA39= 46      ( 95)   c$-6 = 9.3     ( 92)   AcDst= 69     ( 71)
    P/E  = 24      ( 75)   RelPE= 93      ( 95)   Price= 32     ( 87)
 4> CCBF   - CCB FINANCIAL                        .TBS
    GrpRk= 106     ( 93)   EPSRk= 90      ( 82)   $Rank= 107    ( 84)
    GrpCh3Wk= 2.6  ( 92)   EPSCh13Wk=19   ( 90)   c$-1 = 1.9    ( 83)
    AcDst= 74      ( 81)   cEA26= 27      ( 88)   c$-3 = 1.6    ( 80)
    cEA39= 13      ( 69)   c$-6 = 3.5     ( 78)   AcDst= 74     ( 81)
    P/E  = 11      ( 24)   RelPE= 62      ( 76)   Price= 41     ( 90)
 5> EFII   - ELECTRONICS FOR IMAGING             .TSO
    GrpRk= 103     ( 84)   EPSRk= 96      ( 93)   $Rank= 114    ( 92)
    GrpCh3Wk= 2.4  ( 90)   EPSCh13Wk=2.0  ( 61)   c$-1 = 4.6    ( 93)
    AcDst= 71      ( 75)   cEA26= 20      ( 82)   c$-3 = 4.4    ( 90)
    cEA39= 30      ( 87)   c$-6 = 16      ( 97)   AcDst= 71     ( 75)
    P/E  = 17      ( 59)   RelPE= N/A     (   )   Price= 22     ( 78)
 6> CCXLA  - CONTEL CELLULAR'A'                   .TTC
    GrpRk= 104     ( 89)   EPSRk= 93      ( 87)   $Rank= 108    ( 85)
    GrpCh3Wk= -0.6 ( 42)   EPSCh13Wk=21   ( 92)   c$-1 = 1.9    ( 83)
    AcDst= 76      ( 85)   cEA26= 31      ( 91)   c$-3 = 3.2    ( 87)
    cEA39= 18      ( 75)   c$-6 = 6.9     ( 88)   AcDst= 76     ( 85)
    P/E  = N/A     (   )   RelPE= N/A     (   )   Price= 19     ( 73)
 7> PTZ    - PULITZER PUBLISHING                  .TTV
    GrpRk= 104     ( 86)   EPSRk= 91      ( 84)   $Rank= 106    ( 82)
    GrpCh3Wk= -0.4 ( 47)   EPSCh13Wk=14   ( 84)   c$-1 = 1.1    ( 76)
    AcDst= 71      ( 75)   cEA26= 32      ( 91)   c$-3 = 1.3    ( 78)
    cEA39= 31      ( 88)   c$-6 = 3.3     ( 77)   AcDst= 71     ( 75)
    P/E  = 18      ( 60)   RelPE= 36      ( 54)   Price= 38     ( 89)
 8> NTN    - NTN COMMUNICATIONS                   .TTV
    GrpRk= 104     ( 86)   EPSRk= 97      ( 95)   $Rank= 118    ( 94)
    GrpCh3Wk= -0.4 ( 47)   EPSCh13Wk=3.0  ( 64)   c$-1 = 6.1    ( 95)
    AcDst= 70      ( 73)   cEA26= 14      ( 74)   c$-3 = 8.6    ( 95)
    cEA39= 19      ( 76)   c$-6 = 20      ( 98)   AcDst= 70     ( 73)
    P/E  = N/A     (   )   RelPE= N/A     (   )   Price= 8.5    ( 29)
 9> MCSY   - MEDIC COMPUTER SYSTEMS               .TIC
    GrpRk= 110     ( 99)   EPSRk= 92      ( 85)   $Rank= 121    ( 96)
    GrpCh3Wk= -3.1 ( 16)   EPSCh13Wk=14   ( 84)   c$-1 = 2.5    ( 87)
    AcDst= 73      ( 79)   cEA26= 48      ( 97)   c$-3 = 5.1    ( 91)
    cEA39= 71      ( 99)   c$-6 = 13      ( 95)   AcDst= 73     ( 79)
    P/E  = 26      ( 77)   RelPE= 41      ( 58)   Price= 20     ( 74)
10> PSFT   - PEOPLESOFT INC                       .TSO
    GrpRk= 103     ( 84)   EPSRk= 98      ( 98)   $Rank= 112    ( 90)
    GrpCh3Wk= 2.4  ( 90)   EPSCh13Wk=1.0  ( 57)   c$-1 = 8.3    ( 97)
    AcDst= 65      ( 64)   cEA26= 2.0     ( 55)   c$-3 = 8.6    ( 95)
    cEA39= 2.0     ( 53)   c$-6 = 7.3     ( 89)   AcDst= 65     ( 64)
    P/E  = 47      ( 90)   RelPE= N/A     (   )   Price= 38     ( 89)
```

Exhibit 5.6 (continued)

```
11> YRK     - YORK INTERNATIONAL                .TAC
      GrpRk= 107      ( 94)    EPSRk= 93    ( 88)    $Rank= 105    ( 80)
      cGRP3= 0.3      ( 57)    cEA13= 2.0   ( 61)    c$-1 = 1.4    ( 79)
      AcDst= 74       ( 81)    cEA26= 12    ( 72)    c$-3 = 4.5    ( 90)
      cEA39= 10       ( 65)    c$-6 = 7.9   ( 90)    AcDst= 74     ( 81)
      P/E  = 18       ( 61)    RelPE= N/A   (   )    Price= 41     ( 90)
12> TNL     - TECHNITROL INC                     .TPM
      GrpRk= 104      ( 89)    EPSRk= 95    ( 92)    $Rank= 110    ( 88)
      cGRP3= 0.4      ( 59)    cEA13= 3.0   ( 64)    c$-1 = 2.4    ( 86)
      AcDst= 75       ( 83)    cEA26= 21    ( 83)    c$-3 = 0.2    ( 67)
      cEA39= 40       ( 93)    c$-6 = 0.9   ( 54)    AcDst= 75     ( 83)
      P/E  = 15       ( 50)    RelPE= 64    ( 77)    Price= 39     ( 90)
13> TER     - TERADYNE INC                       .TEI
      GrpRk= 105      ( 91)    EPSRk= 97    ( 95)    $Rank= 106    ( 82)
      cGRP3= 2.6      ( 92)    cEA13= 1.0   ( 57)    c$-1 = 6.3    ( 96)
      AcDst= 64       ( 62)    cEA26= 3.0   ( 57)    c$-3 = 0.9    ( 75)
      cEA39= 5.0      ( 58)    c$-6 = 3.5   ( 78)    AcDst= 64     ( 62)
      P/E  = 20       ( 65)    RelPE= 0.9   (  1)    Price= 28     ( 84)
14> TCB     - TCF FINANCIAL                      .TSL
      GrpRk= 107      ( 98)    EPSRk= 94    ( 89)    $Rank= 108    ( 86)
      cGRP3= 2.1      ( 87)    cEA13= -1.0  ( 45)    c$-1 = 2.7    ( 88)
      AcDst= 65       ( 64)    cEA26= 4.0   ( 60)    c$-3 = 2.4    ( 84)
      cEA39= 21       ( 79)    c$-6 = 6.3   ( 87)    AcDst= 65     ( 64)
      P/E  = N/A      (   )    RelPE= N/A   (   )    Price= 38     ( 89)
15> FSII    - FSI INTERNATIONAL                  .TSM
      GrpRk= 103      ( 82)    EPSRk= 97    ( 96)    $Rank= 112    ( 90)
      cGRP3= 1.3      ( 75)    cEA13= 1.0   ( 57)    c$-1 = 0.9    ( 74)
      AcDst= 67       ( 68)    cEA26= 1.0   ( 52)    c$-3 = 5.7    ( 92)
      cEA39= 5.0      ( 58)    c$-6 = 11    ( 94)    AcDst= 67     ( 68)
      P/E  = 14       ( 42)    RelPE= N/A   (   )    Price= 14     ( 62)
```

higher current P/E (15) but is otherwise comparable to CCB. However, when we look at their long-term price trends (Exhibits 5.7 and 5.8), Technitrol is a far more attractive candidate than CCB Financial.

As you can see, CCB Financial is currently near the top of its LSQ trading channel[1], which is a red flag. Technitrol, on the other hand, is well down in the bottom channel but has similar momentum to CCB. So why buy the one that is near the top of a long-term trend? We're not saying that stocks don't occasionally break through the top of their trading channels. They do. But common sense tells us there's more risk involved.

At the risk of offending all the momentum investors, we suggest that even momentum stocks be viewed through various lenses to see whether they are right for your portfolio.

---

[1] LSQ trading channels are discussed in Chapter 8. In a nutshell, the LSQ line divides the price action in half (based on a complex mathemathical formula); parallel lines form a trading channel based on stock tops and bottoms.

Exhibit 5.7 A long-term stock graph for Technitrol, Incorporated, with an overlay of LSQ trading channels. Note that Technitrol was selling (in August 1994) just slightly above the bottom of its long-term LSQ channel.

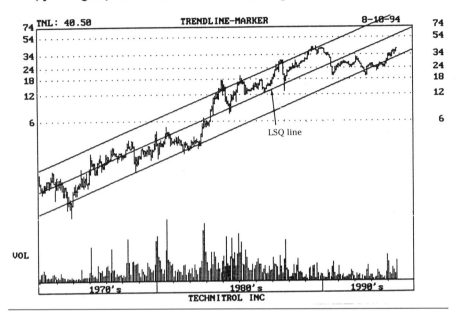

INSIDERS + UNDERVALUED GROWTH + MOMENTUM = SUPER SEARCH?

Can you combine searches? Certainly. But be careful how you do it. We always add the insider trading indicator to our undervalued growth search, at least as a list-only tool. In that way, it doesn't affect the search, but we can consult it during our analysis (as you'll see in Chapter 7). Combining the undervalued growth and momentum searches is a little trickier. Stocks would get high scores for being low priced, for having high growth, *and* for having a lot of momentum. It seems to us that is trying to do too many things in one search. In our experience, the results tend to be a bit of a hodgepodge.

There's a better way, we think, to reap the benefits of both searches. Run the momentum search and the undervalued growth search separately. You'll end up with two lists of stocks. When a stock turns up on both lists, you may have a winner. It probably won't happen very often—undervalued

Exhibit 5.8 A long-term stock graph for CCB Financial with an overlay of LSQ trading channels. (CCB has been public for only 10 years.) Note that CCB Financial was selling (in August 1994) at the very top of its long-term LSQ channel.

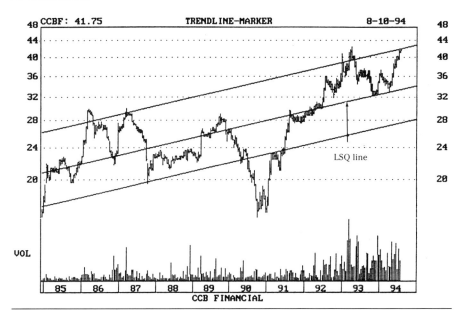

PROSPECTING WITH THE PROS

Investment newsletters are an alternative way to identify prospects. It is especially helpful if the newsletter is published online so that the comments and advice are timely. Your Cyber-Investing Kit offers a 30-day trial subscription to more than 20 online newsletters, plus free issues of several that are not online. This sampler gives you a chance to taste each one, so to speak, without buying the whole box. We advise against taking anyone's recommendations on faith, however, even our own. Put any recommended stock through the same evaluation that we suggest for a "hot stock tip" in Chapter 8, at least until you become completely comfortable with the editor's strategy and techniques.

stocks rarely display very high momentum—but it does happen. Remember the retired dentist in Chapter 1 who uses separate searches such as these? He says he doesn't find a stock on both lists very often, but it has happened often enough to generate an annual return of over 40 percent!

YOU MUST REMEMBER THIS . . .

A computerized search can increase the odds that the stocks you find will have a greater-than-average potential for price increase (or, if your strategy is to short stocks, a greater-than-average potential for price decrease). Keep these thoughts in mind when creating a search:

- Use your most important goals as score-and-rank indicators to bring the most desirable stocks into your search report.

- Use your minimum requirements to eliminate unacceptable stocks from the search universe.

- Supplement your major goals with score-and-rank indicators to help move the best stocks to the top of the list. (Use lower weighting for these.)

- An indicator can be used to eliminate stocks *and* to score and rank stocks in the same search.

- Before buying stocks found by a search, evaluate them along the lines described in Chapters 7 and 8. Use list-only indicators to retrieve information needed for the evaluation.

- Many different kinds of searches can be created with computerized search programs. Experiment with the indicators to find those that best match your investment goals.

In the next chapter, we'll show you how to determine if a particular search will produce good results. We'll demonstrate a tool that allows you to go back in time and test your search in different kinds of markets. You'll be able to see for yourself how the stocks from a search would have performed over time. After that, we'll move on to analyzing the stocks from our undervalued growth stock search.

6

THE TIME MACHINE

How would you like to see the actual performance of stocks found by your search? In this computerized age, you can do just that. In effect, you can travel back in time, run a search, and see how the stocks from that search performed over time.

This is called "backtesting," and it is one of the most exciting of the computerized tools because it lets you peer into the future from the vantage point of the past. It is like asking, "What if Ross Perot had won the 1992 Presidential race?"—and being able to see what the consequences would have been. It's even better than that. We can use "what if" with any number of different search strategies, which is more like asking, "What if the Republican ticket had been a Bush/Baker ticket instead of Bush/Quayle?" "What if Colin Powell had run instead of Ross Perot?" "What if, what if, what if . . . " Backtesting is like a time machine, and we have to warn you: *It can be addictive.*

DIVINING THE FUTURE

Backtesting follows the advise of Confucius: "Study the past if you would divine the future." It is based on the assumption that if a search strategy worked consistently in the past, it should work comparably in the future.

The backtesting procedure is simple. After you create a search, simply select the backtesting option, specify the date you wish to start the test, enter the time period of the test, and then run the search. (There are two restrictions with ProSearch: You can test a search only over the past 23 months, and you must start the test on the first day of one of those 23 months.) A backtested search evaluates the stocks on the basis of their qualities at the time of the search, as opposed to their present qualities. This is what gives backtesting its power and validity.[1]

We always backtest a search strategy before using it. Backtesting is one of the most valuable features of any search product because it gives you a chance to develop some confidence in your searches *before* you "place your bets."

SEARCHES THAT BEAT THE MARKET: THREE FOR THREE

For illustration, we backtested all three searches from the previous chapter, using 8/1/93 as the date for the backtest (one year prior to the time of writing). For the undervalued growth search and insider trading search, we asked the computer to test the results over the 200 days (40 weeks) following the date of the test. These kinds of searches require a relatively long period to judge performance since undervaluation doesn't correct overnight and insiders usually act well in advance of events that may affect their company. We tested the performance of the momentum search over just 45 days (nine trading weeks) because we would expect momentum stocks to achieve results more quickly than stocks based on value.

Exhibits 6.1, 6.2, and 6.3 summarize the results of our three backtested searches. In every case, they beat the market by a substantial margin. Look at the summary information at the bottom of the search report. In each test, the average total return of all 25 stocks was considerably more than any of the market averages. The insider trading search (Exhibit 6.1) returned an average of 20.3 percent over 200 days versus a Nasdaq return of 4.7 percent and against a virtually flat return for the New York Stock Exchange index and the S&P 500. The undervalued growth search (Exhibit 6.2) generated an average return of 9.1 percent over the same period, more than double the Dow, almost double the Nasdaq market. The momentum search (Exhibit 6.3) returned an average of 15.2 percent in only 45 days. On an annualized basis, that's over 100 percent per year!

---

[1] ProSearch uses Telescan's online database for its backtest; other programs allow you to backtest technical trading theories based on the data that you've accumulated on your own computer.

Exhibit 6.1   The top 25 stocks from the insider trading backtest for the 200-day period from 8/1/93 through 5/5/94.

ProSearch 4.0 Top Stock Report
Backtesting Report
8/01/93–5/05/94

Stock Symbol/Company Name	Industry Group	Percent Gain over Period Tested
1> GPI—GUARDSMAN PRODS INC	.TPN	−7.9%
2> WAMU—WASHINGTON MUT SVGS BK SEATT	.TBW	−27.1
3> GROV—GROVE BK FOR SVGS MASS	.TBN	26.3
4> BKSO—BANK SOUTH CORP	.TBS	32.4
5> PZL—PENNZOIL CO	.TUI	−26.3
6> SBK—SIGNET BKG CORP	.TBS	46.6
7> WMS—WMS INDS INC	.TRG	4.6
8> KSF—QUAKER ST OIL REFNG CORP	.TOR	6.8
9> ITG—INTEGRA FINL CORP COM	.TBN	−3.2
10> INTC—INTEL CORP	.TSM	11.3
11> FFB—FIRST FID BANCORPORATION NEW	.TBN	−5.7
12> ONPR—ONE PRICE CLOTHING STORES IN	.TSS	50.1
13> NCBC—NATIONAL COMM BANCORPORATION	.TBS	13.1
14> BBY—BEST BUY INC	.TDS	177.6
15> UCIT—UNITED CITIES GAS CO	.TGD	−14.3
16> GUN—GUNDLE ENVIRONMENTAL SYS INC	.TPC	−15.7
17> FRTH—FOURTH FINL CORP	.TBM	−3.0
18> BBB—BALTIMORE BANCORP	.TBS	74.1
19> OKE—ONEOK INC	.TGD	−23.3
20> PKE—PARK ELECTROCHEMICAL CORP	.TEZ	95.1
21> ELK—ELCOR CORP	.TMG	−9.3
22> MTL—MERCANTILE BANCORPORATION IN	.TBM	9.2
23> BBI—BARNETT BANKS FLA INC	.TBS	−4.8
24> SUNBURST SYS CORP	.TBS	−11.2
25> SPGLA—SPIEGEL INC CL A	.TRZ	112.8

Average Total	=	20.3
Dow Jones Industrial Average Total	=	3.6
New York Stock Exchange Total	=	0.4
S&P 500 Total	=	0.2
NASDAQ Total	=	4.7
American Stock Exchange Total	=	1.1

Note: Scores for the indicators used in the search have been omitted to save space.

Exhibit 6.2   The top 25 stocks from the undervalued growth backtest for the 200-day period from 8/1/93 through 5/5/94.

ProSearch 4.0 Top Stock Report
Backtesting Report
8/01/93—5/05/94

Stock Symbol/Company Name	Industry Group	Percent Gain over Period Tested
1> CDIC—CARDINAL DISTR INC	.TDW	58.5%
2> DHR—DANAHER CORP	.THH	19.4
3> HRB—BLOCK H & R INC	.TFB	20.4
4> WFSL—WASHINGTON FED SVGS & LN ASS	.TSL	−14.0
5> CRDB—CRAWFORD & CO	.TIP	−12.3
6> STBK—STATE ST BOSTON CORP COM	.TBN	12.2
7> VALN—VALLEN CORP	.TPS	−11.3
8> EFX—EQUIFAX INC	.TFB	32.5
9> PAYC—PAYCO AMERN CORP	.TFB	21.2
10> LAWS—LAWSON PRODS INC	.TMX	−15.8
11> WILM—WILMINGTON TRUST CORP COM	.TBN	−10.9
12> TCAT—TCA CABLE TV INC	.TCT	0.0
13> CASC—CASCADE CORP	.TMY	−8.7
14> PMS—POLICY MGMT SYS CORP	.TSO	5.7
15> DAPN—DAUPHIN DEP CORP	.TBN	1.0
16> LADF—LADD FURNITURE INC	.TFU	−2.8
17> AMZ—AMERICAN LIST CORP	.TFB	11.7
18> CATA—CAPITOL TRANSAMERICA CORP	.TIP	1.4
19> KRI—KNIGHT RIDDER INCSPAPERS INC	.TNP	10.2
20> LEE—LEE ENTERPRISES INC	.TNP	24.2
21> BC—BRUNSWICK CORP	.TLP	81.4
22> SZ—SIZZLER INTL INC	.TRT	−30.4
23> TWBC—TRANSWORLD BANCORP CALIF	.TBW	7.6
24> TNL—TECHNITROL INC	.TPM	37.8
25> SPW—SPX CORP	.TAO	−7.0

Average Total	=	9.1
Dow Jones Industrial Average Total	=	3.6
New York Stock Exchange Total	=	0.4
S&P 500 Total	=	0.2
NASDAQ Total	=	4.7
American Stock Exchange Total	=	1.1

Note: Scores for the indicators used in the search have been omitted to save space.

Exhibit 6.3   The top 25 stocks from the momentum backtest for the 45-day period from 8/1/93 through 9/30/93.

ProSearch 4.0 Top Stock Report
Backtesting Report
8/01/93–9/30/93

Stock Symbol/Company Name	Industry Group	Percent Gain over Period Tested
1> CU—CUC INTL INC	.TRZ	14.8%
2> SVM—SERVICEMASTER LTD PARTNERSHI	.TMS	3.6
3> ALGR—ALLIED GROUP INC	.TIM	21.3
4> TROW—PRICE T ROWE & ASSOCIATES	.TIN	13.6
5> ATML—ATMEL CORP	.TSM	35.3
6> WHO—WATERHOUSE INV SVCS INC COM	.TIB	49.6
7> SMP—STANDARD MTR PRODS INC	.TAT	−3.4
8> CMH—CLAYTON HOMES INC	.TMB	1.4
9> EAVN—EATON VANCE CORP	.TIN	6.9
10> BMC—BMC INDS INC MINN	.TPM	9.9
11> BQR—QUICK & REILLY GROUP DEL	.TIB	17.4
12> LLTC—LINEAR TECHNOLOGY CORP	.TSM	7.8
13> AB—ALEX BROWN INC COM	.TIB	24.8
14> MRCY—MERCURY GEN CORP NEW	.TIP	5.4
15> SCH—SCHWAB CHARLES CORP NEW	.TIB	17.9
16> JEFG—JEFFERIES GROUP INC	.TIB	16.1
17> BSC—BEAR STEARNS COS INC	.TIB	8.8
18> FAHC—FIRST AMERN HEATH CONCEPTS	.THM	10.8
19> ABX—AMERICAN BARRICK RES CORP	.TGM	−17.4
20> MDD—MCDONALD & CO INVTS INC	.TIB	5.6
21> BV—BLOCKBUSTER ENTMT CORP	.TRX	13.3
22> AMAT—APPLIED MATLS INC	.TSM	12.1
23> FNF—FIDELITY NATL FINL INC COM	.TIP	40.6
24> INTV—INTERVOICE INC	.TCX	52.1
25> HS—HEALTHSOURCE INC COM	.THM	12.0

Average Total	=	15.2
Dow Jones Industrial Average Total	=	−0.4
New York Stock Exchange Total	=	2.3
S&P 500 Total	=	1.9
NASDAQ Total	=	7.8
American Stock Exchange Total	=	5.4

Note: Scores for the indicators used in the search have been omitted to save space.

During that 45-day period, the Dow was down, and in fact, the only market index that even approached our return was the Nasdaq at 7.8 percent. Keep in mind, you are judging the stocks' performance against the market's performance. All we can ask of any search is that the stocks it finds outperform the market. Also note that all 25 stocks were used in the calculations; in real life, we would evaluate the search and select only those stocks that appear to have the best chances for growth, which should improve these returns.

HOW GOOD IS GOOD?

There are several ways to determine how good a backtested search is, before you try it out in real time. First, compare the average return of the stocks with the market returns, as we did here. The best search is one that outperforms the market by the largest percentage.

Next, look at the individual percentage gain or loss figures for each stock. If the search is valid, the stocks should move from highest gain to lowest gain (more or less) as you go down the list (this assumes a list of 25 or more stocks). In other words, the better-performing stocks should be collected near the top of the list, although you should, of course, allow for considerable variation among the individual stocks. If there doesn't seem to be any pattern at all, the search could possibly be improved, especially if your report contained at least 100 stocks.

Two of our backtests look very good in this regard. The first five stocks from both the momentum search (Exhibit 6.3) and undervalued growth search (Exhibit 6.2) have a higher average percentage return than their respective groups as a whole. The average return of the first five momentum stocks is 17.7 percent versus an average of 15.2 percent for group; the average return of the top five undervalued growth stocks is 14.4 percent versus 9.1 percent for the group.

The stocks from the insider buying search are less than ideally ranked. The first five stocks have an average loss of .5 percent versus an average gain of 20.3 percent for the group as a whole. But there are some outstanding performers, with returns of 50 to 177 percent. The fact that these are ranked 12 or lower would prompt us to take a careful look at their scores to see which indicators seem to be holding them down. Then we would refine the search to try to move these stocks closer to the top of the list. (See "Refining a Search" in this chapter.) Keep in mind that these three searches were backtested only on one market period. To prove any kind of real validity, a search should be tested over many different markets, as we discuss later in this chapter. The insider buying search, incidentally, was tested by others against many market periods, and despite its relative simplicity, it outperformed the market in all eight time periods tested.[2]

Another way to review a backtested search is to observe the number of losses versus the number of gains. This reveals the volatility of the search. Certain kinds of searches tend to produce a list of stocks with a considerable variance in the returns: a large number of big gainers but a larger number of big losers. If such a search produces a good overall result, it is probably a valid search, but you may not like its volatility. You would need to have considerable confidence in your ability to pick the winners from the losers. You might prefer to look for searches that produce more consistent results.

In our three backtested searches, the momentum search gave the most consistent results: Only two stocks out of 25 were negative. It would be easier to pick a winner from this group than from the insider trading search which produced six stocks that had gains over 40 percent (one exceeded 177 percent), but overall contained almost as many losers as winners.

REFINING A SEARCH

When evaluating a ProSearch report, it is only natural to pay more attention to the higher ranked stocks at the top of the list. After all, the stocks are ranked by how well they meet a set of objectives. But the ranking may not predict future performance as well as we would like. That's why we backtest a search: to verify its ability to predict future performance. After the initial backtesting, however, you may need to refine the search to improve its predictive ability.

The purpose of refining a search is to move the best-performing stocks—the ones with the highest percentage returns over the backtested period—as close as possible to the top of the list. Look at the backtested insider trading search in Exhibit 6.1. Several stock which have performed very well over the backtested period are ranked below the middle of the list: Best Buy, with a return of 177 percent, is ranked

---

[2] Mark Draud and Paul Alvim, *ProSearch Strategy Handbook, Volume II* (Houston: Telescan, 1994).

14; Baltimore Bancorp, with 74 percent is ranked 18; Park Electrochemical, with 95 percent, is ranked 20, and Spiegel, with 112 percent, is ranked 25. Closer inspection of these stocks revealed two anomalies. One, their relative P/E ratios were somewhat higher than stocks near the top of the list (we had asked for low scores on this indicator); and two, they had excellent one-month changes in projected earnings (we had asked for high scores but had weighted this indicator only 60 percent). Both of these indicators were used to score and rank the stocks, so we had two options: we could increase the weight on the one-month change indicator, so that ProSearch would use a higher percentage of that score in the ranking. Or, we could change the relative P/E ratio indicator to list-only, thereby eliminating it as a factor in the ranking.

We did both. As a result, three of the four high-performing stocks moved closer to the top of the list (Exhibit 6.4). Baltimore Bancorp moved from number 18 to number 2; Park Electrochemical, from number 20 to number 7; and Spiegel, from number 25 to number 15. (Best Buy remained at number 14.)

In general, when high-performing stocks are ranked below lesser performing stocks on a backtest, it is because they have lower scores on criteria for which you wanted high scores *or* have higher scores on criteria for which you wanted low scores, or both. To correct the situation, first try increasing or decreasing the weighting percentage on the score-and-rank indicator that to be at fault. Then rerun the search to see if the high-return stocks move up the list. If that doesn't do the job, eliminate the indicator or eliminate its effect on the search by changing it to list only. Be sure to rerun the backtest after each change so you can assess cause and effect.

Don't ignore the elimination indicators. The ranking of stocks is affected only by the score-and-rank indicators, but an indicator used to eliminate stocks might not be restrictive enough. Narrowing its range might weed out some of the less desirable stocks and allow the better stocks to move up. In contrast, switching an indicator from elimination to score-and-rank or list-only will widen the universe of stocks and might defeat your purposes.

Another way to test the effectiveness of a refinement is to look at the average performance of the top five stocks. It should increase after the refinement. In the original insider trading backtest (Exhibit 6.1), the top five stocks averaged a .5 percent loss; with the two refinements mentioned previously, the top five stocks in Exhibit 6.4 averaged 15.6 percent,

Exhibit 6.4   The top 25 stocks from the "refined" insider trading backtest for the 200-day period from 8/1/93 through 5/5/94.

ProSearch 4.0 Top Stock Report
Backtesting Report
8/01/93–5/05/94

Stock Symbol/Company Name	Industry Group	Percent Gain over Period Tested
1> GPI—GUARDSMAN PRODS INC	.TPN	−7.9%
2> BBB—BALTIMORE BANCORP	.TBS	74.1
3> BKSO—BANK SOUTH CORP	.TBS	32.4
4> KSF—QUAKER ST OIL REFNG CORP	.TOR	6.8
5> WAMU—WASHINGTON MUT SVGS BK SEATT	.TBW	−27.1
6> BBI—BARNETT BANKS FLA INC	.TBS	−4.8
7> PKE—PARK ELECTROCHEMICAL CORP	.TEZ	95.1
8> GROV—GROVE BK FOR SVGS MASS	.TBN	26.3
9> OKE—ONEOK INC	.TGD	−23.3
10> ONPR—ONE PRICE CLOTHING STORES IN	.TSS	50.1
11> GUN—GUNDLE ENVIRONMENTAL SYS INC	.TPC	−15.7
12> ITG—INTEGRA FINL CORP COM	.TBN	−3.2
13> VFBK—EASTERN BANCORP INC	.TSL	24.0
14> BBY—BEST BUY INC	.TDS	177.6
15> SPGLA—SPIEGEL INC CL A	.TRZ	112.8
16> UCIT—UNITED CITIES GAS CO	.TGD	−14.3
17> GY—GENCORP INC	.TDO	−17.5
18> ATVC—AMERICAN TRAVELLERS CORP	.TIA	9.7
19> PZL—PENNZOIL CO	.TUI	−26.3
20> SBK—SIGNET BKG CORP	.TBS	46.6
21> FRTH—FOURTH FINL CORP	.TBM	−3.0
22> INTC—INTEL CORP	.TSM	11.3
23> WMS—WMS INDS INC	.TRG	4.6
24> FFB—FIRST FID BANCORPORATION NEW	.TBN	−5.7
25> PLIT—PETROLITE CORP	.TCY	−3.7

Average Total	=	20.8
Dow Jones Industrial Average Total	=	3.6
New York Stock Exchange Total	=	0.4
S&P 500 Total	=	0.2
NASDAQ Total	=	4.7
American Stock Exchange Total	=	1.1

Note: Scores for the indicators used in the search have been omitted to save space.

significantly outperforming the market. Obviously, our refinements improved the search for the market on which it was tested.

It is not wise, however, to rely on a search that was backtested on a single market period. Once you have refined a search, test it again on several different time periods. Otherwise, you might be artificially forcing stocks to the top of the list in one time period when that adjustment might produce poor results over other time periods.

Refining a search is mostly a matter of trial and error. Make a few changes, and rerun the search after each change to see if the better stocks have moved toward the top of the list. Then test the refined search over different time periods. The better a search works on historical markets, the more confidence you will have when you use it in real life.

No Pain, No Gain?

Refining search may also mean weeding out highly volatile stocks. Look at the stock graph for Best Buy (Exhibit 6.5) from our insider trading search. It returned over 177 percent in 200 days, but you would have had a fairly bumpy ride from October 1993 through February 1994. Could you, would you, have held on for the whole ride? If the answer is no, it might be a good idea to check for volatility by viewing stock graphs of the highest performing stocks on your list. Backdate the graphs to the date of your theoretical purchase and take a look at the next six months to a year. You can see at a glance how much volatility you would have had to endure. If you decide you can handle the volatility, the stock graphs will give you some idea of how much leeway to give a stock when it starts to drop. If a search produces good results but delivers highly volatile stocks, you may want to put a volatility indicator in your search and require "the lower, the better."

TEST, TEST, AND TEST AGAIN

The most important test of a search's validity is how well it performs over *many* historical periods. Be sure to test it on some past bearish markets and flat markets and see what happens. You might have accidently backtested a roaring bull market (like the one that began in September 1992), when most stocks did well. A search that does well in a bull market might stumble in a flat market and fall flat on its face in front of the bears.

Exhibit 6.5   A graph for Best Buy Company from the insider trading back-test. Note the volatility in the middle of the test period (November 1993 to February 1994).

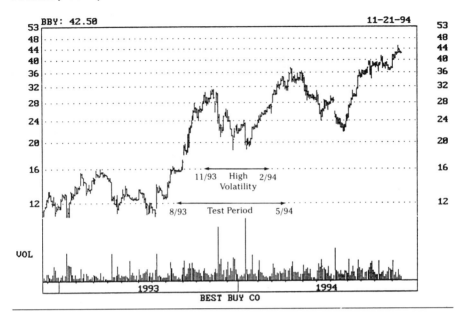

We recommend using at least six periods for every backtest:

- A short bullish market.
- A long bullish market.
- A short bearish market.
- A long bearish market.
- Two flat markets.

If your search is designed to find quick, short-term profits, as the momentum search is, it probably doesn't make sense to test it on the two long periods. Furthermore, you may want to consider developing a search that does particularly well in a specific kind of market, such as a good bull market search or a good bear market search. If so, you would test the bull market search only against bullish periods and the

HOW DO YOU TELL A BULL FROM A BEAR?

In real life, it is sometimes hard to know whether you are in a bull market, a bear market, or a sideways market. A 20-point drop might be a
correction in a bull market, a dip in a sideways market, or the first
growl of the approaching bears. In hindsight, however, we all have
20-20 vision. To find past bull and bear markets, all you have to do is
look at a graph of one of the market indexes, which can be done with
any stock analysis program.

   If you like smaller cap stocks, print a graph of the Nasdaq index
(Chart 1) over the past two years, or whatever period of time is available for backtesting. If you're interested in large cap stocks, use the
New York Stock Exchange Index (Chart 2) or the S&P 500 index. (The
Dow, with only 30 blue chip stocks, is too narrow an index for market analysis.) Use a pencil to mark on the graph the down periods,
the up periods, and the sideways periods. Then backtest your search
over the various periods.

**Chart 1   A two-year graph of the Nasdaq market index showing bullish,
bearish and flat market periods.**

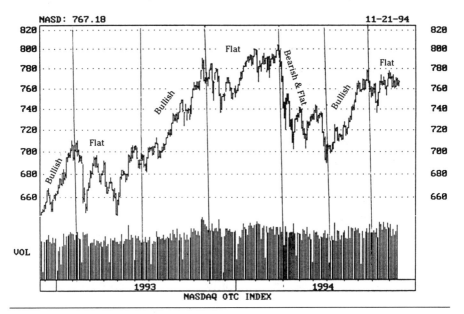

Chart 2   A two-year graph of the New York Stock Exchange index showing bullish, bearish and flat market periods.

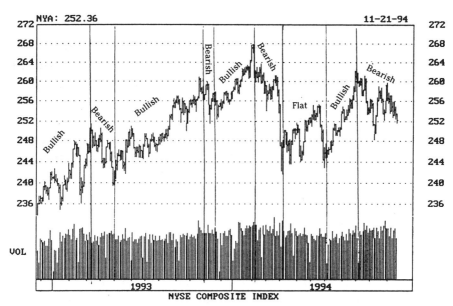

bear market search only against bearish periods. We prefer a search that works well over various markets, because it is often difficult, in a current market, to tell the bulls from the bears. Nevertheless, you may wish to try.

When you are backtesting a search, keep in mind that almost any search will appear to do well in a bull market. The question becomes one of degree. Whatever profits you make, you can expect to make most of them during bull markets, so you want a search that will double or re-double your efforts during those prime markets. A good bull market search, then, should outperform the market; an outstanding bull market search should outperform it by a large degree. A bear market is a different story. You're basically just trying to hold on to your capital when the market is retreating, and a search that simply breaks even should serve you well.

YOU MUST REMEMBER THIS . . .

Here are some hints for successful backtesting:

- In general, technical indicators are predictive over shorter periods than fundamental indicators. So judge them accordingly when you backtest a search. (Technical indicators measure price movement and price patterns; fundamental indicators measure the basic health and viability of a company.) For example, if you're using a technical indicator that generates buy and sell signals every two weeks, test the performance over 15 days or so. For searches based on fundamental indicators, such as the insider buying or undervalued growth searches, test the results over six months or a year.

- Start with a simple search using your favorite indicator. Then add one indicator at a time to see how it changes the results.

- Tailor the backtest to your own goals. If you are particularly averse to risk, be sure to test your searches against a number of bear markets.

- Notice whether a search produces widely varying results—big losers as well as big gainers. Such volatility may or may not suit your taste.

- If the higher performing stocks are clustered near the bottom of the list, refine your search strategy to coax them toward the top.

- Test a search against six or more market periods, being sure to include bear markets and sideways markets.

- If you're technically inclined, have a backtesting contest among the various technical indicators (testing one indicator at a time). You'll quickly see which ones have done well in the past.

- Discard searches that don't backtest well. If you backtest a search over half a dozen periods and it never does well, forget it. No matter how much you like it, if it doesn't do well in the past, it probably won't do well in the future when you're putting your money on it.

- A good search is one that outperforms the market. That's really all you're looking for in a backtest. You can match the market, remember, by throwing darts or buying broad-based mutual funds. So the best search is the one that consistently outperforms the market.

Keep in mind that backtesting results assume the purchase of every stock on the list. In the next chapter, we will discuss various tools that can be used to try to eliminate what would be the "worst" companies on a search report, and thereby, improve the results. The point is, if you can find a search that tests better than the market, it should do even better when you qualify the stocks on the list.

7

STAGE ONE EVALUATION

A search report is like a list of job candidates being considered for an important position. They represent the top one-half of one percent of all candidates. They all meet the basic qualifications: Each has the education, the skills, and the experience to do a good job. Each embodies the personal qualities needed for success. They seem to be equal in most respects, but there is only one job. Obviously, the candidates musts be evaluated further to find one who has an edge over the others. It is the same with a search report. With stocks, as well as with job candidates, some are more equal than others.

In Chapters 7 and 8, we are going to show you some computerized tools that make this evaluation process easy. We have divided the process into two stages. In this chapter, which describes Stage One, we will use the information retrieved during the search to compare various characteristics of each stock. The 10 to 12 stocks that make the first cut will become candidates for the hands-on evaluation of Stage Two, described in the next chapter. There, we'll introduce several research and analysis tools to help further narrow the list to three or four finalists. Finally, in Chapter 9, we'll show you how to decide which one of the finalists to buy.

GATHERING THE DATA

In Stage One of our evaluation, we will let the search program gather the data. We will add several list-only indicators to our original search in order to retrieve information for the evaluation. Then we will compare each score for all the stocks on the list. Stocks with the most negative scores will be eliminated; stocks with the most positive scores will become candidates for the Stage Two evaluation.

In our original undervalued growth search, we used 13 indicators to eliminate undesirable stocks and then to score and rank the remaining stocks. Those indicators represented our most important objectives, and they gave us a working list of 25 top stocks that match our goals. (We limited the list to 25 stocks for this book; it is better to look at 50 or even 100 stocks from each search.) For this Stage One evaluation, we will add a group of list-only indicators that we consider secondary in importance in their ability to meet our goals, but important nevertheless. They will help us determine which of the stocks are the better candidates for our purposes. Please note that we are not doing two searches here. The list-only indicators are selected at the same time as the primary indicators that control the search, and only one search is run. We are explaining them separately for clarity.

The indicators that we've chosen to list information for our Stage One evaluation are:

Debt-to-equity ratio.

5-year earnings growth rate.

5-year cash flow growth rate.

One-month change in projected EPS growth rate.

P/E ratio.

Relative P/E ratio.

Company growth ratio.

Insider trading.

No. of analysts following the company.

Price rank.

EPS rank.

5-day-to-30-day average volume.

Accumulation/distribution.

Like the other indicators in our strategy, these list-only indicators represent a purely arbitrary selection on our part; we'll explain each one as we go through the evaluation. If you're more technically inclined, you might wish to add several technical indicators. Or you may prefer different ones altogether—there's plenty of room to add your favorites.

The entire search strategy appears in Exhibit 7.1. It contains the 13 indicators from the previous chapter and the 13 indicators shown above, plus stock price. The search report (see Exhibit 7.3 on pages 105–108) lists 25 stocks, instead of 10, and all 27 indicators; otherwise, it is identical to the previous undervalued growth search. The list-only indicators did not affect the search, but they retrieved information to help us in our evaluation.

LOW-TECH TOOLS IN A HIGH-TECH WORLD

The Stage One evaluation is very low tech. At this point, we will set aside our computerized tools and pick up a pen. We will circle good scores and X-out bad scores on our working list of stocks. You may use any kind of system for this evaluation: checkmarks, pluses and minuses, pink and yellow highlight pens, whatever. The point is to be able to easily distinguish the good scores from the bad scores. If your search returned 50 or 100 stocks (as we recommend), you will need a system that makes it easy to spot the potential winners.

A Few Pointers before We Continue . . .

Before we go on, we would like to point out several things:

- Don't concentrate only on the top several stocks on the list. All the stocks are all *relatively* good. All scored well on the standards imposed by the search, so there may be only a very fuzzy line between the merits of, say, number 4 and number 14. As we go through the two-stage evaluation, that fuzzy difference should come into sharper focus. The point is, these stocks are the top 25

Exhibit 7.1   The complete search request for undervalued growth stocks, including the list-only indicators.

Indicators	Action: The Basic Search
10-Yr LSQ Deviation (10Ldv)	Eliminate stocks that aren't at least 10% below their LSQ line
10-Yr LSQ Deviation (10Ldv)	The lower, the better 100%
10-Yr Price Growth Rate (10$Gr)	The higher, the better 80%
5-Yr Projected EPS Growth Rate (5yPEG)	The higher, the better 100%

Indicators	Action: Narrow the Universe
8/17/9 Weekly MACD (Mc8wC)	Eliminate stocks that aren't technically positive
3-Week Relative Performance (3-Wk)	Eliminate stocks that have not had a positive move within the past 3 weeks
Group Rank (GrpRk)	Eliminate stocks below 50% ranking

Indicators	Action: Seasoning
3-Yr LSQ Deviation (3LDv)	The lower, the better 60%
Quarter-over-Quarter Earnings—Most Recent Quarter (%cELt)	The higher, the better 80%
Quarter-over-Quarter Earnings—Second Most Recent Quarter (%cE-2)	The higher, the better 60%
3-Wk Price Rank Change (c$-3)	The higher, the better 80%
6-Wk Price Rank Change (c$-6)	The higher, the better 40%
3-Wk Group Rank Change (cGRP3)	The higher, the better 20%

Indicators	Action: List Information
Debt-to-Equity Ratio (%D/Eq)	List only
5-Yr Earnings Growth Rate (5YrEg)	List only
5-Yr Cash Flow Growth Rate (5YrCf)	List only
One-Month Change in Earnings Estimates (1mEGC)	List only
P/E Ratio (P/E)	List only
Relative P/E Ratio (RelPE)	List only
Company Growth Ratio (GrRat)	List only
Insider Buying (Insdr)	List only
Number of Analysts Following Company (#AnCF)	List only
Price Rank ($Rank)	List only
EPS Rank (EPSRk)	List only
5-to-30-Day Average Volume (5-30)	List only
Accumulation/Distribution (Ac/Dst)	List only
Stock Price (Price)	List only

stocks out of 9,000 (top one-half of one percent of all listed stocks); therefore, there are relatively small differences between the number 1 stock and the number 25 stock.

- During this Stage One evaluation, we are considering only the scores for the list-only indicators. The other scores have already done their jobs by eliminating or ranking the stocks. And, we're looking only for extremes. In our rating system, very good scores merit a circle; very bad scores, an X. Some scores may not fit either extreme, so we may end up with a number of stocks without circles or X's. We'll probably ignore those, because in picking our top 10 or 12 candidates—the semifinalists—we will be looking for stocks that have a preponderance of extremely good scores (lots of circles).

- The ProSearch report lists two scores for each indicator: the "raw score," such as the actual P/E ratio, and the "percentile rank," which is always shown in parentheses. The percentile rank reveals where the stock is ranked on that indicator, compared with all other stocks; possible rankings are 0 to 99. In the following evaluation, we will tell you whether to judge the raw score or the percentile rank.

- With regard to the percentile rank, if "higher is better," 99 would be the best score; if "lower is better," zero (0) would be the best score.

- When we evaluate a stock based on its raw score, such as relative P/E ratio, we will tell you what we consider to be an acceptable score.

- Space limitations prevent us from including our evaluation of all 25 stocks from the undervalued growth search. So we'll use just two stocks to illustrate the low-tech analysis: Telephone & Data Systems (TDS), listed as number 1 on the report, and CML Group (CML), listed as number 3. The completed evaluation of these two stocks is shown in Exhibit 7.2.

We now have a list of undervalued growth stocks in front of us. We have a pen at the ready. Let's begin.

Exhibit 7.2   Two stocks from the undervalued growth search reflecting the Stage One evaluation.

1> TDS—TELEPHONE & DATA SYS

Debt/Equity	41	(77)
5Yr Earnings Growth	10	(55)
5Yr Cash Flow Growth	8.7	(63)
Upward Revision in Earnings Est.	(2.3)	(91)
P/E Ratio	✗	(91)
Relative P/E	41	(58)
Growth Ratio	0.9	(30)
Insider Buying	0.0	(87)
Number of Analysts	(7.0)	(74)
Price Rank	100	(59)
EPS Rank	89	(80)
5-30-Day Average Volume	80	(42)
Accumulation/Dist.	59	(52)
Stock Price	41	(91)

3> CML—CML GROUP

Debt/Equity	25	(72)
5Yr Earnings Growth	(44)	(85)
5Yr Cash Flow Growth	(77)	(98)
Upward Revision in Earnings Est.	−✗	(5)
P/E Ratio	(7.3)	(7)
Relative P/E	(17)	(30)
Growth Ratio	(2.9)	(93)
Insider Buying	0.0	(87)
Number of Analysts	(12)	(86)
Price Rank	83	✗
EPS Rank	94	(89)
5-30-Day Average Volume	✗	(12)
Accumulation/Dist.	✗	(13)
Stock Price	9.4	(37)

TOOLS TO CONFIRM FUNDAMENTAL STRENGTH

We will start with the nine indicators that we used to extract more information about the fundamental strength of a company: debt-to-equity ratio, 5-year earnings growth rate, 5-year cash flow growth rate, one-month change in projected EPS growth rate, P/E ratio, relative P/E ratio, company growth ratio, insider trading, and the number of analysts following the company.

Low Debt

If you have two equally good stocks, why buy the one with the extra risk of high debt? ProSearch states the debt-to-equity ratio as a percentage; a score of 100 means that the company's debt is 100 percent of its equity, or 1 to 1; a score above 100 means the debt-to-equity is more than 1 to 1; a score below 100, less than 1 to 1. We consider as high a debt-to-equity ratio of more than 1 to 1, so we'll draw a big X over any score above 100 percent; we'll circle scores of 20 percent or lower.

On our list, both TDS, at 41 percent, and CML, at 25 percent, fall between our extremes; neither gets a mark.

Good Earnings Trend

Good growth stocks generally have a history of good earnings, so we'll check out the 5-year earnings growth indicator. Circle any scores above 20 percent; X out any scores below 10 percent. Ignore scores of "N/A," which means that 5-year earnings weren't available. If such a stock should make it to the next stage because of other high scores, we suggest that you take a look at its earnings over the past year or two.

On our list, TDS scrapes by with a 10 (no mark); CML gets a circle for its 5-year growth rate of 44 percent.

Cash Counts

The bottom line in business is to generate cash. So we like to compare a company's cash flow growth rate with its earnings growth rate. If the growth of cash flow is substantially higher than the growth of earnings—for example, cash flow at 25 percent and earnings at 15 percent—that's good. If cash flow is significantly lower—say, 5 percent to earnings of 20 percent—that's bad.

TDS's cash flow growth rate is only slightly below its 10 percent earnings growth rate for five years, so it doesn't get any mark. CML has a 5-year cash flow growth rate that is almost double its 5-year earnings growth (77 to 44), which gets it a circle.

Up with Estimates

In our insider trading search, we talked about the importance of upward revisions of earnings estimates by Wall Street analysts. A revision upward may cause the stock price to go up; a revision downward may take the stock price down. It makes sense, then, to take a hard look at this score. Circle any positive number; X-out any negative number. (Many stocks will have zeros for this indicator because there were no revisions of the estimates.)

TDS wins a circle, with a 2.3 percent upward revision; CML is branded X for its substantial downward revision of 14 percent.

P/E Again

The importance of P/E ratio was established in Chapter 2, along with the danger of extremely high or extremely low P/E's. For this evaluation, we will consider P/E ratios under 5 and over 35 to be undesirable (give them an X). Circle any P/E ratio from 7 to 14; in general, that would be below the market multiple and thus have a better than average chance of moving up. (The average market P/E has ranged from 5 to 20 or so; as of this writing, it is about 14.)

TDS gets an X for its P/E ratio of 53; CML gets a circle for a low P/E of 7.3.

. . . and Again

We talked about relative P/E ratio in the insider trading search in Chapter 5. Relative P/E tells us how a stock's current P/E ratio measures up against its own history, whether it is higher or lower than it has ever been. We've used it in this search to confirm a company's undervaluation (the lower the relative P/E, the more likely the stock is undervalued). Thus, we'll circle relative P/E ratios of 30 or below and draw an X through scores of 70 or above.

We can ignore TDS's relative P/E of 41 percent: too high for a circle, too low for an X. CML's P/E ratio is only 17 percent of its all-time high; it has lots of room to grow, so we'll give it a circle.

. . . and Again

How much bang do you get for your buck? The company growth ratio will tell you. Basically, it is the price you pay for growth. It is calculated by dividing the 5-year projected earnings growth rate by the projected P/E ratio. (Projected P/E is the P/E ratio that will exist at the end of the next fiscal year if the company meets its earnings projections.) A projected EPS growth rate of 10 over a projected P/E ratio of 10 would give a company growth ratio of 1; a projected EPS growth rate of 20 over a projected P/E of 10 would give a company growth ratio of 2. The higher growth ratio is better. Most stocks fall in the 0.6 to 2.0 range, so in our evaluation, we'll circle any score above 1.2 and cross out anything below 0.8.

In our examples, TDS is in the average range, at 0.9, (no mark) while CML is higher than average, at 2.9 (circle).

The Magic Touch

We have already extolled the merits of insider buying, which is why we want to look at what the insiders are doing. Recall that ProSearch's inside trading indicator subtracts insider sales from insider purchases to give the *net* insider purchases for a company. Thus, a positive figure indicates more insider buying than selling; a negative figure, more insider selling than buying. We will circle any positive figure and draw an X through any negative figure.

What if you find insider selling on an otherwise virtuous stock? Don't be too quick to throw it out. People often sell stocks just because they need the money. Insider selling should be considered a red flag that tells you to check out the conditions. Look at the insider text report (if you're using Telescan) to find out who is selling and how much. If the president, vice president, and chairman are unloading half their shares, that's cause for alarm. If a couple of insiders are selling a small percentage of their holdings, it's probably a nonevent.

Neither TDS nor CML has insiders buying their stock.

How Many Elves Does It Take to . . .

As discussed earlier, this indicator tells us how many analysts follow the company. The more there are, the more confidence we have in the projected earnings growth of a company. If five or six different analysts say that the company's earnings are going to grow at a certain rate, that is more credible than if only one or two say it. How many analysts we require for comfort—and how we distribute our circles and X's—depends on how conservative we are. Some investors might feel better with 8 or 10 analysts; we would be happy with 5. Therefore, we'll circle scores of 5 or higher and X out scores of zero or N/A.

Both TDS and CML are well represented by analysts. Both get circles with 7 and 12, respectively.

TOOLS TO CONFIRM PERFORMANCE

Next we'll look at a couple of performance indicators—price rank and EPS rank—to see if the stock is indeed on its way up.

The Price Is Right

We talked about price rank in our earlier momentum search. It measures a stock's quarterly price performance over a year, with a bias to the most recent three months, and compares its momentum with all other stocks. If the price rank is in the top 25 percent, the stock is a performance leader; if the price rank is in lower 25 percent, the stock has lost its steam. With that in mind, we will circle *percentile ranks* (the number in parentheses) of 75 and above, and give X's to ranks of 25 or below.

TDS has a price rank of 59, not high enough for a circle; CML is ranked in the 6th percentile, which rates an X.

. . . So Are Earnings

Just as the price rank indicator measures price momentum, the EPS rank indicator measures a company's earnings momentum against all other companies. It uses the weighted sum of various EPS growth rates over the past five years, biased for the most recent quarter. Look at the *percentile rank:* 75 or above gets a circle; 25 or below gets an X.

Both TDS and CML have considerable earnings momentum, with percentile ranks of 80 and 89, respectively. Both get circles.

TOOLS TO DETECT INSTITUTIONAL INTEREST

Finally, we'll look at two tools that point to an increasing level of interest by institutional investors: the 5-to-30-day average volume indicator and the accumulation/distribution indicator. This is important to know

because when institutions move into a stock en masse, P/E's often rise—
and finding stocks with rising P/E's is the ultimate goal of our search.

High Volume Rising

Increasing volume is obviously a sign of increasing interest in a stock, be
it institutional or otherwise. The 5-to-30-day average volume indicator
compares the average volume over the last five days with the average volume over 30 days. Any number much over 150 percent would be a sign of
increasing interest and would get a circle. A number under 50 percent
would get an X because, right now at least, the stock isn't attracting much
attention.

CML gets an X for its low volume of 39 percent; TDS falls in the neutral range, at 80.

Here Come the Big Guns

The accumulation/distribution indicator, which we used in the momentum search in Chapter 5, tells us whether money is flowing into or out of
a stock, as compared with all other stocks. Generally speaking, if the highest volume occurs on up days, money is flowing into the stock. We interpret this to mean institutions are accumulating the stock. On the other
hand, if the highest volume occurs on down days, money is flowing out of
the stock (institutions are selling, we assume). Scores 60 or above get a
circle; 40 or below, an X.

At 59, TDS is only slightly below the minimum. If it came down to
the wire, however, we would take a closer look. CML is clearly under distribution with its score of 20, which earns it an X.

THE TOP TEN LIST

We now have a search report filled with circles and X's (we could show
only two stocks as examples in Exhibit 7.12). To select candidates for the
next stage of the evaluation, we will:

- Cross off stocks that have a preponderance of X's in their scores.
- Circle stocks that have multiple circles. These are the candidates
  that we'll take on to the next stage.

And the winners are:

No. 1	Telephone & Data Systems (TDS)
No. 4	Wausau Paper Mills (WSAU)
No. 5	Wal-Mart Stores (WMT)
No. 6	Surgical Care (SCA)
No. 11	Lin Broadcasting (LINB)
No. 12	Nordson Corp (NDSN)
No. 15	Paxar Corp. (PXR)
No. 19	Kroger Co. (KR)
No. 20	Stryker Corp. (STRY)
No. 21	Datascope Corp. (DSCP)

Notice that of the two stocks we used to illustrate this process, only TDS made the cut. So what happened to CML? It had 7 circles to TDS's three! Did CML's four X's outweigh TDS's single bad score? Not really. It was the importance of one particular bad score that eliminated CML. As you will see, the factors that affect our decision are not always equal.

The X that eliminated CML was the downward revision in its earnings estimates. If you'll recall, an upward revision in estimates is one of the best harbingers of stock price increases. The reverse is also true. A downward revision signals a possible drop in stock price. If 12 experts say they don't think the company's earnings are going to increase as much as they previously thought, as in CML's case, that's bad news for the stock. CML also had another fairly important negative: the small showing of institutional interest, based on its low volume and low accumulation/distribution score.

A mixture of good and bad scores in this evaluation process is common. Very often, even the best stocks have one or two bad scores, and in fact, six of our ten finalists had one or more X's. Of course, you don't have to limit your finalists to ten at this stage, which we did for space considerations. There were other stocks from the search which we normally would have evaluated more closely. For example, Research Industries scored very well on all our criteria, but there were more insiders selling than buying and no upward revision in earnings estimates. A closer look might have overridden these negatives.

In the end, you have to weigh the importance of the bad scores against the preponderance of the good. If a relatively unimportant score gets thumbs down, you can safely ignore it. But take heed if it is a factor you consider important. After all, you might buy a car without air bags, but you wouldn't buy one without brakes.

YOU MUST REMEMBER THIS . . .

Never take a search at face value. Computerized search products are valuable and powerful tools, but they simply compare or calculate raw data. Any list of stocks found by a search should be evaluated further, whether you use our method or one of your own. Here are a few points to keep in mind.

- All the tools described in this chapter reflect our philosophical bent.

- Use as many list-only indicators as you have room for in a search. (For space considerations, we limited ourselves to 14 in this chapter.) If you use 10 or 12 indicators to eliminate and rank stocks, you could conceivably use as many as 28 to 30 to list information for evaluation.

- In the Stage One evaluation, concentrate only on extreme scores. The objective is to eliminate the very worst stocks on the list and carry the very best ones on to the next evaluation.

- Be sure you're judging the right score. In some cases, you'll want to look at the raw score; in other cases, at the percentile rank.

- In most cases, an "N/A" score means that the data was not available, or there were pieces of data (such as negative numbers) which make up a calculation that cause the score to be invalid.

- Use common sense in evaluating the list-only scores. There are no "right" answers, except in retrospect.

- As you gain experience, you should get a feel for which secondary indicators are the most important. At some point, you might consider using some of the more important ones to eliminate or score the stocks on your list, rather than just to list information.

- Remember, you can judge the value of individual indicators by backtesting them against previous markets.

Let's go on to the analysis tools that we use to judge the stocks that made our top ten list. Our goal, remember, is to end up with the crème de la crème—the three or four finalists in the search for spectacular returns.

Exhibit 7.3   The top 25 stocks from the undervalued growth search. This is the same as the search report in Exhibit 5.4, except it includes 25 stocks, instead of 10, and shows the list-only indicators.

ProSearch 4.0 Top Stock Report

8/02/94

```
1> TDS      - TELEPHONE & DATA SYS                .TTE
     %cELt= 44       ( 91)    10LDv= -42    (  6)    10LDv= -42    (  6)
     %cE-2= 28       ( 86)    3LDv = -11    ( 32)    Mc8wC= 98     ( 96)
     c$-3 = 5.4      ( 88)    5yPEG= 31     ( 93)    3-Wk = 115    ( 92)
     c$-6 = 3.8      ( 81)    10$Gr= 29     ( 95)    GrpRk= 101    ( 76)
     cGRP3= -0.3     ( 26)    %D/Eq= 41     ( 77)    5YrEg= 10     ( 55)
     5YrCf= 8.7      ( 63)    1mEGC= 2.3    ( 91)    P/E  = 53     ( 91)
     RelPE= 41       ( 58)    GrRat= 0.9    ( 30)    Insdr= 0.0    ( 87)
     #AnCF= 7.0      ( 74)    $Rank= 100    ( 59)    EPSRk= 89     ( 80)
     AcDst= 59       ( 52)    Price= 41     ( 91)    5/30= 77.7    ( 41)
2> GGTI     - GTI CORP                              .TEZ
     %cELt= -60      ( 62)    10LDv= -29    ( 13)    10LDv= -29    ( 13)
     %cE-2= -57      ( 63)    3LDv = -54    (  1)    Mc8wC= 132    ( 98)
     c$-3 = 7.2      ( 91)    5yPEG= 20     ( 74)    3-Wk = 117    ( 93)
     c$-6 = 8.8      ( 91)    10$Gr= 24     ( 92)    GrpRk= 98     ( 55)
     cGRP3= 2.8      ( 84)    %D/Eq= 5.0    ( 64)    5YrEg= 53     ( 88)
     5YrCf= N/A      (   )    1mEGC= -16    (  4)    P/E  = 12     ( 32)
     RelPE= 3.1      (  6)    GrRat= 2.2    ( 87)    Insdr= 1.0    ( 92)
     #AnCF= 5.0      ( 65)    $Rank= 88     ( 10)    EPSRk= 54     ( 46)
     AcDst= 48       ( 44)    Price= 12     ( 54)    5/30= 41.1    ( 14)
3> CML      - CML GROUP                             .TLP
     %cELt= 13       ( 81)    10LDv= -53    (  3)    10LDv= -53    (  3)
     %cE-2= 14       ( 80)    3LDv = -60    (  0)    Mc8wC= 7.0    ( 19)
     c$-3 = 5.2      ( 88)    5yPEG= 19     ( 68)    3-Wk = 104    ( 74)
     c$-6 = 1.4      ( 68)    10$Gr= 31     ( 95)    GrpRk= 100    ( 67)
     cGRP3= -1.8     ( 14)    %D/Eq= 25     ( 72)    5YrEg= 44     ( 85)
     5YrCf= 77       ( 98)    1mEGC= -14    (  5)    P/E  = 7.3    (  7)
     RelPE= 17       ( 30)    GrRat= 2.9    ( 93)    Insdr= 0.0    ( 87)
     #AnCF= 12       ( 86)    $Rank= 83     (  6)    EPSRk= 94     ( 89)
     AcDst= 20       ( 13)    Price= 9.4    ( 37)    5/30= 46      ( 17)
4> WSAU     - WAUSAU PAPER MILLS                    .TPA
     %cELt= 9.3      ( 79)    10LDv= -39    (  8)    10LDv= -39    (  8)
     %cE-2= 6.2      ( 77)    3LDv = -16    ( 22)    Mc8wC= 39     ( 83)
     c$-3 = 2.6      ( 78)    5yPEG= 16     ( 59)    3-Wk = 104    ( 74)
     c$-6 = 1.4      ( 68)    10$Gr= 39     ( 97)    GrpRk= 104    ( 87)
     cGRP3= 5.3      ( 96)    %D/Eq= 14     ( 68)    5YrEg= 16     ( 65)
     5YrCf= N/A      (   )    1mEGC= 2.4    ( 91)    P/E  = 15     ( 47)
     RelPE= 58       ( 72)    GrRat= 1.4    ( 62)    Insdr= 1.0    ( 92)
     #AnCF= 3.0      ( 50)    $Rank= 96     ( 24)    EPSRk= 76     ( 71)
     AcDst= 29       ( 25)    Price= 24     ( 81)    5/30= 51.8    ( 26)
5> WMT      - WAL-MART STORES                       .TDP
     %cELt= 10       ( 79)    10LDv= -37    (  8)    10LDv= -37    (  8)
     %cE-2= 15       ( 81)    3LDv = -5.2   ( 57)    Mc8wC= 54     ( 90)
     c$-3 = 2.5      ( 77)    5yPEG= 19     ( 67)    3-Wk = 104    ( 76)
     c$-6 = 1.5      ( 69)    10$Gr= 29     ( 95)    GrpRk= 98     ( 52)
     cGRP3= 1.7      ( 63)    %D/Eq= 86     ( 86)    5YrEg= 21     ( 71)
     5YrCf= 22       ( 85)    1mEGC= 0.0    ( 81)    P/E  = 24     ( 74)
     RelPE= 34       ( 51)    GrRat= 1.1    ( 44)    Insdr= 0.0    ( 87)
     #AnCF= 38       ( 99)    $Rank= 99     ( 48)    EPSRk= 90     ( 81)
     AcDst= 60       ( 54)    Price= 25     ( 82)    5/30= 85.4    ( 48)
6> SCA      - SURGICAL CARE AFFIL                   .THC
     %cELt= 10       ( 79)    10LDv= -62    (  1)    10LDv= -62    (  1)
     %cE-2= 5.0      ( 76)    3LDv = 21     ( 92)    Mc8wC= 73     ( 94)
     c$-3 = 13       ( 97)    5yPEG= 18     ( 67)    3-Wk = 113    ( 91)
     c$-6 = 15       ( 96)    10$Gr= 50     ( 97)    GrpRk= 100    ( 71)
     cGRP3= 2.6      ( 81)    %D/Eq= 34     ( 75)    5YrEg= 41     ( 84)
     5YrCf= 38       ( 94)    1mEGC= 0.0    ( 81)    P/E  = 18     ( 58)
     RelPE= 6.6      ( 13)    GrRat= 1.4    ( 62)    Insdr= 8.0    ( 99)
     #AnCF= 18       ( 93)    $Rank= 106    ( 82)    EPSRk= 91     ( 83)
     AcDst= 52       ( 47)    Price= 15     ( 66)    5/30= 83.6    ( 47)
```

Exhibit 7.3 (continued)

```
 7> CCON   - CIRCON CORP                        .TMI
    %cELt= 450    ( 99)   10LDv= -44    (  5)   10LDv= -44    (  5)
    %cE-2= -45    ( 63)   3LDv = 0.0    ( 74)   Mc8wC= 27     ( 76)
    c$-3 = 6.3    ( 90)   5yPEG= 18     ( 67)   3-Wk = 108    ( 85)
    c$-6 = 4.0    ( 81)   10$Gr= 14     ( 78)   GrpRk= 99     ( 61)
    cGRP3= 2.0    ( 72)   %D/Eq= 0.0    ( 58)   5YrEg= 86     ( 94)
    5YrCf= N/A    (   )   1mEGC= -22    (  3)   P/E  = 38     ( 86)
    RelPE= 8.9    ( 17)   GrRat= 1.4    ( 62)   Insdr= -2.0   (  7)
    #AnCF= 2.0    ( 38)   $Rank= 95     ( 22)   EPSRk= 58     ( 50)
    AcDst= 23     ( 17)   Price= 9.5    ( 37)   5/30= 24.8    (  5)
 8> CEFT   - CONCORD EFS                         .TFB
    %cELt= 10     ( 79)   10LDv= -45    (  5)   10LDv= -45    (  5)
    %cE-2= -3.6   ( 71)   3LDv = 4.1    ( 80)   Mc8wC= 38     ( 82)
    c$-3 = 8.0    ( 92)   5yPEG= 22     ( 80)   3-Wk = 113    ( 90)
    c$-6 = 2.9    ( 77)   10$Gr= 52     ( 97)   GrpRk= 98     ( 55)
    cGRP3= -0.5   ( 24)   %D/Eq= 3.8    ( 63)   5YrEg= 26     ( 76)
    5YrCf= 14     ( 76)   1mEGC= -0.9   ( 20)   P/E  = 27     ( 78)
    RelPE= 42     ( 59)   GrRat= 1.2    ( 50)   Insdr= 0.0    ( 87)
    #AnCF= 5.0    ( 65)   $Rank= 102    ( 72)   EPSRk= 78     ( 74)
    AcDst= 44     ( 41)   Price= 25     ( 82)   5/30= 145.8   ( 75)
 9> GPI    - GUARDSMAN PRODUCTS                  .TPN
    %cELt= 43     ( 91)   10LDv= -27    ( 15)   10LDv= -27    ( 15)
    %cE-2= 25     ( 85)   3LDv = -20    ( 17)   Mc8wC= 22     ( 69)
    c$-3 = 3.0    ( 80)   5yPEG= 27     ( 88)   3-Wk = 106    ( 80)
    c$-6 = -2.2   ( 20)   10$Gr= 8.6    ( 56)   GrpRk= 99     ( 58)
    cGRP3= 1.8    ( 68)   %D/Eq= 41     ( 77)   5YrEg= -7.5   ( 27)
    5YrCf= -4.5   ( 25)   1mEGC= 0.0    ( 81)   P/E  = 15     ( 49)
    RelPE= 16     ( 30)   GrRat= 2.4    ( 89)   Insdr= 2.0    ( 95)
    #AnCF= 2.0    ( 38)   $Rank= 94     ( 18)   EPSRk= 96     ( 94)
    AcDst= 22     ( 16)   Price= 10     ( 46)   5/30= 70.9    ( 36)
10> TSS    - TOTAL SYSTEMS SVCS                  .TBU
    %cELt= 13     ( 81)   10LDv= -14    ( 28)   10LDv= -14    ( 28)
    %cE-2= 16     ( 81)   3LDv = -22    ( 14)   Mc8wC= 26     ( 75)
    c$-3 = 7.8    ( 92)   5yPEG= 17     ( 63)   3-Wk = 112    ( 89)
    c$-6 = -1.5   ( 24)   10$Gr= 17     ( 85)   GrpRk= 98     ( 55)
    cGRP3= 1.7    ( 63)   %D/Eq= 1.7    ( 61)   5YrEg= 15     ( 63)
    5YrCf= N/A    (   )   1mEGC= 0.0    ( 81)   P/E  = 33     ( 84)
    RelPE= 17     ( 31)   GrRat= 0.7    ( 18)   Insdr= 2.0    ( 95)
    #AnCF= 5.0    ( 65)   $Rank= 96     ( 25)   EPSRk= 89     ( 80)
    AcDst= 44     ( 41)   Price= 22     ( 78)   5/30= 34      (  9)
11> LINB   - LIN BROADCASTING                    .TTC
    %cELt= 66     ( 94)   10LDv= -14    ( 29)   10LDv= -14    ( 29)
    %cE-2= -0.7   ( 72)   3LDv = 0.9    ( 76)   Mc8wC= 176    ( 98)
    c$-3 = 0.9    ( 60)   5yPEG= 24     ( 83)   3-Wk = 103    ( 72)
    c$-6 = 1.9    ( 72)   10$Gr= 22     ( 91)   GrpRk= 102    ( 78)
    cGRP3= 2.4    ( 78)   %D/Eq= N/A    (   )   5YrEg= N/A    (   )
    5YrCf= N/A    (   )   1mEGC= 0.0    ( 81)   P/E  = N/A    (   )
    RelPE= N/A    (   )   GrRat= 0.2    (  2)   Insdr= 0.0    ( 87)
    #AnCF= 15     ( 91)   $Rank= 106    ( 83)   EPSRk= 90     ( 82)
    AcDst= 66     ( 66)   Price= 125    ( 95)   5/30= 60.5    ( 27)
12> NDSN   - NORDSON CORP                        .TMG
    %cELt= 21     ( 85)   10LDv= -20    ( 21)   10LDv= -20    ( 21)
    %cE-2= 17     ( 82)   3LDv = -2.2   ( 69)   Mc8wC= 10     ( 23)
    c$-3 = 2.7    ( 78)   5yPEG= 15     ( 53)   3-Wk = 102    ( 61)
    c$-6 = 2.9    ( 77)   10$Gr= 27     ( 94)   GrpRk= 100    ( 71)
    cGRP3= 5.0    ( 94)   %D/Eq= 23     ( 71)   5YrEg= 11     ( 57)
    5YrCf= 9.0    ( 63)   1mEGC= 0.4    ( 83)   P/E  = 24     ( 74)
    RelPE= 78     ( 87)   GrRat= 0.8    ( 24)   Insdr= -1.0   ( 11)
    #AnCF= 5.0    ( 65)   $Rank= 105    ( 80)   EPSRk= 87     ( 79)
    AcDst= 62     ( 58)   Price= 55     ( 93)   5/30= 33.8    (  9)
13> MCIC   - MCI COMMUNICATIONS                  .TTZ
    %cELt= 15     ( 82)   10LDv= -26    ( 16)   10LDv= -26    ( 16)
    %cE-2= 16     ( 81)   3LDv = -22    ( 15)   Mc8wC= 47     ( 88)
    c$-3 = 1.4    ( 69)   5yPEG= 15     ( 54)   3-Wk = 104    ( 76)
    c$-6 = 1.5    ( 69)   10$Gr= 24     ( 92)   GrpRk= 98     ( 55)
    cGRP3= -0.3   ( 26)   %D/Eq= 65     ( 83)   5YrEg= 9.8    ( 55)
    5YrCf= 3.3    ( 47)   1mEGC= 0.0    ( 81)   P/E  = 19     ( 62)
    RelPE= 17     ( 31)   GrRat= 1.1    ( 44)   Insdr= -2.0   (  7)
    #AnCF= 33     ( 99)   $Rank= 96     ( 26)   EPSRk= 76     ( 71)
    AcDst= 52     ( 47)   Price= 23     ( 80)   5/30= 107.2   ( 67)
```

Exhibit 7.3   (continued)

```
14> POSS    - POSSIS MEDICAL                      .TDO
      %cELt= 53      ( 92)   10LDv= -20    ( 21)   10LDv= -20     ( 21)
      %cE-2= -750    ( 56)   3LDv = -15    ( 24)   Mc8wC= 27      ( 76)
      c$-3 = 5.6     ( 89)   5yPEG= 20     ( 74)   3-Wk = 101     ( 57)
      c$-6 = 2.6     ( 76)   10$Gr= 5.3    ( 43)   GrpRk= 100     ( 74)
      cGRP3= 3.4     ( 89)   %D/Eq= 11     ( 67)   5YrEg= N/A     (   )
      5YrCf= N/A     (   )    1mEGC= 0.0    ( 81)   P/E  = N/A     (   )
      RelPE= N/A     (   )   GrRat= N/A     (   )    Insdr= 0.0     ( 87)
      #AnCF= 1.0     ( 21)   $Rank= 92     ( 14)   EPSRk= 28      ( 21)
      AcDst= 63      ( 60)   Price= 6.4    ( 25)   5/30= 73.6     ( 37)
15> PXR     - PAXAR CORP                          .TMG
      %cELt= -16     ( 68)   10LDv= -18    ( 23)   10LDv= -18     ( 23)
      %cE-2= -24     ( 66)   3LDv = -27    ( 10)   Mc8wC= 13      ( 27)
      c$-3 = 1.5     ( 70)   5yPEG= 20     ( 74)   3-Wk = 104     ( 76)
      c$-6 = -1.3    ( 25)   10$Gr= 36     ( 96)   GrpRk= 100     ( 71)
      cGRP3= 5.0     ( 94)   %D/Eq= 13     ( 68)   5YrEg= 28      ( 77)
      5YrCf= N/A     (   )    1mEGC= 2.5    ( 92)   P/E  = 21      ( 68)
      RelPE= 25      ( 41)   GrRat= 1.4    ( 62)   Insdr= 0.0     ( 87)
      #AnCF= 1.0     ( 21)   $Rank= 101    ( 65)   EPSRk= 62      ( 55)
      AcDst= 50      ( 45)   Price= 13     ( 61)   5/30= 167.8    ( 89)
16> MDT     - MEDTRONIC, INC                      .TMI
      %cELt= 18      ( 84)   10LDv= -23    ( 18)   10LDv= -23     ( 18)
      %cE-2= 25      ( 85)   3LDv = 13     ( 88)   Mc8wC= 160     ( 98)
      c$-3 = 3.4     ( 82)   5yPEG= 16     ( 58)   3-Wk = 105     ( 79)
      c$-6 = 4.9     ( 84)   10$Gr= 29     ( 95)   GrpRk= 99      ( 61)
      cGRP3= 2.0     ( 72)   %D/Eq= 3.0    ( 62)   5YrEg= 20      ( 70)
      5YrCf= 17      ( 80)   1mEGC= 0.0    ( 81)   P/E  = 21      ( 68)
      RelPE= 26      ( 41)   GrRat= 1.0    ( 37)   Insdr= -3.0    (  4)
      #AnCF= 27      ( 98)   $Rank= 110    ( 88)   EPSRk= 93      ( 88)
      AcDst= 38      ( 36)   Price= 87     ( 94)   5/30= 129.5    ( 78)
17> OII     - OCEANEERING INT'L                   .TOS
      %cELt= -47     ( 63)   10LDv= -31    ( 12)   10LDv= -31     ( 12)
      %cE-2= -34     ( 65)   3LDv = -7.0   ( 45)   Mc8wC= 44      ( 86)
      c$-3 = 2.1     ( 74)   5yPEG= 18     ( 64)   3-Wk = 104     ( 76)
      c$-6 = 5.3     ( 85)   10$Gr= 28     ( 94)   GrpRk= 106     ( 98)
      cGRP3= -1.3    ( 18)   %D/Eq= 0.3    ( 59)   5YrEg= 20      ( 70)
      5YrCf= N/A     (   )    1mEGC= -1.2   ( 19)   P/E  = 22      ( 70)
      RelPE= 31      ( 48)   GrRat= 1.4    ( 62)   Insdr= 0.0     ( 87)
      #AnCF= 11      ( 84)   $Rank= 104    ( 76)   EPSRk= 47      ( 39)
      AcDst= 68      ( 70)   Price= 14     ( 62)   5/30= 62.3     ( 29)
18> RBD     - RUBBERMAID, INC                     .TIR
      %cELt= 9.3     ( 79)   10LDv= -31    ( 12)   10LDv= -31     ( 12)
      %cE-2= 3.2     ( 75)   3LDv = -5.3   ( 56)   Mc8wC= 60      ( 91)
      c$-3 = 2.4     ( 76)   5yPEG= 13     ( 42)   3-Wk = 108     ( 85)
      c$-6 = 5.8     ( 86)   10$Gr= 19     ( 88)   GrpRk= 102     ( 82)
      cGRP3= 2.3     ( 76)   %D/Eq= 3.0    ( 62)   5YrEg= 11      ( 57)
      5YrCf= 10      ( 67)   1mEGC= 0.0    ( 81)   P/E  = 20      ( 66)
      RelPE= 40      ( 57)   GrRat= 0.8    ( 24)   Insdr= 3.0     ( 96)
      #AnCF= 18      ( 93)   $Rank= 100    ( 61)   EPSRk= 75      ( 70)
      AcDst= 31      ( 27)   Price= 28     ( 85)   5/30= 88.3     ( 50)
19> KR      - KROGER CO                           .TSU
      %cELt= 6.7     ( 78)   10LDv= -15    ( 28)   10LDv= -15     ( 28)
      %cE-2= 187     ( 97)   3LDv = 14     ( 89)   Mc8wC= 44      ( 86)
      c$-3 = 1.4     ( 69)   5yPEG= 18     ( 64)   3-Wk = 103     ( 69)
      c$-6 = 2.6     ( 76)   10$Gr= 25     ( 93)   GrpRk= 100     ( 71)
      cGRP3= 2.0     ( 72)   %D/Eq= N/A     (   )    5YrEg= 158     ( 98)
      5YrCf= 14      ( 75)   1mEGC= 0.4    ( 83)   P/E  = 14      ( 40)
      RelPE= 6.0     ( 12)   GrRat= 1.9    ( 80)   Insdr= 5.0     ( 98)
      #AnCF= 13      ( 88)   $Rank= 109    ( 86)   EPSRk= 90      ( 81)
      AcDst= 65      ( 64)   Price= 25     ( 82)   5/30= 74.8     ( 40)
20> STRY    - STRYKER CORP                        .TMI
      %cELt= 20      ( 85)   10LDv= -31    ( 12)   10LDv= -31     ( 12)
      %cE-2= 20      ( 83)   3LDv = 17     ( 91)   Mc8wC= 134     ( 98)
      c$-3 = 0.7     ( 53)   5yPEG= 19     ( 69)   3-Wk = 102     ( 64)
      c$-6 = 6.1     ( 87)   10$Gr= 31     ( 95)   GrpRk= 99      ( 61)
      cGRP3= 2.0     ( 72)   %D/Eq= 11     ( 67)   5YrEg= 33      ( 80)
      5YrCf= 30      ( 90)   1mEGC= 0.0    ( 81)   P/E  = 22      ( 71)
      RelPE= 20      ( 33)   GrRat= 1.1    ( 44)   Insdr= 1.0     ( 92)
      #AnCF= 18      ( 93)   $Rank= 106    ( 83)   EPSRk= 94      ( 89)
      AcDst= 54      ( 48)   Price= 30     ( 86)   5/30= 73.4     ( 37)
```

Exhibit 7.3   (continued)

```
21> DSCP   - DATASCOPE CORP               .TMI
      %cELt= 30      ( 88)   10LDv= -34   (  9)   10LDv= -34    (  9)
      %cE-2= 14      ( 80)   3LDv = 32    ( 95)   Mc8wC= 11     ( 24)
      c$-3 = 3.8     ( 83)   5yPEG= 21    ( 76)   3-Wk = 112    ( 89)
      c$-6 = -0.6    ( 30)   10$Gr= 17    ( 84)   GrpRk= 99     ( 61)
      cGRP3= 2.0     ( 72)   %D/Eq= 0.0   ( 58)   5YrEg= 10     ( 55)
      5YrCf= 11      ( 69)   1mEGC= 0.0   ( 81)   P/E  = 14     ( 44)
      RelPE= 13      ( 24)   GrRat= 1.5   ( 66)   Insdr= -1.0   ( 11)
      #AnCF= 6.0     ( 70)   $Rank= 105   ( 80)   EPSRk= 87     ( 79)
      AcDst= 66      ( 66)   Price= 16    ( 68)   5/30= 104.8   ( 60)
22> PLL    - PALL CORP                     .TMZ
      %cELt= 9.0     ( 79)   10LDv= -25   ( 17)   10LDv= -25    ( 17)
      %cE-2= 533     ( 99)   3LDv = -4.3  ( 62)   Mc8wC= 28     ( 77)
      c$-3 = 4.8     ( 87)   5yPEG= 13    ( 39)   3-Wk = 106    ( 81)
      c$-6 = 3.7     ( 81)   10$Gr= 13    ( 74)   GrpRk= 99     ( 58)
      cGRP3= 1.0     ( 50)   %D/Eq= 29    ( 73)   5YrEg= 8.5    ( 52)
      5YrCf= N/A     (   )   1mEGC= 0.0   ( 81)   P/E  = 19     ( 62)
      RelPE= 24      ( 39)   GrRat= 0.8   ( 24)   Insdr= -1.0   ( 11)
      #AnCF= 10      ( 82)   $Rank= 99    ( 53)   EPSRk= 90     ( 81)
      AcDst= 39      ( 37)   Price= 16    ( 69)   5/30= 130.3   ( 78)
23> SMLS   - SCIMED LIFE SYSTEMS           .TMI
      %cELt= -38     ( 64)   10LDv= -74   (  0)   10LDv= -74    (  0)
      %cE-2= -287    ( 57)   3LDv = -3.6  ( 65)   Mc8wC= 136    ( 98)
      c$-3 = 5.7     ( 89)   5yPEG= 14    ( 46)   3-Wk = 109    ( 86)
      c$-6 = 9.4     ( 92)   10$Gr= 62    ( 98)   GrpRk= 99     ( 61)
      cGRP3= 2.0     ( 72)   %D/Eq= 0.0   ( 58)   5YrEg= 9.2    ( 53)
      5YrCf= 33      ( 91)   1mEGC= -4.8  ( 10)   P/E  = 90     ( 95)
      RelPE= 16      ( 29)   GrRat= 1.7   ( 74)   Insdr= 1.0    ( 92)
      #AnCF= 18      ( 93)   $Rank= 88    ( 10)   EPSRk= 11     (  6)
      AcDst= 61      ( 56)   Price= 31    ( 87)   5/30= 68.7    ( 34)
24> BMS    - BEMIS CO                      .TPP
      %cELt= 20      ( 84)   10LDv= -29   ( 14)   10LDv= -29    ( 14)
      %cE-2= 23      ( 84)   3LDv = 2.4   ( 78)   Mc8wC= 20     ( 43)
      c$-3 = 3.1     ( 80)   5yPEG= 13    ( 42)   3-Wk = 108    ( 85)
      c$-6 = 1.3     ( 67)   10$Gr= 23    ( 91)   GrpRk= 103    ( 83)
      cGRP3= 3.6     ( 90)   %D/Eq= 44    ( 78)   5YrEg= 1.3    ( 39)
      5YrCf= 2.9     ( 46)   1mEGC= 0.7   ( 85)   P/E  = 24     ( 74)
      RelPE= 88      ( 93)   GrRat= 0.8   ( 24)   Insdr= 0.0    ( 87)
      #AnCF= 10      ( 82)   $Rank= 104   ( 76)   EPSRk= 72     ( 67)
      AcDst= 63      ( 60)   Price= 24    ( 81)   5/30= 81.6    ( 45)
25> REIC   - RESEARCH INDUS                .TMZ
      %cELt= 14.2    ( 82)   10LDv= -42.4 (  6)   10LDv= -42.4  (  6)
      %cE-2= 15.3    ( 81)   3LDv = -3.4  ( 67)   Mc8wC= 25.0   ( 75)
      c$-3 = 3.5     ( 83)   5yPEG= 20.7  ( 75)   3-Wk = 104.6  ( 77)
      c$-6 = 2.5     ( 77)   10$Gr= 17.5  ( 85)   GrpRk= 100.4  ( 68)
      cGRP3= 2.5     ( 79)   %D/Eq= 1.2   ( 60)   5YrEg= 46.2   ( 86)
      5YrCf= 33.2    ( 91)   1mEGC= 0.0   ( 81)   P/E  = 13.9   ( 39)
      RelPE= 4.3     (  8)   GrRat= 1.9   ( 80)   Insdr= -1.0   ( 11)
      #AnCF= 4.0     ( 58)   $Rank= 93.7  ( 17)   EPSRk= 93.0   ( 87)
      AcDst= 35.0    ( 32)   Price= 8.4   ( 32)   5/30= 37.9    ( 11)
```

8

STAGE TWO EVALUATION

We are now half-way through our evaluation. Let's take some time out to review how we got to this point.

Up to now, everything has been done with a stock search tool, specifically with ProSearch. We created a search strategy that accomplished four broad objectives: First, we narrowed our search universe by eliminating undesirable stocks; next, we chose indicators that matched our most important objectives and used them to score and rank the stocks in our narrowed universe; then, we selected other indicators to enhance certain qualities and coax stocks with those qualities to the top of the list (we called this "seasoning the search"); and finally, we included a number of "secondary" indicators to list information on the search report that we could use in our Stage One evaluation. Ten stocks made it through this search and evaluation process. Now we are ready to put them through the second stage of our evaluation.

This time we will look at stock graphs and various information on the company itself. We'll use certain technical analysis tools on the stock graphs to determine whether or not the stock has sufficient room to grow. We will also be able to see the volatility of the stock, which could affect our purchase decision. Then we'll take a qualitative look at each company (through company information tools) to make sure some important event has not occurred that might affect the stock price. The stocks that make it through this evaluation are the ones we will consider buying, upon the appropriate technical buy signal.

In this Stage Two evaluation, we like to give each stock a "grade" for each of the items we examine. We will use letter grades (A through F, as in school); you may wish to use ratings of 1 to 5 or 1 to 10. At the end of this chapter, we will tally up the grades and pick our winners.

A BRIEF ENCOUNTER WITH TECHNICAL ANALYSIS

The technical analysis tools for our Stage Two evaluation are based on concepts that have been shown by many traders to be effective. We will use Telescan Analyzer™, which is included on the disk with this book. We will not discuss the technical concepts at length, which would be a book in itself. Instead, we will describe the concept briefly and show you how it is used as a computerized tool. For more in-depth information on technical analysis, we refer you to *The Encyclopedia of Technical Market Indicators* by Robert W. Colby and Thomas A. Meyers.[1]

The Long . . .

The technical analysis tool for this evaluation is our old friend, the LSQ line. We used it as a search tool in our original undervalued growth search to eliminate stocks that were not at least 10 percent below their LSQ lines. But it is one thing to read that Kroger has an LSQ deviation of 14.4 percent; it is a different experience to see what that looks like on a stock graph. Plotting an LSQ line on a graph allows us to *see* how the current stock price relates to its historical trend. We can judge for ourselves how much room the stock has to grow.

First, we'll download a long-term stock graph for each of our candidates. A short-term graph may not give a true representation of a company's history, but keep in mind that some companies have not been public as long as others. Use the longest period that is available in your analysis program, which is more than 20 years in many cases. Next, we'll draw an LSQ line on the graph to find out the current position of the stock

---

[1] Robert W. Colby and Thomas A. Meyers, *The Encyclopedia of Technical Market Indicators* (Homewood, IL: Business One Irwin, 1988).

Exhibit 8.1   This long-term stock graph shows Kroger's LSQ line flanked by the parallel lines which form the LSQ trading channel. Note that Kroger is just above the LSQ line.

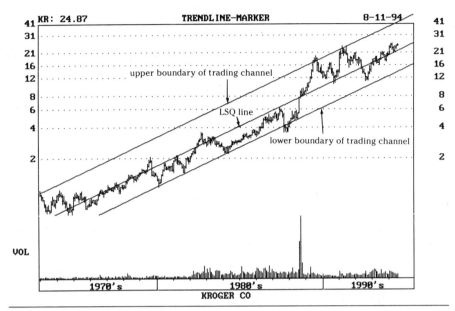

with respect to its long-term trend.[2] (This is a simple menu selection or one keystroke in most programs.) Finally, we'll draw parallel lines on either side of the LSQ line to form a trading channel, as shown in the 20-year Kroger graph in Exhibit 8.1. The lines can be drawn automatically after you mark a point through which each line should go. One line should go through several stock tops and one through several stock bottoms, with as many touches and as few significant penetrations as possible. The parallel lines need not be equal distance from the LSQ line.

What should you look for in the trading channel? How far the current stock price is below the LSQ line. We prefer those stocks that are the farthest below their LSQ lines because, according to their long-term trend, they have more room to grow. This is only true, however, if the company's projected earnings are comparable to its past growth. Otherwise, the company may be headed for bankruptcy. It is possible, of course, for a

---

[2] An LSQ line divides the price action roughly in half. If your program doesn't have an LSQ line, draw a simple trendline through the data to mimic the LSQ.

company to break out of a long-term trend. But if it hasn't broken out of it in 20 years or longer, why place your bet on its breaking out now? The risk is high and the potential reward, small. Now that we have the tools to assess such things, we think it unnecessary to take that risk.

All 10 of our semifinalists received an "A" for their LSQ deviation because we used the LSQ deviation indicator in our search to eliminate stocks above the LSQ line. Had we not done this, we would be even more interested in these graphs. For example, had Motorola (from the insider trading search) been one of our candidates, it would not have passed muster (Exhibit 8.2). As you can see, it is well above its long-term trend, so we would throw it out, even if it were to meet the other criteria.

And the Short of It

We like to look at a one-year graph for each of our candidates because each day's trading is represented by a single bar (in Telescan), which lets us see clearly the day-to-day activity. With graphs longer than two years,

Exhibit 8.2   A long-term LSQ channel for Motorola showing a possible excessive valuation.

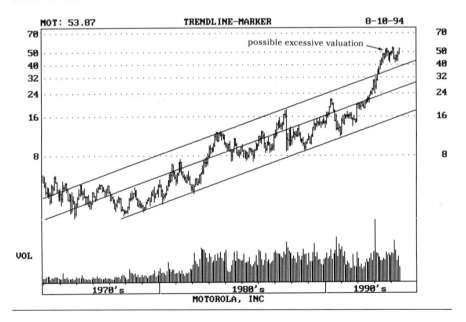

the price data is compressed; one bar may represent four days to several weeks. We look for two things on the graph: the recent price trend and the volatility. If the stock has been falling more or less steadily for several months or a year and has shown no sign of turning up, we would give it an "F." If the most recent action is all downhill, this isn't the time to jump in. Most of our searches are structured to preclude this situation, but yours may not be.

You should also consider a stock's volatility. (Actually, volatility should be noted on both the long-term graph and the short-term graph.) Does the stock make wild swings that would be tough on your tummy as it moves to new highs? Unless you like roller coaster rides, you might want to avoid highly volatile stocks like Datascope in Exhibit 8.3. This is a personal decision, of course. If the company is volatile but has a history of success—steep drops followed by sharp rises—you might want consider it; just be aware that you may have to hang on through some wild gyrations.

Exhibit 8.3   Datascope shows a fair amount of volatility: Several times during the year, price swings exceeded 20 percent.

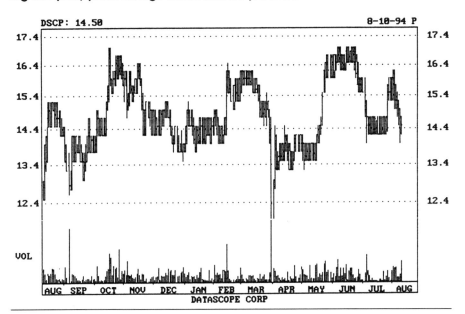

RESEARCHING THE COMPANY

There are a number of company information tools that provide a variety of information about public companies. They range from filings with the Securities and Exchange Commission to research reports from Wall Street analysts to quantitative data on earnings estimates to the latest stories from the newswires. The three tools we consider particularly important are the news stories, analysts' earnings estimates, and company profiles published by independent services.

All the News That's Worth a Byte

Jumping into a stock without looking at the news is like boarding a plane without looking at a flight schedule: you may end up in a place where you really don't want to be. With cyber-investing, you can check the news electronically, which means you may often see an event announced before you see it in the regular media.

Most online services offer electronic news from various newswires, such as Reuters, Comtex, and the Associated Press. Usually, a list of headlines appears first; you may then select the article you wish to read. The headlines themselves will do for starters. At this point, we're simply looking for late-breaking news that might be important to our decision.

Exhibit 8.4 shows recent headlines for Telephone & Data Systems. The most recent one, which says "Telephone and Data Raised to a Nomura Buy," would certainly make us want to take a look at the whole article, which is shown in Exhibit 8.5. This would get top marks on our rating system. On the other hand, the news for one of our stocks, Wausau Paper Mills, announced that the CEO had recently resigned, which could disqualify the stock at least for the time being. Common sense should tell you which news might affect a stock positively or negatively.

A Consensus of Analysts

Among the most valuable computerized tools are reports that summarize earning estimates from Wall Street analysts. They provide a consensus of what Wall Street thinks about the future earnings prospects for a particular stock (which is why they are called *consensus* earnings estimates). The major online suppliers for these reports are Zacks Investment

Exhibit 8.4   Headlines from Reuters on August 1, 1994. The full article may be viewed by selecting the corresponding letter key.

Reuters News—8/01/94

A>	7/20/94	Telephone and Data (TDS.A) raised to a Nomura buy
B>	7/19/94	TDS (TDS.A), units Q2 net boosted by expansion
C>	7/19/94	Telephone & Data Systems Inc (TDS.A) Q2 net up
D>	7/07/94	American Paging (APP.A) buys Sunshine Beeper
E>	6/07/94	Telephone and Data (TDS.A) sets qtly payout
F>	6/07/94	Telephone and Data (TDS.A), Arvig merger approved
G>	6/06/94	American Paging (APP.A) gets paging frequency
H>	5/06/94	Telephone and Data (TDS.A) succeeds in litigation
I>	4/18/94	Telephone & Data (TDS.A) unit to spend $110 mln
J>	4/18/94	Telephone & Data Systems Inc (TDS.A) Q1 net rises
K>	3/31/94	Telephone & Data Systems (TDS.A) upgraded
L>	3/30/94	Court vacates FCC's LaStar Cellular decision
M>	3/10/94	Telephone & Data Systems(TDS.A) lowered by Gruntal
N>	3/07/94	Telephone & Data Systems (TDS.A) raises dividend
O>	3/07/94	Telephone & Data Systems (TDS.A) says increases qtly div
P>	2/09/94	Telephone & Data Systems Inc (TDS.A) Q4 net down
Q>	2/04/94	FCC orders hearing on TDS(TDS.A) Wisconsin license
R>	12/17/93	Telephone & Data (TDS.A) acquires Vernon Telephone
S>	12/17/93	Telephone & Data (TDS.A) to acquire (Vernon Tel)
T>	12/16/93	Telephone & Data (TDS.A) acquiring Minnesota firm
U>	12/08/93	Telephone & Data (TDS.A) unit offering shares

Source: Courtesy of Reuters, Inc. and Telescan.

Research, I-B-E-S, and First Call. Their business is collecting the earnings estimates from research reports published by Wall Street analysts and tabulating the information in various ways. Zacks, which is available through Telescan, follows almost 5,000 companies.[3] (Normally, there is a

---

[3] Zacks reports are also available directly from Zacks Investment Research (see listing in Appendix A) and through Internet (see Chapter 16).

Exhibit 8.5   The article behind one of Reuters' headlines dated July 20, 1994.

Telephone and Data (TDS.A) raised to a Nomura Buy

NEW YORK, July 20 (Reuter)—Nomura Equity Research said analyst Patrick Jurczak upgraded Telephone and Data Systems Inc. to buy from hold.

A Nomura report said the stock is now about 16 percent undervalued. Based on a 9-10 multiple of cash flow, the stock is worth about $44 now and about $50 in a year, the report said. It was off ½ to 37½.

Cellular fundamentals appear strong and are driving cellular stocks higher, the report added. Cellular stocks on average have risen 15.1 percent since March 31 while Telephone and Data Systems has risen only 0.6 percent, the report said.

—Wall Street Bureau, 212-912-7195

REUTER   Rtr   12:17   07-20-94

End of Text

Source: Courtesy of Reuters, Inc., and Telescan.

---

surcharge for the Zacks report; however, with your Cyber-Investing Kit, you may obtain free Zacks reports through Telescan for 30 days.)

A Zacks report contains an abundance of information, as shown for Kroger in Exhibit 8.6. For our Stage Two evaluation, we will concentrate on the following:

- *Earnings Projections.* The Zacks report tabulates earnings projections for the next two quarters and next two years. An annualized earnings growth for the next five years is given, if available. Be sure to look at the quarterly earnings, as well as the longer term; if the short term is not good, you may have to wait several years for your profits. Unless you're willing to do that, you should probably discard that stock. Also, pay attention to the 5-year earnings growth rate, especially if it wasn't used as an indicator in your search. In Exhibit 8.6, Kroger shows positive earnings forecasts for the next two quarters, plus an 18 percent growth rate over the next five years.

Exhibit 8.6   Selected information from Zacks Estimate Service for Kroger, dated August 6, 1994.

KROGER CO   8/6/94

WALL STREET ESTIMATES

		Mean	High	Low	Number Est	Mean Chg Last Mnth ($)
Fisc yr end	9412	2.23	2.37	2.00	12	0.03
Fisc yr end	9512	2.53	2.69	2.25	11	0.03
Quarter end	9406	0.53	0.58	0.41	11	0.00
Quarter end	9409	0.40	0.49	0.34	7	0.00
Next 5 yr grth (%)		18.16	23.00	10.00	11	0.00

COMPANY VS INDUSTRY

	EPS Growth Rates				
		(Cur FY=9412)			P/E on
	Last 5 Yrs Actual (%)	Cur/Last (%)	Nxt/Cur (%)	Nxt 5 Yrs (%)	Cur Yr EPS
Company	11.0	26.8	13.6	18.2	11.1
Ind: Retail-Supermk (T=267)	10.6	13.6	15.6	12.7	15.1
S & P 500	4.1	15.0	9.3	8.7	14.8
Company/Industry	1.0	2.0	0.9	1.4	0.7
Company/S&P	2.7	1.8	1.5	2.1	0.8

QUARTERLY EARNINGS SURPRISES

	Last	Previous Four Qtrs			
	Qtr0	Qtr1	Qtr2	Qtr3	Qtr4
Month FQ End	Jun 94	Mar 94	Dec 93	Sep 93	Jun 93
Mean Estimate	0.54	0.45	0.62	0.26	0.32
Actual EPS	0.62	0.50	0.79	0.26	0.41
	Qtr0	Qtr1	Qtr2	FY1	FY2
30 Day Median	N/A	0.44	0.75	2.29	2.57

Primary Shares Outstanding as of Jun 94: 112,966,400

Recent Reported EPS—Last Report Qtr Date: Jun 94

Last Qtr	Prev Qtr	Last 12 Mth	Last Rprtd FY
0.62	0.50	2.17	1.76

CURRENT RATINGS:

Strong Buy (1)	5
Moderate Buy (2)	1
Hold (3)	7
Moderate Sell (4)	0
Strong Sell (5)	0
Mean Rating (1 to 5 scale) =	2.1

Source: Courtesy of Zacks Investment Research and Telescan.

- *Revisions.* Each Zacks report includes a column which shows the average revision in each estimate, upward or downward, over the past 30 days. Kroger shows an upward revision for the current and next fiscal years.

- *Number of Analysts.* If you don't use the number of analysts as a search tool, you can get it from the Zacks report. Kroger has 11 for the 5-year earnings growth rate projection.

- *P/E Comparisons.* Zacks compares a company's current P/E ratio and projected P/E ratio (the P/E it will earn if estimates are met) with the industry average and S&P 500 companies. At 11.1, Kroger's projected P/E ratio is below both the industry average of 15.1 and the S&P 500 average of 14.8, which means it has room to grow.

- *Earnings Surprises.* The report compares a company's actual earnings to the analysts' estimates and calculates "earnings surprises." Surprises, of course, can be good or bad. Positive surprises occur when the actual earnings exceed the estimates; negative surprises, when the actual earnings fail to meet the estimates. If we see a steady stream of negative earnings surprises, we'll avoid the stock. On the other hand, a company like Kroger, which had positive earnings surprises in three of the past four quarters, would find a warm spot in our hearts.

- *Buy, Hold, and Sell Recommendations.* Zacks also tabulates the number of buy, hold, and sell recommendations by analysts. If a Zacks report lists a dozen sell recommendations and no buys or holds, we probably would not want to swim against the tide. Kroger, however, has six Buy ratings (five of them "Strong Buys"), seven Hold ratings, and no Sells.

The Company Profile

It is important to look at a company profile to get a feel for what the company does and how well it is doing it. A number of services offer profiles, including Standard & Poor's (S&P), Market Guide, and Value Line. Value Line has an extensive hard copy service and is available online to a limited degree, but it only covers about 2,000 companies. Market Guide, available through Telescan and other online services, offers comprehensive financial data and extensive ratio analysis, but provides no qualitative recommendations. A three-page synopsis of a company's financials is also available.

Standard & Poor's has an extensive database which is free for 30 days as part of your Cyber-Investing Kit. The company profile offered by S&P is the MarketScope® report. It includes a brief synopsis of a company's business, commentary (usually) on the expected earnings trend and cash flow, and summary financial information.

One of the reasons we like the S&P MarketScope® is its "stock appreciation ranking system"—a sort of corporate report card that it calls "STARS." S&P gives 5 STARS to companies that it particularly recommends, 4 STARS to ones that are almost as good, all the way down to 1 STAR, which is given to stocks that it recommends avoiding.

Exhibit 8.7 shows the S&P MarketScope for Wal-Mart. We gave it an "A" in our evaluation for several reasons. It has 4 STARS; its earnings have grown steadily over the past three years; its P/E ratio is 19.5, which is well below its 1993 high of 33.5 and even further below its pre-1990 high of 42.8. Moreover, 25 analysts recommend Wal-Mart as a Buy, 11 recommend a Hold, and none recommend a Sell.

None of our 10 stocks had a 1-STAR rating, but we would probably disqualify a stock with one STAR, regardless of its other merits. With all the other good stocks, why bother with one that S&P says to avoid? Maybe they know something we don't.

A stock without a STAR rating is not necessarily bad, because S&P doesn't rate all stocks. If one of your stocks doesn't have a STAR rating, read the report to see if it contains anything negative or particularly positive and act accordingly. Four of our 10 stocks were not rated; we gave them all a "C" because there was nothing exciting or alarming on their S&P reports. Nevertheless, Surgical Care (SCA) turned out to be one of *our* top-rated stocks, despite its lack of an S&P STAR.

Why not buy just stocks with 5-STAR S&P ratings and forget about all this searching and analysis? First of all, at any given time there are several hundred stocks with 5-STAR ratings. Second, the ratings are not good for early signals because they tend to lag the market significantly (at least in our experience). We prefer to consider the S&P STAR ratings in context with the rest of our evaluation.

Analyzing a company profile, as you can see, is highly qualitative. But it can reveal important information about a company, and it gives you a chance to act on any bias you might have. This is the stage at which you

Exhibit 8.7   An S&P MarketScope report for Wal-Mart dated August 4, 1994.

WAL-MART STORES ★★★★

Operates 1,953 Wal-Mart discount department stores, 68 Supercenters, 419 Sam's Wholesale Clubs in 49 states . . . 3/17/94 acquired about 122 Woolco stores across Canada from Woolworth Canada . . . FY 94 EPS up 17% on 21% sales rise . . . 1Q FY 95 EPS up 10% on 27% higher sales . . . helped by stores acquisition in Canada . . . 38% closely held.

★★★★Outlook: FY 96 (Jan.) EPS estimated $1.45, FY 94's seen $1.25 vs. FY 94's $1.02 . . . Raised Apr. '94 quarterly dividend 31% to $0.0425.

Tel.# 501-273-4000

–0– WMT $ (1222)   08-05-94   02:29 PM EST

WAL-MART STORES ★★★★ 04-AUG-94—STATS

Share Earnings		Market Action—NYSE			
3 Mo Apr	.22/.20	: 94 Rng	29.25–22.37		: S&P Rank A+
Last 12 Mos	1.04	: Avg Vol	1995934		
P/E	19.5	: Beta	1.1		
5-Yr Growth %	+18	: Inst Holdings	29%		

Dividends			Balance Sheet		BV/SH	
Rt&Yd	.17	0.6%	: Cur Ratio	1.64	: 93	4.68
Last Div Q		.042	: LT Dt(M)	8460	: 92	3.81
Ex-Date		06/07	: Shs(M)	2298.76	: 91	3.04
PayDate		07/08/94	: Rpt.of	01/31/94	: 90	2.35

S&P 500. CBOE:Cycle 3. 2-for-1,'90,'93.

Yr	High	Low	P/E	Range	Div	EPS	Rev(M)	Net(M)
93	34.12	23.00	33.5	22.5	.12	1.02	67344.5	2333.2
92	32.93	25.06	37.9	28.8	.10	.87	55483.7	1994.7
91	29.93	14.25	42.8	20.4	.08	.70	43886.9	1608.4

–0– WMT $ (1223)   08-05-94   02:29 PM EST

WAL-MART STORES—Earnings Estimates—07/24/94

	New	Old	High	Low	Ests
Current Quarter (Q3-95)					
Consensus Estimate	0.25	N/A	0.27	0.24	22
Current Year 1995 (JAN)					
Consensus Estimate	1.21	N/A	1.25	1.15	41
Next Year 1996 (JAN)					
Consensus Estimate	1.45	N/A	1.60	1.35	35
Next EPS Report Date: 08/09/94					

Street Guidance:	Buy	Buy/Hold	Hold	Hold/Sell	Sell
	19	6	11	0	0

Source: Reprinted by permission of Standard & Poor's, a division of McGraw-Hill, Inc.

may wish to boycott a company just because you found out it manufactures widgets that go against your political sympathies!

Et Cetera

There are many other company information tools that you might wish to use. For example, SEC Online™ (available through Telescan), Disclosure™ (available through Dow Jones) and others publish the various forms filed by public companies with the Securities & Exchange Commission, including the full text of annual reports. If you don't mind reading lengthy documents, you may wish to look at these reports. Our experience tells us that this kind of information has already been digested by the analysts and by services such as S&P and Market Guide, and included in their reports. Nevertheless, such tools are available for those who have the time and wish to expend the effort.

The full text and a summary of research reports written by analysts who follow a company are available through Investex™ (via Dow Jones News Retrieval®, Telescan, and other online services). These offer lengthy commentaries by the analysts but are much more expensive than the Zacks reports, which contain the raw numbers but no text. We predict that, in the tradition of online information, the costs of the full research reports will come down and will eventually be practical for most investors.

The trend toward lower prices has already begun. Market Guide has the lower-priced three-page synopsis, mentioned earlier, and Standard & Poor's recently announced a price reduction for its expanded research reports. (At seven pages, these reports are much more in-depth than the less expensive S&P MarketScope reports.) This should make them more attractive to individual investors, but the prices aren't yet quite low enough that we can strongly recommend them. But if you want to spend the money, research reports can be a valuable supplement to your evaluation.

The Envelope, Please!

From our top 10 candidates, 5 stocks made the final cut: Telephone & Data Systems (TDS), Wal-Mart (WMT), Surgical Care (SCA), Lin Broadcasting (LINB), and Kroger (KR). (Five is not a magic number; you may have more or fewer.) Their ratings are shown in Exhibit 8.8. In Chapter 9, we will view these five stocks through other technical lenses. We'll be looking for technical buy signals that will help us enter the market at the most propitious time.

WHAT TO DO WITH A HOT STOCK TIP

It's inevitable. You know it's going to happen. One day, you'll get a stock tip from your brother-in-law or your dentist or a friend. "You gotta get in on this thing," they'll tell you in an admirable gesture to share the wealth. Before you do, put the stock through a little computerized evaluation. Searches won't work here. There's a more direct way to go about it.

- Read the news headlines and check out any recent story. If your "scoop" is in the news, the market has already discounted it. Even if it is not in the news, there's a good chance that "those in the know" already know.

- Look at the LSQ trading channels on a long-term and short term stock graph. Note where the stock is with relation to the LSQ line.

- Plot a couple of technical indicators: MACD, trading bands, stochastics, or trendlines. Assess the technical condition of the stock.

- Note the current volume level and compare it with the past 15 to 30 days. If the stock is moving up on increasing volume, that's good.

- Look at the analysts' earnings estimates, and check all the items discussed in this chapter, including P/E ratio and P/E comparisons.

- What are the insiders doing? Are they buying or selling?

- Look at a company profile. Note any buy and sell recommendations, as well as any comments about future earnings.

- Check out the industry group graph (the industry group is listed on the stock's fact sheet in Telescan). Is it trending upward or downward? To compare its rank with other industry groups, run the industry group search described in Chapter 14.

- Download the Telescan valuation report and look at the relative P/E ratio and other fundamentals.

Once you have done all this, you can make a decision based on information, not on emotion. The same kind of evaluation should be done on a stock that is being touted in the media or a market letter. The news is obviously out already, so evaluate the stock thoroughly to make sure you're not the last one on the bandwagon!

Exhibit 8.8   A typical "report card" from our Stage Two evaluation. From these ratings, we will select the finalists in our search for the best undervalued growth stocks.

Stock Symbol	LSQ Deviation	Price Pattern	Volatility	News	S&P MarketScope	Zacks Report
TDS	A	C	B	A	B (3-STARS)	B
WASU	A	F	C	F	A (5-STARS)	C−
WMT	A	C	C	B	A (4-STARS)	B
SCA	A	A	B	A	C (no STARS)	B
LINB	A	A	B	B	B (4-STARS)	B
NDSN	A	C	B	B	B (no STARS)	D
PXR	A	C	C	C	C-(no STARS)	F
KR	A	A	B	C	A (4-STARS)	A+
STRY	A	C	C	A	C (3-STARS)	C
DSCP	A	F	C	D	C (no STARS)	B

We used the following rating system:
A	=	Excellent
B	=	Good
C	=	Average
D	=	Below Average
F	=	Unacceptable

YOU MUST REMEMBER THIS . . .

The Stage Two evaluation is just as important as the evaluation in Stage One.

- Look at the long-term LSQ trading channels to make sure the stock has room to grow; look at the short-term trend to make sure it is going in the right direction.
- Consider the stock's volatility in light of your investing personality.
- Make sure there is no late-breaking news that might adversely affect the stock.
- Carefully analyze the earnings estimates report.

- Review a company profile from an independent source. Beware of any sell recommendations.

- If you get a "hot stock tip," check it out thoroughly. It may be as "cold" as last night's pizza.

There are many other search tools and evaluation tools you could use. In previous chapters, we used only 31 search tools, out of more than 200 that are available in ProSearch; in this chapter, we used only two technical analysis tools and three company information tools, out of the several dozen that are available. The important thing is not which tools you use but that you use them. As powerful as it is, a search tool alone cannot do a proper job.

Next up: timing your entry to maximize your returns.

9

TO BUY
OR NOT TO BUY

Choosing among half a dozen excellent stocks may not seem much of a dilemma. If you have followed the investing process thus far, the surviving stocks have met all your investment goals, as defined by your search strategy. They have all passed a rigorous technical and fundamental evaluation. They are the "best of the best," the crème de la crème. The question now is not so much *which* stock to buy, but *when* to buy it. You could probably buy any or all five of the stocks at this point and do just fine, as long as you held them long enough. But based on our experience and backtesting, technical timing can add as much as three percentage points to your returns. If you recall what three percentage points can be worth, you'll agree that it is worthwhile to wait for a good technical "buy" signal.

Because of space considerations, we can only discuss a few of the technical timing tools out of the dozens that are available. We will briefly describe the technical concept employed by the tools we use and show you how to interpret the indicator on a few stock graphs. At the end of the chapter, we will use these technical tools to do an abbreviated analysis on each of the top five stocks from our Stage Two evaluation. To learn more about technical analysis, you may wish to consult any of the excellent books on technical analysis, including the Colby and Meyers book mentioned earlier. User's manuals for any technical analysis program also provide helpful information.

WHAT'S IT ALL ABOUT?

Stocks do not move in a straight line in their progression from one price level to the next. They move up for a while, then down; they surge forward, then fall back; sometimes they seem to pause for breath and move sideways for a while. These movements are apparent in most of the figures in this chapter. The uptrends and downtrends are generally fueled by institutional investors (who represent about 70 percent of all trading) moving into or out of a stock. In theory, once a stock starts moving in a one direction and gains momentum, it doesn't easily reverse direction. However, the reversal will occur eventually. At some point in an uptrend, buyers will dry up, which will result in an overbought condition making the stock susceptible to a downward correction. Likewise, at some point in a downtrend, sellers will dry up, resulting in an oversold condition with the stock susceptible to a reversal. Obviously, the best time to buy stocks is when the period of selling is over and the downward trend reverses. This is the point at which the stock would tend to be the most undervalued.

Technical analysis helps identify the point at which an existing trend is likely to reverse or find support, which allows us to buy the stock at the most propitious time and increase our odds for success. Fortunately, there are dozens of technical tools that can help identify the likelihood of a trend reversal. In this chapter, we will discuss three of our favorites: the moving average convergence/divergence (MACD) indicator, the stochastics index, and trading bands. In addition, we'll talk about trendlines and the popular support and resistance lines, all of which are easy to use. This will lead into a brief discussion of basing period breakouts, which typically signal the beginning of a new trend. We suggest that you use some of your free online time with Telescan to experiment with these and other indicators.

THE AUGUST ANCESTOR

The moving average is so basic to most technical indicators that it should precede any discussion of the more complex indicators. A moving average smooths out the fluctuations in stock prices to show a smooth directional trend. It can be plotted for any time period, but the simplest is the 30-day moving average, the grandaddy of technical analysis.

To calculate a simple 30-day moving average, total the closing prices of a stock over 30 days and divide the sum by 30. That's the average. To make it "move," add the most recent closing price to the 30-day total and subtract the oldest closing price and divide the remainder by 30. In the old days, analysts had to do this by hand, laboriously plotting the stock price on a graph and then plotting the moving average. Personal computers can now do it all instantaneously.

The 30-day moving average indicator is based on the idea that when a stock breaks through its 30-day moving average headed upward (Exhibit 9.1), the stock is more likely to continue to move up, due to momentum, than to reverse direction. And vice versa: When a stock breaks through the moving average headed *downward* (Exhibit 9.2), the stock is more likely to continue to fall than to turn back up.

These movements are based on market psychology. When a stock is above its 30-day moving average, it is higher than the price at which most

Exhibit 9.1   This graph shows a positive breakout above the 30-day moving average for the Gap.

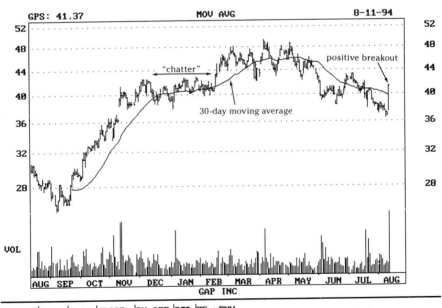

Exhibit 9.2   Here's a negative breakout below the 30-day moving average for 20th Century Industries.

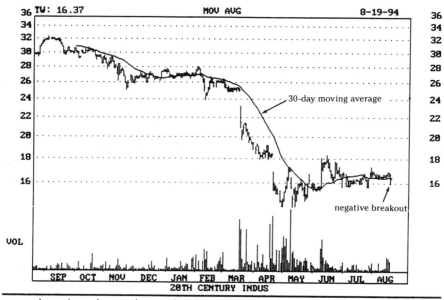

30 DY |0 DY |0 DY |CLOSE |SH-OFF |STD |75 %ENV

people have recently bought. Thus, they feel reassured about their investment. As long as it stays above its 30-day moving average, there is a positive tone to the stock. However, when it falls below the 30-day moving average, there are more and more people who bought at prices higher than the current price. So fear sets in and is likely to drive the price down further.

Moving averages can be plotted for any number of days. One of the more popular is the 200-day moving average. It is used with the 30-day indicator in this way: If a stock is *already* above its 200-day moving average when it moves above its 30-day moving average, the stock is even more likely to continue moving upward. The positive longer trend is said to help buoy the shorter trend. The reverse is also true.

There is nothing magic about the 30-day moving average, except that it is the most widely followed of all the averages and therefore the most likely to create psychological impairment when the stock falls below that line. But there is a major problem with using it for buy and sell signals. It tends to give a lot of false breakouts (referred to as "chatter" or "whipsaws") where the stock jumps back and forth across the

MORE ABOUT MACD

In the MACD indicator, the 8/17/9 refers to the length of the three moving averages: On a daily 8/17/9 MACD, the short moving average would be 8 days; the long one, 17 days; and the signal line, 9 days. On a weekly 8/17/9 MACD, the periods would be 8, 17, and 9 weeks. A daily MACD (a short-term signal) is based on daily data and generates many more signals than the weekly MACD (a longer-term signal), which is based on weekly durations. Thus, the weekly indicator has fewer whipsaws. Most technical gurus who use daily indicators trust them only if the weekly is pointing in the same direction. In other words, they will trust a positive breakout from a daily MACD only if the weekly MACD is also positive. Only the very short-term players depend strictly on daily signals.

Gerald Appel, who developed the MACD indicator, has a system for defining the quality of the MACD breakout, although this is more of a pure technical trader's "game." If you wish to pursue this, ProSearch offers a number of MACD indicators that can help find and rank stocks in order of the quality of their MACD breakouts.

moving average. This is probably caused by the competing interest of short-term traders and longer term investors. A good illustration of chatter is the period from December to May in Exhibit 9.1. Many brilliant minds have applied themselves to this problem over the past 30 years and have come up with a number of technical tools that reduce the whipsaw effect and generate more reliable signals. Our personal favorite is the moving average convergence/divergence indicator—the "MACD," as it is commonly known.

BREAKING OUT WITH MACD

The MACD trading method was developed and popularized by Gerald Appel, publisher of *Systems & Forecasts*, a market letter that has one of the best long-term records for market timing. The MACD is said to measure the intensity and direction of the market's mood and to confirm a trend reversal. The MACD uses three exponential moving averages:[1] a short one,

---

[1] An exponential moving average is similar to a simple moving average except it gives more weight to the most recent closing prices.

a long one, and a third that plots the moving average of the *difference* between the other two and forms a "signal line" on an MACD graph. Trend reversals are signaled by the convergence and divergence of these moving averages, thus the name: moving average convergence/divergence. Exhibit 9.3 shows an MACD histogram with its buy and sell signals. (Breakouts are easier to read on a histogram than on an MACD graph.) A positive breakout (a buy signal) occurs when the histogram crosses the zero line upward; a negative breakout (a sell signal) occurs when the histogram crosses the zero line downward.

Many short-term traders use Appel's trading theory as follows: They look for stocks that are positive (above the zero line) on an 8/17/9 *weekly* MACD; then they look for *daily* breakouts with the 8/17/9 MACD. Why? Because the weekly MACD offers a longer perspective on the price movement of the stock and prevents acting on false signals. For example, look at the two graphs for Pyxis Corporation (Exhibits 9.4 and 9.5). During the decline from early to mid-1994, the daily MACD (Exhibit 9.4) gave numerous buy

Exhibit 9.3 An MACD histogram is plotted in the lower graph. The "false" buy signals in early March, early April and early July would have been overridden by a negative weekly MACD.

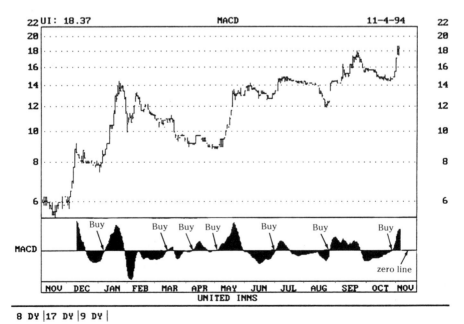

Exhibit 9.4   This graph shows the daily 8/17/9 MACD for Pyxis Corporation. Note a positive daily MACD breakout on the date of the report. (The weekly MACD was also negative, as shown on Exhibit 9.5.) Notice also that the whipsaws in the daily MACD which gave false signals from January through June would have been overridden by the fact that the weekly MACD (Exhibit 9.5) was negative during the same period.

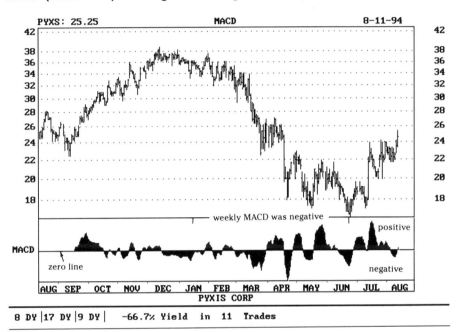

signals, but the weekly MACD (Exhibit 9.5) was negative from January through most of June. Requiring the weekly MACD to be positive would have avoided those false signals. On the date the graph was made, Pyxis had a positive daily MACD breakout with a positive weekly MACD, which we would take as a good signal. No indicator is perfect, of course, but requiring the weekly MACD to be positive before acting on a daily MACD breakout helps avoid the chatter or false signals.

STALKING THE STOCHASTICS

The stochastics index, developed by George C. Lane of Investment Educators, is an overbought/oversold indicator built out of relative strength

Exhibit 9.5 **This graph shows the weekly 8/17/9 MACD for Pyxis Corporation. Compare it with the daily MACD in Exhibit 9.4.**

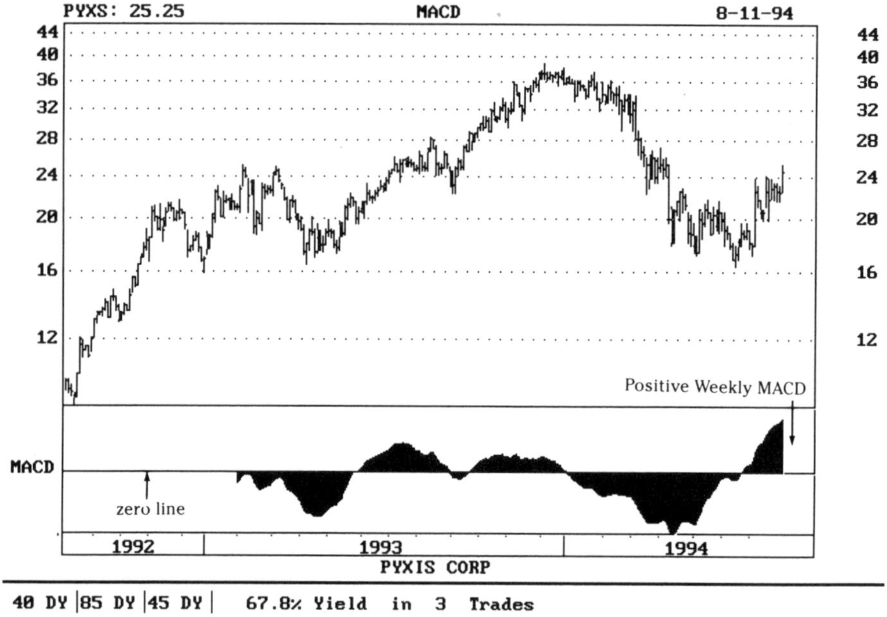

PYXS: 25.25   MACD   8-11-94

Positive Weekly MACD

MACD

zero line

1992   1993   1994

PYXIS CORP

40 DY |85 DY |45 DY | 67.8% Yield in 3 Trades

concept and moving averages. It is a child of the personal computer age because, as William F. Eng says, "It is hard to imagine someone even having the idea for something like Lane's Stochastics without a PC at hand."[2] With a PC, the stochastic index is a valuable and easy-to-use tool.

In simple terms, the stochastic index is expressed as a percentage of the difference between the low and the high during the period of the stochastic. A 14-day stochastic means that you are going to consider the low point in price versus the high point for the past 14 days: The stochastic on the day calculated is the percentage that the price represents of that difference between the low and high. In other words, if the stock has traded between $10 and $15 in a 14-day period, at a price today of $10 the stochastic reading is zero. It is at the very bottom of the range. At $15, the stochastic reading is 100, the very top of the range. At $12½, the stochastic would be 50; at $13, it would be 60. It is simply the percentage of the difference between the low and high.

[2] William F. Eng, *The Technical Analysis of Stocks, Options and Futures: Advanced Trading Systems and Techniques* (Chicago: Probus Publishing, 1988), p. 95.

Exhibit 9.6   The popular 14/5 stochastic for Snapple Beverage is in neutral territory.

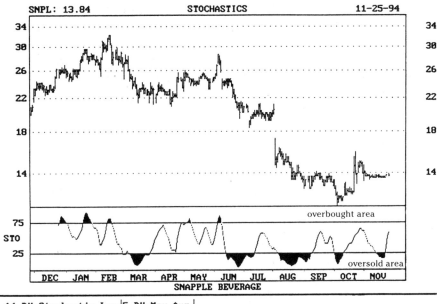

SNPL: 13.84   STOCHASTICS   11-25-94

14 DY-Stochastic Len |5 DY-Mov Avg |

In actual usage, the stochastic index takes a slightly more complex but more useful form. It uses a moving average of the simple stochastic to plot the indicator. For example, the popular 14-5 stochastic shown in Exhibit 9.6 is calculated over a 14-day period with the final plot of the index based on a 5-day moving average of the simple stochastic. Eng gives a detailed exposition of Lane's stochastics in *The Technical Analysis of Stocks, Options & Futures.*

On a stochastics graph, the 75 percent line and the 25 percent line measure oversold and overbought conditions as follows:

- *Oversold.* When the stochastic falls below the 25 percent line, it generally indicates an oversold condition; then, when the index crosses the 25 percent line upward (a "positive breakout"), a new uptrend is anticipated.

- *Overbought.* An overbought condition is generally indicated when the stochastic goes above the 75 percent line; then, when it crosses the 75 percent line downward (a "negative breakout"), a new downtrend is signaled.

We prefer to use the MACD for actual buy signals and the stochastic to confirm an oversold condition. We should point out that in trending markets, which represent a majority of recent market history, the MACD is the superior indictor, according to our backtesting. During a trading market, however (as in most of 1994), the stochastic appears to give a better result.[3] Beginners will do well to use both indicators.

THE ALVIM STOCHASTIC

Luiz Alvim, a futures trader and colleague, has developed a unique two-stage application of the 21-5 stochastic, which we like to use. Twenty-one refers to the length of time over which the stochastics is being calculated; 5 refers to the number of days of a moving average used to plot the stochastics reading. After a positive breakout at the 25 percent line, Alvim recommends waiting until the stochastic crosses the 50 percent line upward (Exhibit 9.7). At that point, he enters half of his position. When and if the index crosses the 75 percent line upward, he enters the rest of his position. This application appears to give good results, perhaps because the delay ensures a continuation of the trend before more money is expended.

Alvim's selling strategy is to retrace his steps. After a negative breakout at the 75 percent line, he sells half his holdings, with the remaining position to be closed when the 50 percent line is crossed downward. This prevents being taken completely out of a stock when the stochastic dips below the 75 percent line and then heads back upward, as often happens.

Like most investors, Alvim requires confirmation from other technical signals. Specifically, he requires:

- To enter a position, the 20-day moving average must be sloping upward when the stochastic crosses the 50 percent and 75 percent lines.

- To close a position, the 20-day moving average must *not* be sloping upward but can be horizontal. This prevents an early exit of

---

[3] A trending market is one in which a clear uptrend or downtrend is discernible. A trading market, also called a "sideways" or "flat" market, is virtually trendless.

Exhibit 9.7 This is the Alvim 21/5 stochastic. Note the buy and sell points. The places marked "X" would be a Sell, *except* for the fact that the 20-day moving average is still sloping upwards.

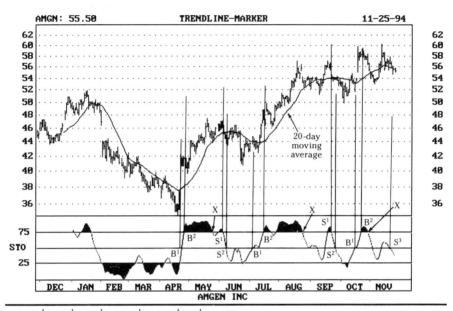

20 DY |0 DY |0 DY |CLOSE |SH-OFF |STD |75 %ENV

B^1 = Buy first half of position.
B^2 = Buy second half of position.
S^1 = Close first half of position.
S^2 = Close second half of position.
S^3 = Close all open positions if the moving average turns down, after the index has crossed through the 75 and 50 percent lines.

a good move, which is the major disadvantage of using stochastics in trending markets. However, if the moving average turns down after the stochastic crosses the 75 or 50 percent lines, all open positions are closed.

TRADING WITH TRADING BANDS

We generally use trading bands to confirm an MACD buy signal. The trading band concept is based on the tendency of a stock to trade within a

Exhibit 9.8   Trading bands for Chiron Corporation. Notice the positive failure swing in July and the negative failure swing in September.

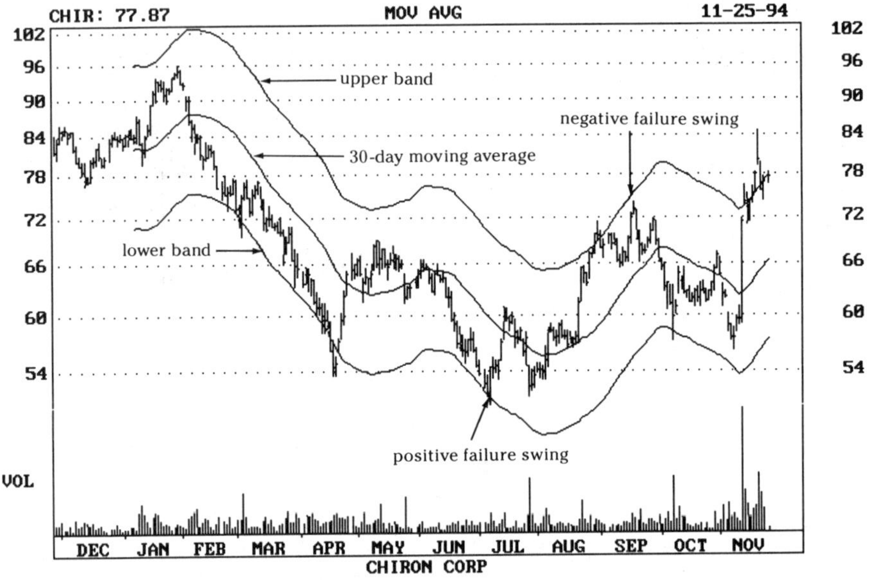

predictable range around its moving average. Thus, we can draw an "envelope" around the moving average to encompass the trading range of the stock (Exhibit 9.8) and predict with some confidence which way the stock will go next and how far it might go. Trading bands can be drawn automatically with almost any technical analysis program.[4]

Interpreting trading bands is more of an art than a science. Like all technical indicators, this one is based on market psychology. As the stock approaches the top of the band, a tug of war tends to set up between short-term and long-term traders. Short-term traders begin to take their profits, which slows down the stock's momentum. If nothing happens to offset this, there will be a "failure swing" at the top band (the stock will reverse without touching the band). If, however, the stock makes it all the way to the top band, short-term sellers may be shaken out while long-term investors continue to add to their positions. When this happens with sufficient strength, the stock may break loose from the pull of the short-term

[4] A special kind of trading bands, called "Bollinger bands," was developed by John Bollinger, the popular technical analyst who appears on CNBC. Bollinger bands are drawn a certain number of standard deviations away from the moving average.

traders and shoot through the top of the band. A *significant* penetration of the top band indicates gathering momentum and a likely continuation of the trend. This is often a good entry point.

What happens next, generally speaking, is that the stock "climbs the band": It will ride along the top of the band as the band itself moves up with the stock price. Finally, a point will be reached when even the long-term traders start selling, either to take their profits or in fear of the inevitable reversal. At this point, the stock will start to fall. If it finds support at the 30-day moving average (which it normally does in strong stocks as short-term traders reenter their positions), it may renew its charge toward the top, which is a good buy confirmation. If it does not find support at the 30-day moving average, what happened at the top band will be mirrored at the bottom band. If the stock penetrates the bottom band *significantly,* it is likely to continue its downtrend. On the other hand, a failure swing at the bottom—where the stock reverses without touching the bottom band—is a sign of strength. If the stock continues upward, it may meet resistance at the 30-day moving average, but if it pushes on through, that is a sign of continuing strength.

To recap, the three best confirmations of a buy signal are (1) a failure swing at the bottom band; (2) bouncing off the 30-day moving average *after* a penetration of the top band, and (3) a fresh penetration of the top band. It may take a while to become confident with your interpretations. The more charts you study, the better you will be able to read the signals.

THE TRENDSETTERS

Among the most widely used technical tools are trendlines. There have been many volumes filled with chart patterns depicting trendline analysis, but we have not found a great deal of value in such complicated patterns as "head and shoulders," "double tops," "cup and handles," and the like. We do, however, think simple trendline analysis is very helpful, and in this section we will talk about how to use rising and falling trendlines and horizontal support and resistance lines to time entry and exit points in a stock. (Trendlines are part of every technical analysis package and are easy to draw.)

Rising Trendlines

The foundation of trendline analysis is the simple rising trendline and falling trendline. A simple rising trendline is drawn diagonally through

Exhibit 9.9 Motorola shows an uptrend starting in late 1991.

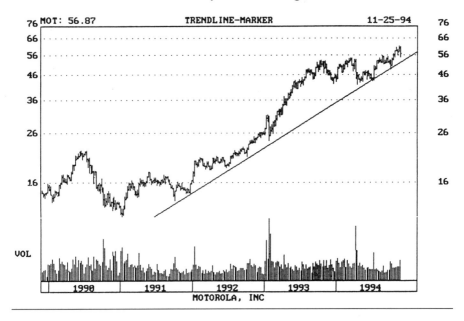

Exhibit 9.10 Micron Technology's long upward trend began in 1987. A sharper uptrend began in 1993 which was broken in November 1994.

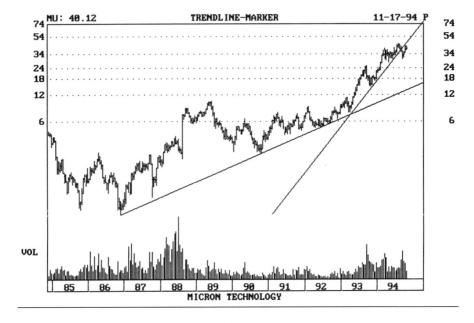

stock bottoms. It represents an important support zone on a stock's upward climb. The more times the stock touches the rising trendline, the stronger the support and the more valid the trend.

Rising trendlines are shown for Motorola (Exhibit 9.9), Micron Technology (Exhibit 9.10), and Amgen (Exhibit 9.11). All three of these uptrends are fairly well defined. Motorola repeatedly found support over three years as it reached its trendline. Micron had established a very long-term uptrend (since 1987), but at the beginning of 1993 it seems to have begun an even sharper uptrend. This latest trend would be more visible on a 2-year graph. Amgen shows a well-defined upward trend over eight months. The stock touched or approached the trendline a number of times on its way from $35 to $60. These rising trendlines are generally fueled by the same factors we have discussed previously: expectations of increased earnings and/or rising P/E ratios.

A good time to buy during a rising trend is when the stock hits support and reverses direction to continue its upward climb. At every test of the rising trendline, however, there is a chance that the trend will fail, so you should await the rebound from the trendline, as well as consider other

Exhibit 9.11   Amgen's uptrend is well defined: Notice the number of times it approached or touched the trendline in just 8 months.

signals. When a stock finally breaks its upward trend and drops below the rising trendline, it is a negative sign and a reason to consider selling.

Falling Trendlines

A simple falling trendline is drawn diagonally through stock tops and represents an area of resistance. Trendline analysts generally consider an upward break through a falling trendline as a good opportunity to buy, particularly if the trend break is confirmed by other technical signals. IBM (Exhibit 9.12), Merck (Exhibit 9.13) and Digital Equipment (Exhibit 9.14) are good examples. Many stocks do not exhibit such well-defined trends as we've shown here, but when one does, it is a good reinforcement of other buy signals.

Here are some points to keep in mind when drawing rising and falling trendlines:

- Rising trendlines should be drawn through stock bottoms; falling trendlines, through stock tops.

- The more tops or bottoms that a trendline touches, the more valid the trend.

Exhibit 9.12   **IBM broke through its 4-year downtrend in mid-1994.**

Exhibit 9.13   Merck & Co. broke through its 3-year downtrend in mid-1994.

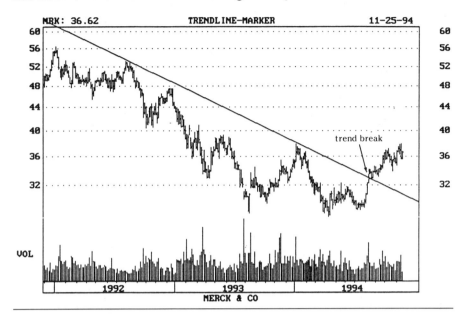

Exhibit 9.14   Digital Equipment broke through its 8-year downtrend in late 1994 on strong volume.

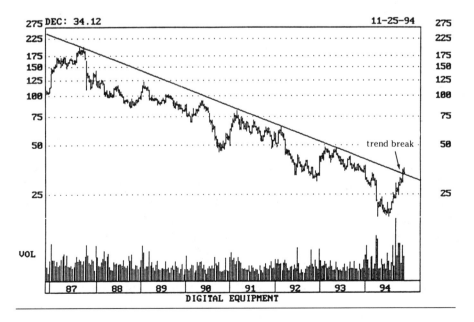

- A trend break that occurs on large volume is a more important signal than one that occurs on low volume.

- A trend break accompanied by buy signals from other technical indicators is particularly significant.

- Trends can be long-term as well as short-term.

- In a long uptrend, the ideal time to enter a new position would be a successful test of the trendline: when the stock approaches the rising trendline and reverses direction. Be sure to check to see whether the MACD remains positive. A bad time to enter in an uptrend would be when the stock is farthest from the rising trendline.

- In a long downtrend, an ideal time to enter a new position would be at a significant breakthrough of the falling trendline, with confirmation by other indicators.

SUPPORT AND RESISTANCE: FLOORS AND CEILINGS

Horizontal support and resistance lines are also helpful in assessing entry points. A support line is a horizontal line drawn across stock bottoms—it represents a short-term or long-term "floor" which supports the stock at that price level. A resistance line is a horizontal line drawn across stock tops—it represents a "ceiling" or area of resistance which the stock has difficulty penetrating. Pushing through a resistance line is a positive signal; a breakdown of a support line is negative.

Support

A support level is normally caused by one or more large institutions establishing that point as the price at which they will buy the stock. Being the patient investors they have to be, they will wait months (even years) to accumulate the stock at the price they've established as their entry point. Every time the stock reaches that level, the institutions step in and the stock rebounds. As a result, a floor forms under the stock at that point. The more times a stock has reached a support level and rebounded in the past, the more people are willing to trust the support level and enter at that point, and the more solid the floor becomes. For example, Micron Technology (Exhibit 9.15) has an eight-month support level at about $30; eight or nine times during the eight months it reached that level and reversed directions. Intel Corp. (Exhibit 9.16) has a year-long support level at about $56. Calgene (Exhibit 9.17) had fairly long-term support around $10 until mid-1994, when it breached that support once, rebounded, then fell below support and stayed there (through November 1994). Thus, a support line can be a good point of entry *if* the stock has reversed direction and *if* there are positive signals from other indicators.

Resistance

A resistance level that a stock has difficult penetrating is also caused by institutions in something of a self-fulfilling prophecy. When a stock reaches a price that represents a target level for many investors (especially institutions), the stock will have difficulty going beyond that point because these investors will sell every time it reaches that price. This sends the stock into a reversal and strengthens the resistance to that

Exhibit 9.15   Micron Technology has an 8-month support level at about $30.

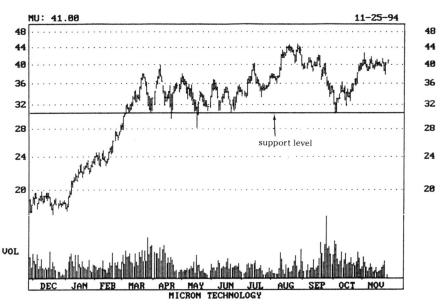

Exhibit 9.16   Intel Corporation has strong support at about $56.

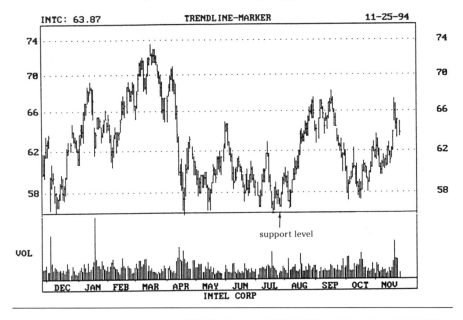

Exhibit 9.17   Calgene had strong support at about $10, which it broke through in July 1994. It recovered briefly and then fell through the floor again in September.

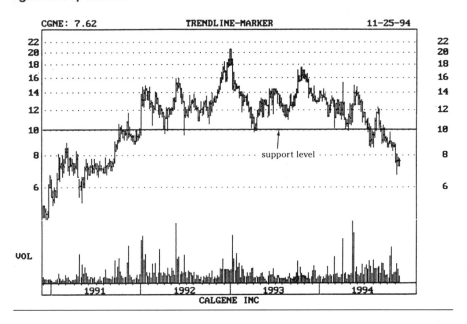

particular price level. The stock is unlikely to break through that resistance until the selling dries up, which is not likely to occur until earnings prospects, P/E ratios, or the market in general improves.

The strength of the resistance can be judged by how many times the stock has tested the resistance level and failed. The more approaches and failures, the more important the resistance. Intel (Exhibit 9.18) has a resistance level at about $72, which it has tested six or seven times. It is unwise to buy near a strong resistance level, but a strong breakthrough of a resistance level is an excellent entry point, especially if it is on high volume. Motorola (Exhibit 9.19) broke through a resistance level of about $54 in October of 1994 though not on significant volume. Broderbund Software (Exhibit 9.20) did the same, on higher volume. Breaking through a resistance level is more significant if the stock is in a long-term uptrend.

One final point before we leave this subject. Once a stock breaks through a resistance level that same level most frequently becomes an area of support. You can see that clearly in the Motorola and Broderbund graphs. When resistance and support lines are fairly close together and well defined, a stock may chatter between the two lines for a period of time. This then becomes known as a "basing period."

Exhibit 9.18   Intel has a 2-year resistance level at about $72.

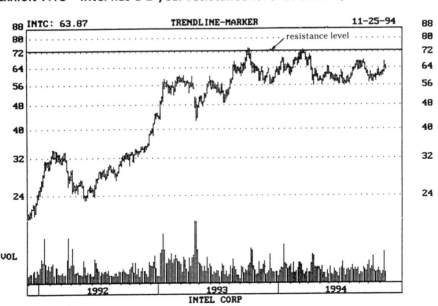

Exhibit 9.19 In October, Motorola broke through a fairly strong resistance level. Notice that support level at $43 was a resistance level in mid-1993.

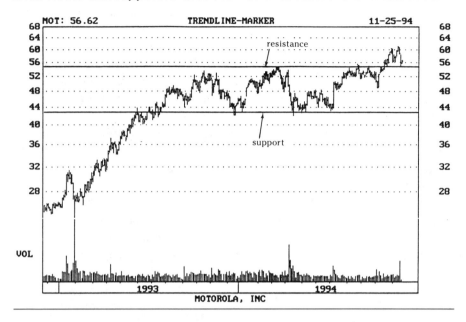

MOTOROLA, INC

Exhibit 9.20 Broderbund Software broke through a resistance level at about $59. Notice that the support level at $32 was a resistance level through most of 1992.

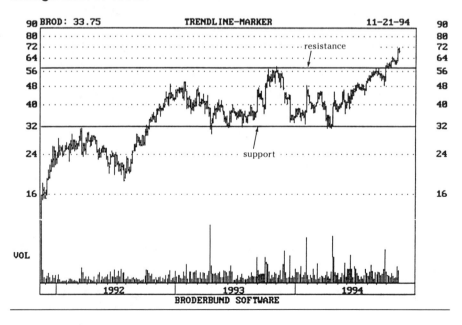

BRODERBUND SOFTWARE

BASING, BASING, BASING . . .

A technical indicator that we find very powerful for buy signals is the "basing period breakout." It is particularly effective for short-term trading.

A basing period takes place when a stock trades in a narrow price range for several days or weeks (Exhibit 9.21). This may occur during an uptrend, when the stock halts along the way as if to catch its breath, and it frequently happens after a "waterfall" decline. During a basing period, supply and demand are more or less equally matched. Every time new buyers move in, there is an overhead supply: Enough sellers are satisfied with the market price and are willing to sell and move on to something else. As new buyers move in, these sellers pour stock into the marketplace, preventing the stock from moving higher. It just sort of treads water—"basing" within a narrow trading range often on low volume. In other words, support and resistance lines come together.

Eventually, the stock will break out of its basing pattern in one direction or the other. A positive breakout (upward) means the selling has basically dried up or more buying has started to come in. A negative

---

Exhibit 9.21   A 10 percent, 13-week basing pattern for Imax Corporation. Notice the breakout on November 16.

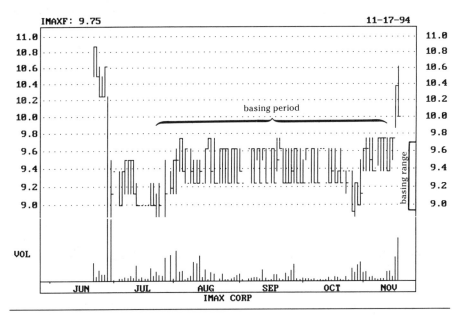

breakout (downward) means the opposite: The buying has dried up and the selling has begun.

The Quality of the Breakout

The quality of the breakout is judged by the pattern of the basing period, the magnitude of the breakout, and the volume on the day of the breakout. The basing pattern consists of the length of the period and the percentage of price range during the period. Investors have different ideas about what constitutes a high quality basing pattern, although a tight pattern is usually considered good. For example, when a stock trades between, say, $20 and $22 for six months, it is in a 10 percent, 26-week basing period, which is considered a very tight pattern.

The longer the stock has stayed in a tight basing pattern (so technicians generally say), the more powerful a move it will make when it breaks out. It seems obvious that a stock which bases for 13 weeks in a 10 percent range and then breaks out is more impressive than a stock which breaks out of a 20-percent, 3-week pattern. We're not aware of any academic studies that correlate the tightness of the basing pattern with the subsequent move, but our observations tend to support it.

The magnitude of the breakout is also important. If the stock that has been basing from $20 to $22 suddenly goes to $22¼, that would be considered a breakout, but ¼ of a point is not particularly exciting. A breakout to $22½ or $22¾ would be more impressive, especially on large volume.

Volume is important in judging the quality of a basing pattern breakout. If a stock breaks out on weak volume, it may drift right back into the basing pattern the next day. Stocks that break out of tight basing patterns on high volume have tended to move significantly higher. The rationale for this is that the high volume associated with the breakout dries up the sellers.

The Search for Basing Pattern Breakouts

Not all basing patterns are as easy to recognize as Imax Corporation's 10-percent, 13-week pattern in Exhibit 9.21. Those with broader bases and wider ranges are harder to distinguish on a stock graph. Many technicians use a search tool to find basing pattern breakouts (the stocks should then be evaluated as described previously). You could also run the basing pattern search and an undervalued growth search, and wait for a stock to appear on both lists. Either approach is valid. Just remember to take a close look at the magnitude of the breakout and the volume.

WATCHING A "WATCH LIST"

Many investors keep a "watch list" of 25, 50, or 100 stocks that they would be willing to purchase on a strong technical buy signal. It becomes cumbersome and time-consuming, however, to plot technical indicators on so many stock graphs. There are two alternative approaches you might use to obtain technical entry signals for a large group of stocks. One way is to run breakout searches; another is to turn your decision over to an "expert system."

Breakout Searches

Breakout searches are an easy way to look for buy signals on a large group of stocks. Simply run a search looking for MACD breakouts, stochastics breakouts, or basing period breakouts. This would be a one-indicator search, eliminating all stocks except those with the designated breakouts. When one of the stocks on your watch list turns up on one of the breakout searches, you have your buy signal. All you need to do is to evaluate the stock along the lines described in earlier chapters, or, if the stocks have already been evaluated, check other technical indicators for confirmation.

The TradingExpert™

An alternative for following a large list of stocks is the AIQ Trading-Expert™ from AIQ Incorporated. This system combines a number of technical trading rules to generate an "expert rating" for each stock in the system. Here's how it works.

First, the stocks are loaded into AIQ (which can be done automatically from ProSearch); then the expert rating is obtained by logging onto an online services that serves AIQ (Dial Data, Dow Jones, or Telescan, among others). Exhibit 9.22 shows a weekly Expert Rating Report. The expert rating, which is based on many technical indicators, predicts the likelihood that each stock in the system will move or continue to move upwards. An accompanying AIQ stock chart for the top-rated stock (Exhibit 9.23) reveals the rules which fired in giving rise to the expert rating.

Exhibit 9.22   The weekly "Expert Analysis" report from AIQ TradingExpert. The same stocks are repeated in both upside and downside ratings because only the top 10 stocks from the undervalued growth search were entered into the system.   Normally, investors would use the TradingExpert to follow a greater number of stocks.

AIQ TradingExpert
Weekly Expert Analysis Report
09/09/94

Ticker	Op	Name	Urc	ER	RSI	Delta		Accum	
Upside Rating									
15 lines of Upside ER GE 0									
WMT	Y	Wal-Mart Stores	WMT	89	55	4	43	26	50
STRY	Y	Stryker Corp	STRY	59	58	84	71	76	68
LINB	Y	LIN Broadcasting	LINB	42	73	71	2	92	100
WSAU	N	Wausau Paper Mills	WSAU	21	62	0	83	5	39
PXR	N	Paxar Corp	PXR	13	77	66	100	34	76
SCA	Y	Surgical Care	SCA	13	41	100	63	100	50
TDS	Y	Telephone & Data Systems	TDS	13	53	54	0	73	84
KR	Y	Kroger Co	KR	7	68	28	25	33	61
NDSN	N	Nordson Corp	NDSN	3	64	15	44	0	0
DSCP	Y	Datascope Corp	DSCP	2	53	30	25	2	44
Downside Rating									
15 lines of Downside ER GE 0									
NDSN	N	Nordson Corp	NDSN	96	64	15	44	0	0
DSCP	Y	Datascope Corp	DSCP	79	53	30	25	2	44
PXR	N	Paxar Corp	PXR	72	77	66	100	34	76
SCA	Y	Surgical Care	SCA	72	41	100	63	100	50
TDS	Y	Telephone & Data Systems	TDS	72	53	54	0	73	84
KR	Y	Kroger Co	KR	67	68	28	25	33	61
WSAU	N	Wausau Paper Mills	WSAU	48	62	0	83	5	39
LINB	Y	LIN Broadcasting	LINB	37	73	71	2	92	100
STRY	Y	Stryker Corp	STRY	11	58	84	71	76	68
WMT	Y	Wal-Mart Stores	WMT	1	55	4	43	26	50
Volume Accumulation									
15 lines of Volume Accumulation % GE 0									
LINB	Y	LIN Broadcasting	LINB	42	73	71	2	92	100
TDS	Y	Telephone & Data Systems	TDS	13	53	54	0	73	84
PXR	N	Paxar Corp	PXR	13	77	66	100	34	76
STRY	Y	Stryker Corp	STRY	59	58	84	71	76	68
KR	Y	Kroger Co	KR	7	68	28	25	33	61
WMT	Y	Wal-Mart Stores	WMT	89	55	4	43	26	50
SCA	Y	Surgical Care	SCA	13	41	100	63	100	50
Volume Distribution									
15 lines of Volume Distribution % GE 0									
NDSN	N	Nordson Corp	NDSN	96	64	15	44	0	0
WSAU	N	Wausau Paper Mills	WSAU	48	62	0	83	5	39
DSCP	Y	Datascope Corp	DSCP	79	53	30	25	2	44

Source: Courtesy of AIQ, Incorporated.

Exhibit 9.23 An AIQ graph for Wal-Mart which was No. 1 on the upside rating in Exhibit 9.22. The MACD indicator is plotted as a graph, rather than a histogram. (Source: Courtesy of AIQ, Incorporated.)

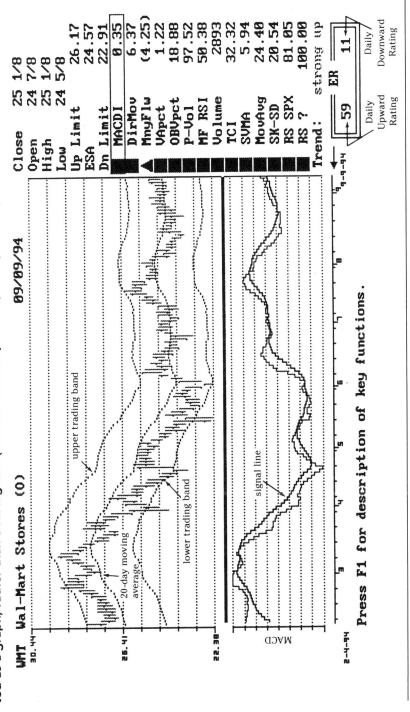

151

The AIQ system is a powerful and very useful program, but it probably doesn't make sense to use it for only 10 stocks, as we did. It is more frequently used to follow 100 or so stocks, and more often by short-term traders than by fundamentally inclined investors.

TO RECAP

Technical timing is the last step before purchasing the stock. The ideal entry point is either of the following conditions:

- An MACD breakout, especially one on good volume, with positive readings on the stochastics (above the 25 percent line and moving upward) and trading bands (above the 30-day moving average headed upward). Confirmation by one of the three trading band signals described earlier makes the breakout especially strong.

- If there is no MACD breakout, go with the preponderance of evidence: a positive reading on the MACD (a recent positive breakout or below the zero line and increasing), plus positive readings on the stochastics and trading bands.

The situations to avoid are technically overbought conditions or a failure swing at the top of the trading bands.

THE SEARCH FOR THE SUPER-INDICATOR

For the died-in-the-wool technician, a number of technical analysis programs, such as MetaStock™, SuperCharts™, and Windows on Wall Street™, allow you to combine indicators for a unique effect and to create your own indicators. (A MetaStock diskette is included with your Cyber-Investing Kit.) Be forewarned that creating your own indicators is extremely time-consuming and can be expensive because of the extensive backtesting that is required. A significant amount of time and money must be expended to obtain the necessary data. Nonetheless, many are fascinated with the search for the superior indicator. If you have the time and the inclination, you may find this fun and potentially rewarding.

MEANWHILE, BACK AT THE RANCH . . .

We haven't forgotten the five finalists from our undervalued growth search. All these stocks were positive on the weekly MACD (a requirement of our original search), so they are all considered generally positive from our technical viewpoint. Therefore, in the following analysis (as of August 11, 1994), we are considering only the very short term—whether we buy the stock immediately or wait for better technical readings.

- Wal-Mart (Exhibits 9.24, 9.25, and 9.26) looks somewhat attractive. It has recently broken above a major downtrend and is at a major support level. The only negative is that it has also broken a minor uptrend. The stochastic is close to giving a buy signal, and the MACD is now headed in the right direction. There was a failure swing at the top of the trading bands, which caused the most recent correction in the stock, but it may be holding just below the 30-day moving average.

Exhibit 9.24   Wal-Mart's MACD is turning upward and could generate a buy signal soon. Note the support level at $24.

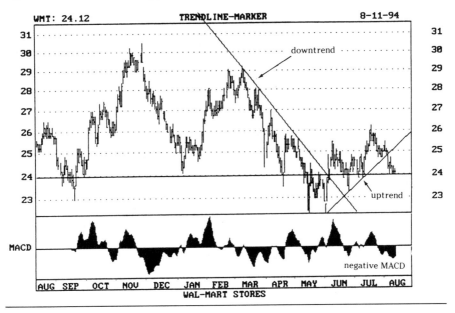

Exhibit 9.25 The 21/5 stochastic for Wal-Mart. A buy signal will occur when the index crosses *above* the 25 percent line.

21 DY-Stochastic Len |5 DY-Mov Avg |

Exhibit 9.26 In July Wal-Mart had a negative failure swing at the top of the trading bands.

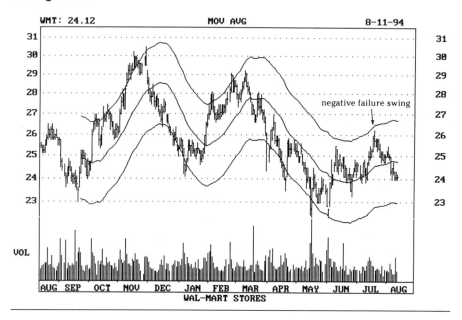

- TDS (Exhibits 9.27, 9.28, and 9.29) has broken out of a major downtrend, but may be in for a short-term correction. Once before it has not been able to break through the resistance at $43. The MACD is very close to a sell signal, and the stochastics is clearly overbought. It is now climbing the trading band after a positive failure swing at the bottom of the band. All in all, TDS is somewhat of a mixed bag, but slightly negative at the moment.

- Kroger (Exhibits 9.30, 9.31 and 9.32), near a 12-month high, appears to be in an uptrend, but it is right at support for that trend. It is also near a major resistance level, which has kept the stock from going higher. The daily MACD is negative and moving even more negative. It has had a negative breakout on the stochastic, a bad sign, and did not even come close to reaching the top of the trading band on its most recent attempt. So, as good as Kroger looked in the Stage Two evaluation, it appears to be on a downward trend, at least for the short term. Remember, though, the weekly MACD is positive, so chances are, any correction will be brief.

Exhibit 9.27   TDS broke its downtrend in late July, but it is at a resistance level with the MACD close to a sell signal.

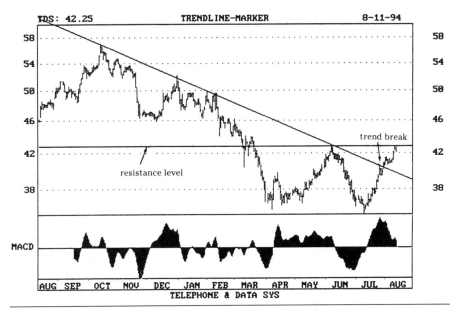

Exhibit 9.28   The TDS stochastic is clearly overbought.

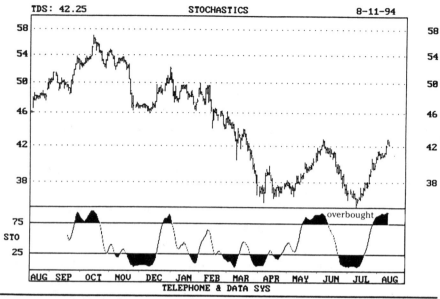

21 DY-Stochastic Len |5 DY-Mov Avg |

Exhibit 9.29   TDS had a positive failure swing at the bottom of the trading bands and is now climbing the band.

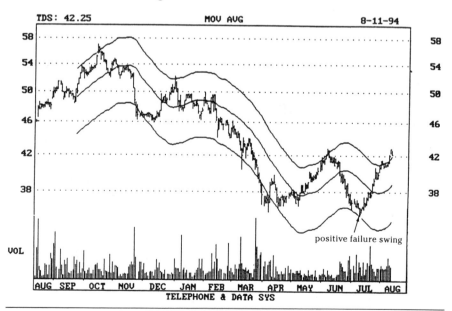

Exhibit 9.30   Kroger is at support on its uptrend but near a major resistance level.

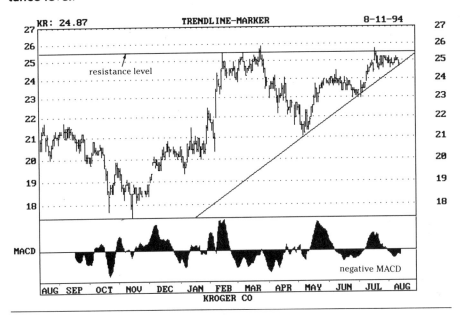

Exhibit 9.31   Kroger had a negative breakout in late July on its 21/5 stochastic.

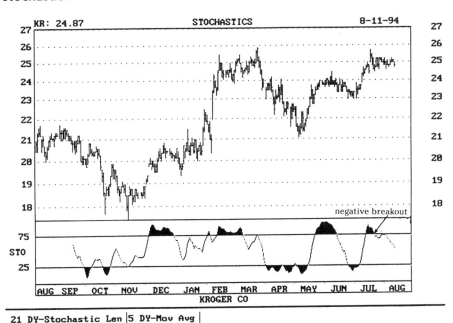

**Exhibit 9.32   Kroger made a run at the top of the trading bands in early
July but failed; now it is around its 30-day moving average.**

- Lin Broadcasting (Exhibits 9.33, 9.34, and 9.35) is near its 12-month
  high. There doesn't seem to be any resistance, at least during the
  past year, and it appears to be holding at support on its uptrend.
  If the daily MACD breaks out positively (which appears likely
  since the weekly MACD is positive), this could be a good time to
  buy. On the other hand, the stochastics is about to generate a sell
  signal, so we would probably await the test of the 30-day moving
  average on the trading bands before making a decision.

- Surgical Care Affiliates (Exhibits 9.36, 9.37, and 9.38) has been on
  a steady upward move and appears to have broken through some
  major resistance and is fighting to stay there. The problems are
  the daily MACD is weakening, it is overbought on the stochastics,
  and there has been a recent failure swing at the top of the trading
  bands. We would await something more positive before buying
  this stock.

Exhibit 9.33 Lin Broadcasting looks close to a buy signal on its daily 8/17/9 MACD and is at support on its uptrend.

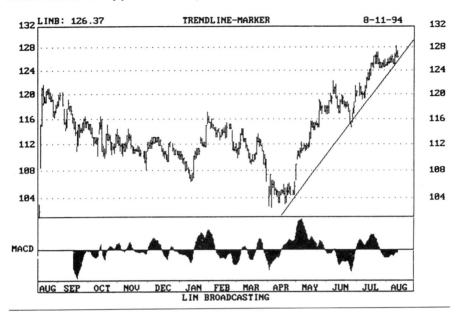

Exhibit 9.34 Lin Broadcasting is overbought according to its stochastics, which could generate a sell signal momentarily, in direct contradiction to the MACD reading in Exhibit 9.33.

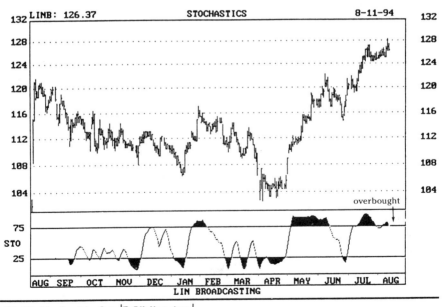

21 DY-Stochastic Len |5 DY-Mov Avg |

Exhibit 9.35 Lin Broadcasting had a negative failure swing in mid-July and is testing the 30-day moving average.

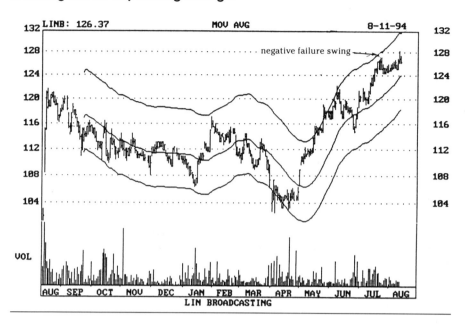

Exhibit 9.36 Surgical Care recently broke through a major downtrend and through resistance, which is a positive sign, but the 8/17/9 daily MACD appears to be weakening.

Exhibit 9.37 The 21/5 stochastics shows Surgical Care as overbought.

21 DY-Stochastic Len |5 DY-Mov Avg |

Exhibit 9.38 Surgical Care has had a negative failure swing at the top of its trading bands.

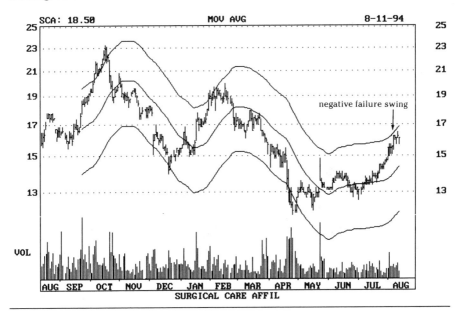

None of the five stocks gave us a clear buy signal, but remember that all we're trying to do is optimize our entry. Since all the stocks are positive on the weekly MACD, one could buy Wal-Mart, because it has a preponderance of evidence on its side. It is also close to its low for the year, so the risk/reward relationship is good. The long-term investor might go ahead and buy Wal-Mart now, although the short-term trader would probably wait a few days to see if Wal-Mart or Lin Broadcasting gives an MACD buy signal. The point is, why hurry? All five stocks have favorable fundamental characteristics and long-term patterns that would make them good buys. Waiting for a signal seems to be prudent for a short-term investor.

As you can see, stocks are not always ready when you are. That's why it is a good idea to keep a "watch list" of stocks that have been thoroughly evaluated. This increases the likelihood of finding a stock that is technically desirable when you are ready to buy.

YOU MUST REMEMBER THIS . . .

In stocks, as in romance, timing is important. Pay attention to the technical condition of the stock when you're ready to purchase it, but don't become obsessed with technical analysis.

- The MACD, in our experience, offers satisfactory exit and entry points, especially when confirmed by a positive stochastics or trading bands.

- In lieu of a clear-cut buy signal, go with the preponderance of evidence: positive readings on two or more indicators.

- Don't try to get large numbers of technical indicators to agree. The effect is not cumulative. One valid signal is often as good as three, as long as it is confirmed by another indicator.

- We have found no evidence that a stock with multiple breakouts—say, an MACD breakout, a stochastics breakout, and a basing period breakout—is more likely to go up than a stock with just one breakout.

- Technical timing is somewhat less critical to long-term investors who plan to hold stocks for six months to several years. Nevertheless, our backtesting has proven the value of technical timing, which often prevents being caught in a meltdown.

- A number of publications have done exhaustive backtesting of technical indicators. One of the best is Colby and Meyers' *The Encyclopedia of Technical Market Indicators* mentioned previously. Generally speaking, they concluded that technical indicators are helpful, with the MACD among the best.

- Trendline analysis with its support and resistance zones is used by many investors with good results.

- It may take several weeks for a stock to give an appropriate buy signal. If even one day has elapsed between your Stage Two evaluation and the technical buy signal, double-check the current news and the S&P report for that stock. We operate in a dynamic market and something could have happened to change your opinion of the stock.

10
THE ART
OF THE PURCHASE

Purchasing a stock involves more than just calling up a broker and saying "Buy 100 shares of IBM." You have to decide whether to use a full service broker or a discount broker, whether to place your trades by telephone or enter them on your computer (which can reduce the broker's commission). You have to open the account, transfer your investment funds into it, and sign a few papers. Once your account is set up, buying a stock becomes fairly routine. Still, with every purchase, you have to decide whether to use a "market order" or a "limit order," how many shares to buy, and where to set your targets and stops. Finally, you need to keep a file of everything that went into your purchase decision so that when it comes time to sell, you will have a basis of comparison. If you're an experienced trader, you may not need any help with these matters. If you're not, this chapter offers some guidance and tools.

CHOOSING A BROKER

Selecting a broker is a personal decision. Full-service brokers offer personal attention and (usually) access to their company's research data;

discount brokers offer lower commissions for investors who like to do their own research. The best thing is to do some comparison shopping: Request sales literature from both and compare their services. Then call a couple of brokers and ask questions. Or talk with friends who trade stocks and ask them about their experience with brokers.

If you have never had a brokerage account, you might find of value a little book called *How to Talk to a Broker* by Jay J. Pack.[1] It provides basic information about selecting a broker, opening an account, types of orders, margin accounts, holding the stock in your name or the broker's name (called *street name*), and more.

ELECTRONIC TRADING

If you're interested in electronic trading—placing buy and sell orders directly to a broker via Touchtone telephone or personal computer—discount brokers are the way to go. Generally speaking, you can prepare the orders offline and then log to the appropriate database (or place the telephone call) and send them all at once.

Electronic trading requires investors who are confident in their investment skills and comfortable with the technology. If this sounds like you, you can save an *additional* 10 percent or more on the already-discounted commissions by entering your trades on your computer or through the broker's interactive telephone system. (The Cyber-Investing Kit contains a special offer from Charles Schwab & Co. Other brokers offering electronic trading are listed in Appendix A.) Trades may be placed 24 hours a day, and most online trading systems offer stock quotes, account balances, and trade status. Some offer research, quasi-portfolio management programs, charting, graphing, and other online services and analytical tools.

Electronic trading is in its infancy, but it is growing rapidly. Stay tuned.

PLACING THE ORDER

Whether you place your order by telephone or by computer, here are a few hints:

---

[1] Jay J. Pack, *How to Talk to a Broker* (New York: Harper & Row, 1985).

- If a day or two has passed since the Stage Two analysis described in Chapter 8, recheck the current news for any story that might have a negative effect on the stock you wish to buy.

- Don't "nickel and dime" your entry point. Unless you are a very, very short-term trader, quibbling over a fraction of a point may only keep you out of a good stock. If you have done your homework, the stock you choose should stand a reasonable chance of increasing as much as 50 percent in less than a year. If it has had a positive technical breakout—which it will have if you're using the guidelines in this book—it *should* be moving upward. The fact that it moves another quarter or half a point while you're trying to buy it should only confirm that you've made the right decision.

- In most cases, use a "market order" rather than a "limit order." A market order tells the broker to buy the stock at the going price; if the stock moves up before your order can be executed, the broker will pay the higher price. A limit order places conditions on the purchase, such as "Don't pay more than X." If a stock's fundamentals are good and the technical signal is right, the stock *should be* moving up smartly. Using a limit order is only advisable on thinly traded stocks (with an average daily volume of, say, fewer than 10,000 shares) and only if you are buying several hundred shares.

- Don't buy on a "pullback." This is a limit order that tells the broker to buy only if the stock drops a quarter or an eighth. *If the stock pulls back, it is going in the wrong direction!* This is a very common mistake of amateur investors. To repeat ourselves, if you've made a good selection, the stock should be moving up, and if you insist on seeing it drop before you buy, you may miss it altogether. Besides, if it heads down instead of up, it may mean you were wrong in your analysis.

TARGET PRACTICE

If you don't know where you're going, how will you know when you arrive? Setting a *target* gives you a destination for your stock—and a gauge against which to measure its progress. As the stock approaches the target, its risk/reward relationship changes dramatically and that can bear on your decision to hold the stock or sell it, as we'll talk about later.

A target is not just some hopeful number plucked out of thin air. Nor is it the overall portfolio goal of a 15 to 20 percent per year return. A target is the price that you expect the stock to achieve based on its historical performance. There are several ways to set a target: LSQ lines, trading bands, trendlines, resistance levels. In actual practice, we consider them all, setting stops (described later in this chapter) as the stock reaches each level. How you set stops will depend in part on whether you're a short-term or long-term investor. In this section, we will use Wal-Mart as an example of the various ways to set a target. In Chapter 12, we'll talk about what to do when a stock approaches its target.

Long-Term LSQ

The top of the long-term LSQ channel can be used with many stocks as a long-term target. However, if a stock has had a dramatic price move in the past, as Wal-Mart did in the 1980s, that can create a steeply angled LSQ line on the long-term chart. Using the top of Wal-Mart's long-term LSQ trading channel (Exhibit 10.1) would set an unrealistic performance goal in the upper $60s, which is more than triple its current price. However, the stock has spent almost eight years near the LSQ line, so using that as a target—somewhere in the upper $40s—might be reasonable. It would just be a doubling of the current price.

Short-Term LSQ

If there has been an anomalous price move in the past, we will also look at a short-term LSQ (Exhibit 10.2). Wal-Mart has spent a fair amount of time at the top of the channel, so it would not be unrealistic to think it could reach that level again. That would give us a target in the low $40s.

Resistance Levels

Short-term traders might look at resistance levels (Exhibit 10.3). The stock has previously reached $34, but there is a fair amount of resistance at about $30. With the stock currently trading around $23, you could set a short-term goal of about $30, which would be a fairly handsome short-term profit.

Exhibit 10.1   A target based on Wal-Mart's long-term LSQ channel would be in the mid-$60 range.

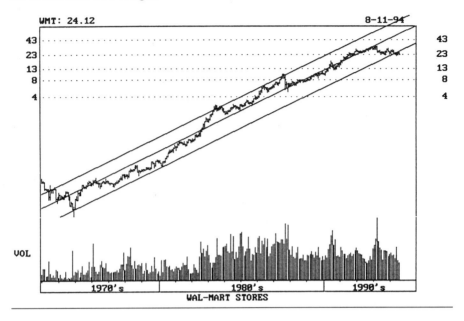

Exhibit 10.2   A target based on Wal-Mart's short-term LSQ channel would be in the low $40s.

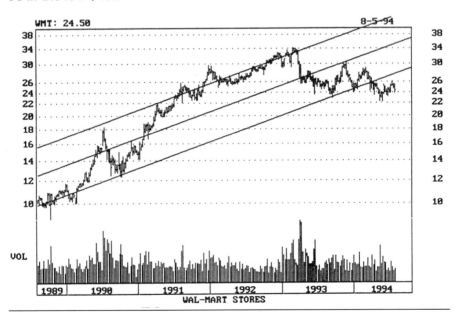

Exhibit 10.3   A short-term target based on Wal-Mart's resistance level would be about $30.

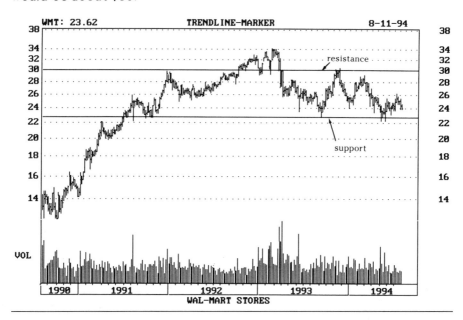

WAL-MART STORES

Trading Bands

Wal-Mart's trading bands (Exhibit 10.4) would more or less confirm a near-term target of around $29 to $30. The stock has recently had a failure swing at the bottom band and is seeking support at the 30-day moving average. If it gets it, the band will turn up as the stock moves up, but it should run into the upper band resistance at around $29 or $30.

Considering these various resistance levels, we might set the following series of targets for Wal-Mart: $30, low $40s, upper $40s, mid-$60s. Assuming the stock makes it through the first resistance level and you remain comfortable with the situation, you can aim at the next target, and then the next, and then the next. However, as the stock moves through the various resistance levels, you will want to focus on all the issues that are brought up in Chapter 12 under "The Positive Sell" (one of which is setting stops at each resistance level to protect your profits). In that chapter, we'll show you how to use computerized tools to assess the progress of a stock as it moves, or fails to move, toward its target.

Exhibit 10.4 A short-term target for Wal-Mart based on trading bands would be around $29 or $30.

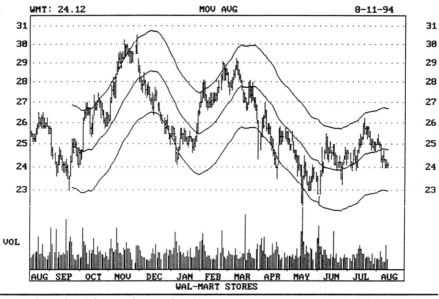

WAL-MART STORES

SETTING STOPS

Stops can be used to limit your losses. There are "hard stops" and "mental stops." A hard stop is a firm order to your broker to sell a stock if it drops to a specified level. Hard stops, in most cases, can protect your downside, but they leave no room for rethinking a decision. If you give your broker a stop order, he or she is legally obligated to sell the stock if the price drops to your stop price, even though it may bounce back five minutes later. This can sometimes force you out of a stock before you're ready or at a disadvantageous price.

We generally prefer mental stops. A mental stop is simply a reminder to yourself to consider selling a stock if it falls to a certain level. (A mental stop can be entered as a "risk level" in the Telescan portfolio management program described in Chapter 11.) A mental stop enables you to reflect on market conditions and consider any extenuating circumstances before making a decision to sell.

When to Use a Mental Stop

It is a good idea to set an initial mental stop at the time of purchase to limit any losses at the outset. We typically set the initial mental stop at approximately 15 to 20 percent below the purchase price (typically , these are set just below important support levels in the 15 to 20 percent zone). In other words, we're suggesting that if we buy a stock at $20 and it drops to $17 or $16, we may have made a mistake. We say "may have" because whether or not the stock should be sold depends in part on what the market is doing. In essence, a mental stop simply tells us it is time to rethink our decision.

When to Use a Hard Stop

There are times when a hard stop is preferred. One is when a stock is near a major support level. For example, look at Wal-Mart's strong historical support level at approximately $23 a share in Exhibit 10.3; that is just $1.00 below the current (August 11, 1994) price. If the stock should drop below a level that hasn't been breached in three years, we would not need to rethink our decision; we would want out. In Wal-Mart's case, we would be inclined to use a initial hard stop at around $22.

Another time we use hard stops is to protect our profits. We always keep a "protective" mental stop about 15 percent below the stock price. However, when the stock nears its target, we switch to a hard stop, which we set (and keep) about 5 percent below the current price or at an important support level. If a stock is near its target, we will be looking for a reason to sell; we won't need to rethink our decision. (We'll talk more about this in the next chapter.)

A hard stop can protect your downside, but it will not fully protect you if a stock "gaps down." A downward gap occurs when a stock opens below its previous day's close or after a "trading halt" due to important news. For example, if a stock should close at $40 and open at $32, a hard stop at $37 would be bypassed. You would sell at $32. (A 20 percent gap, by the way, is not infrequent.)

There is, however, something else to consider. What if it turns out that the market overreacted, that the news wasn't as bad as expected. If you still find the stock attractive and want back in, you might have to pay more than the $32 at which you were stopped out. Plus, you'll have to pay commissions both ways.

In the end, using mental stops versus hard stops is a personal call. Sometimes, experience is the only way to learn which you prefer.

THE PURCHASE LOG

When you're trying to decide whether or not to sell a stock, it helps to know why you purchased it in the first place. Memories are fallible, which is why many investors keep a "purchase log." When you review your decision some months down the road, a purchase log can help illuminate where you made a mistake if things go awry, or what went into a good decision if things go well.

A purchase log should contain all the research material you used to analyze a stock: stock graphs, technical charts, news stories, corporate profiles, earnings estimate reports, any information that you used in your decision. It is also helpful to include handwritten notes such as, why Stock A was chosen over Stock B; how you felt about the market (positive? wary?); what kind of mood you were in at the time (optimistic? apprehensive?). Such information helps clarify what was going on externally and internally at the time you bought the stock.

Purchase logs can take almost any form, from neatly labeled folders to a bunch of sheets stapled together to a catchall box in the corner of your office. One investor says he uses the finest leather-grained diary because it *feels* like money and makes him aware of how serious the process is. The wave of the future is the computerized purchase log, where all data collected electronically can be stored in an electronic file. An electronic log is currently available in some programs, such as AIQ's TradingExpert™.

The major use of the purchase log is as a reference for tracking the stocks in your portfolio. For example, when one of your companies announces its earnings, you can compare them against the earnings estimates that you relied on when selecting the stock. (You may want to sell if the earnings fail to materialize as projected.) If the earnings estimates are not in your purchase log, you may have a hard time finding out what they were because six months from now, new estimates will have replaced the old ones on the database. Having all the information in one place greatly enhances your ability to make informed decisions.

A purchase log can and should be used as a learning aid, so that you can profit from your mistakes and successes. For this reason, we recommend including in the purchase log the search report that generated the stock you purchased (the report with all your notations from the Stage One analysis), along with the research material on all the stocks from that search which made the final cut. In the months that follow, you may wish to check out the runner-up stocks to see whether you did indeed select the right one; if it turns out that you didn't pick the best one, the purchase log may help you to analyze why one stock did better than another.

Investing is a continual learning process, and the purchase log is an invaluable tool. The more information you have at review time, the more meaningful will be your lessons.

YOU MUST REMEMBER THIS . . .

The most important things to remember when buying a stock are:

- Find a broker that matches your needs and style of investing.
- Electronic trading can save you 10 percent or more on commissions, but it requires confidence in your skills and a degree of comfort with the technology.
- Make sure you have checked the news within a day or so of purchase.
- Don't "nickel and dime" your entry point.
- Don't try to buy on a pullback.
- Set a target for each stock in your portfolio.
- Set an initial mental stop 15 to 20 percent below the purchase price, and tighten the stop as the stock nears its target.
- Use hard stops judiciously.
- Keep a purchase log.
- Learn from your successes and your mistakes.

Now let's move on to portfolio management.

11

THE 20-MINUTE MANAGER

Portfolio management is the nuts and bolts of investing. It encompasses the building of the portfolio, keeping abreast of market conditions, regularly monitoring each stock in the portfolio, deciding when to sell or replace a stock, and repeating the whole investment process each time you buy a new stock. The results of good portfolio management show up on the bottom line, in your quarterly and yearly returns. It is a lot like cultivating a garden. If you select quality seeds, plant them at the right time, weed out the sickly specimens, and watch over them with a lot of TLC, you should reap a bountiful crop at harvest time.

Good portfolio management consists of six broad activities:

1. *Asset Allocation.* How much of your total assets should you invest in stocks at a given time? How much in cash? Should you consider bonds? Should you consider other alternatives?

2. *Market Analysis.* What is the general level of the market on a short-term basis? Is it so high you should temporarily cut back on your stock exposure? Is it so low that you should redouble your efforts to find more prospects? (Long-term investors will

find that careful attention to asset allocation obviates the need for much market analysis.)

3. *Diversification.* How many stocks should you own? In which industries? When should you buy them? Which searches should you use?

4. *Monitoring.* How should you monitor your stocks' progress toward their targets? What information will you review? How often should you review it? How much time will it take?

5. *The Sell Decision.* How will you know when to take your profits? When to let your profits run? When to cut your losses? When to substitute one stock for another?

6. *Evaluation.* How well is your portfolio doing? Are you keeping up with market averages? How do you stack up against comparable mutual funds? What can you do to improve?

In this chapter, we'll introduce you to computerized tools and techniques that will help you answer these questions and simplify your management chores. Because of the nature of the selling process and of market analysis, as well as the length of these discussions, these two activities will be discussed separately in Chapters 12 and 13.

DIVVYING UP THE INVESTMENT PIE

Asset allocation has to do with the way you distribute your total investment funds among various asset classes (e.g., U.S. stocks, bonds, mutual funds, cash, and global investments). At the moment, there is not much computerized help for the average investor. Some very sophisticated asset allocation models are used by financial planners, but we know of only one that is really aimed at the individual investor and that is *WealthBuilder*™, published by Reality Technologies, Inc. This program is exceedingly simple and easy to use, but it may have limited use for the serious investor.

MacroWorld Research Corporation is addressing this problem in a dynamic way with its Macro*World™ Investment Plan. This asset allocation program will incorporate the highly respected Macro*World forecasted returns and risk levels into the mix. Thus, the user will end up with a more realistic risk and reward analysis. Undoubtedly, asset allocation programs will, in general, follow MacroWorld's lead and increase in functionality and sophistication over the next few years.

BONDS AND MUTUAL FUNDS IN CYBERSPACE

Most asset allocation programs recommend that a portion of the investment pie go to bonds. Unfortunately, there's not much activity for bonds in cyberspace at the moment. We do not know of any full bond analysis program for the PC, at least for the individual investor. This shortcoming is sure to be remedied in the near future. Meanwhile, those who prefer bonds will have to rely on professional advice or else search for a mutual fund that concentrates in bonds.

As to mutual funds, the cyber-investor can take an active, analytical approach in selecting (or switching among) funds. Search products designed specifically for mutual funds allow you to search for funds that have the best performance record and that match your investment goals. You may specify risk, portfolio composition, fee structure, purchase requirements, performance relative to market averages, and type of fund, among other things. (Try it yourself with Telescan's Mutual Fund Search™, which is part of the Cyber-Investing Kit.)

There is some crossover between stock tools and mutual fund tools. Graphs can be plotted, just as for stocks, although they are useful mainly in comparing the performance of one fund with another because trends are somewhat meaningless. There is no volume related to mutual fund trading, and the price of a fund's shares is based on the aggregate of all the stocks in the portfolio and therefore not as susceptible to market psychology. A popular information report for mutual funds, the Morningstar Report, published by Morningstar, Inc., is available through many online services. It contains a number of rating criteria and lists the top 10 stocks in a fund's portfolio. And, industry group rotation can be applied indirectly to mutual funds by selecting a "sector fund," which specializes in a particular industry, such as Fidelity Aerospace or Fidelity Biotech. First, you would need to identify the industry groups with the most momentum (you can use the search described in Chapter 14); then you would select a fund that specializes in one of those groups.

In this book, we are considering only the slice of the investment pie that has been allocated to stocks. However, we have provided guidelines in Chapter 13 for analyzing market conditions and adjusting your stocks-to-cash ratio at market extremes.

PUTTING YOUR STOCKS IN DIFFERENT BASKETS

Diversification is one of the most important components of portfolio management. It is a way to reduce risk by spreading it over a number of stocks, a number of industries, a variety of searches, and a variety of market conditions.

More Stocks Lower the Risk

Diversification by number of stocks is a frequently debated topic. One market expert may recommend as few as five stocks for a well-balanced portfolio; another may recommend 20 or more. We believe you should own as many as you can manage effectively. The more, the better. Why? With a large portfolio, you have only a fraction of your assets in any one position, which gives you a more generous margin for error. If you have only five stocks in your portfolio, you're betting 20 percent of your total investment on each stock. If one of them should happen to take a 50 percent drop, you will lose 10 percent of your money on just one position (stops can't protect against gaps). If you have 20 stocks, on the other hand, a 50 percent loss on one represents only 2.5 percent of your total investment.

How much time does it take to manage a portfolio of 20 stocks? With computerized tools, about 20 minutes or so a day. Another hour once a week will need to be spent on weekly tasks, plus another hour once a month on monthly tasks (see the breakdown of daily, weekly, and monthly tasks later in this chapter). If you have the time to spend, spread your risk over a number of stocks. With 9,000 possibilities, finding 20 good stocks is not difficult.

More Industries Lower the Risk

Diversifying among industry groups is an excellent way to put your eggs in different baskets. If you have as many as 20 stocks, you should be able to diversify over 5 to 10 industry groups (with two to four stocks in each group). In the Telescan system, there are approximately 200 industry groups, so at any given time, you can probably find at least 10 attractive groups. Chapter 14 describes how to search for the top industry groups and how to find stocks in the top groups.

Different Market Conditions Lower the Risk

As you start to build your portfolio, go slowly. Accumulating stocks over a period of time (rather than all at once) allows you to enter the market under different market conditions. This averages out market highs and lows and prevents an overcommitment at inappropriate times. We suggest that you buy no more than two or three stocks a month (not necessarily at the same time). It may take a year or longer to complete your initial portfolio, but you will be reducing the market risk. Use common sense, however. If the market is low in its LSQ channel and is beginning to show upward momentum, you may wish to buy more stocks than usual. If the market is becoming extended, it might be a good idea to stop adding stocks until the market pulls back. Chapter 13 presents tools for analyzing market conditions. Once you are fully invested, the investing process which we've described should take care of time diversification.

Different Searches Lower the Risk

Computerized investing offers another important way to achieve diversification: You can vary the searches that are used to find stocks. For example, you might buy one stock from a insider buying search, one from a momentum search, and one from an undervalued growth search (or any other combination of your favorite searches). This would also allow you to have both a short-term portfolio (momentum stocks) and a long-term portfolio (insider buying and undervalued growth stocks). By buying stocks based on these different strategies, we will have in fact diversified the type of stocks in our portfolio, which helps make us more neutral to market conditions.

The components of diversification are intertwined, as you can see. To diversify across industry groups, you need to have a large number of stocks. To diversify through time, you can run different searches over several months. In building your portfolio, the important point is to spread the risk among stocks, industries, market conditions, and searches.

THE PORTFOLIO MANAGEMENT TOOL

Managing a portfolio of stocks used to be an exceedingly laborious process. You had to check the stock prices in the newspaper and enter them by hand. You had to use a calculator to determine your gain or loss for the day, the week, the month, the year. You had to prepare by hand reports for accounting and tax reporting purposes. Now, with cyber-investing tools, all this (and more) can be done with minimal time and effort.

Portfolio management tools have made great strides in the past few years, and there are now many excellent programs on the market. Some are stand-alone products, such as Quicken™, published by Intuit, Inc., and CapTool™, published by TechServe, Inc. Others are integrated with discount brokerage services, such as Fidelity Investment's Fidelity Online XPress™ or Charles Schwab's StreetSmart™ (see the Cyber-Investing Kit in this book for a special offer). Still others are supplemental to online services, such as the Telescan Portfolio Manager™ (TPM). Most operate in a similar manner and include such features as:

- Tracking the sale and purchase of stocks and other securities.
- Maintaining goals (targets) and risk levels (mental stops) for each stock.
- Posting alerts when a target or stop (or high or low) is reached.
- Tracking dividends, interest income, and stock splits.
- Maintaining related cash account with automatic debits and credits for each sale or purchase entered.
- Updating portfolio with online quotes (daily or more often).
- Calculating profits and losses to date.
- Preparing numerous reports.
- Capacity for multiple portfolios.

A major benefit of a computerized portfolio management program is the myriad of reports that can be produced with a couple of keystrokes. There are reports that summarize all the activity in each portfolio; reports that summarize all closed positions or all open positions; reports that list all transactions for a specific security; and many more. Two TPM reports that we find particularly valuable are the "price alert report" and the "tax summary report."

Price Alert! Price Alert!

We use TPM's price alert report (Exhibit 11.1) for a daily update of stock quotes and to track our targets and mental stops. This report lists the low, high, and close for the day for every stock in a portfolio (or in all portfolios, depending on how we select the report option). More importantly, the report flags the stocks that have reached a new high or a new low *or* have reached or exceeded their target or mental stop. As long-term investors, we find it helpful to enter a goal that is within 10 percent of our target and a risk level that is within 10 percent of our mental stop (short-term traders might use smaller percentages). This way, we will be alerted when the stock nears one of these levels. When a stock nears its target, we may consider selling it early (see Chapter 12, "The Positive Sell"); if it hits a mental stop, we may reassess its desirability (see Chapter 12, "The Negative Sell").

The price alert report is easy to run on a daily basis and is an efficient way to follow your holdings. If you don't have TPM or a full-fledged portfolio management program, Telescan's "autoquote" feature may be used for a simplified daily portfolio report.

Not a Taxing Matter

The tax summary report (Exhibit 11.2) reduces the hassle of tax preparation (for stock investments, at least) to a simple menu selection. This report presents the gain or loss for each security for the dates selected, using the IRS guidelines for Schedule D. Other tax reports that summarize dividends, interest, and expenses can also be produced.

TO-DO LISTS FOR MONITORING STOCKS

It is all well and good to update stock prices and produce neat reports. But good portfolio management is more than just looking at figures on your computer screen. Each stock should be monitored closely and evaluated periodically with regard to target levels, mental stops, risk/reward relationship, and negative events that might affect its potential. Situations

Exhibit 11.1   A price alert report from Telescan portfolio manager. Notice that Calgene has fallen below its risk level or mental stop (R); that Chiron has exceeded its goal or target (G); and that the Limited has fallen below its risk level (R) and reached a new low (L).

PRICE ALERT REPORT

Portfolio: UNDERVALUED GROWTH   Date 01/26/1995

Description	Goal	Risk	High	Last	Low
Biotechnology Gener	25.000	2.000	2.750	2.375	2.000
Collagen	35.000	20.000	25.500	24.562	21.250
Calgene	25.000	6.500	7.500	6.250	5.750 R
Chiron	65.000	60.000	65.500	65.375	58.500 G
Chantal	15.000	2.000	2.375	2.125	1.938
Home Depot	80.000	43.000	47.625	47.375	44.625
Kroger Co.	35.000	21.000	25.250	24.875	23.625
Limited	40.000	17.000	18.375	17.000	17.000 R L
Microsoft	65.000	57.000	65.250	60.250	59.375
Maxtor	24.000	5.000	6.500	5.500	5.250
Placer Dome	40.000	18.000	22.250	19.750	19.250
Pier 1	15.000	7.000	9.625	9.375	8.375
Research Indus.	25.000	13.000	14.750	14.562	13.000
Starr Surgical	20.000	7.750	10.125	9.125	8.688
St. Jude Medical	68.000	35.500	40.250	38.250	35.875
Unisys	22.000	8.000	9.875	8.875	8.500

R—At or below risk level (mental stop)
G—At or below goal (target)
L—New 52-week low
H—New 52-week high

change, and something could happen to invalidate the reasons for owning the stock.

To monitor stocks, we will use some of the technical analysis and company information tools introduced in Chapters 7, 8, and 9. The review process is outlined in the following daily, weekly, monthly, and quarterly

Exhibit 11.2 A tax summary report from Telescan portfolio manager.

TAX SUMMARY REPORT

Portfolio: UND. GROWTH- SHORT TERM as of 12/31/1994

Realized Gains and Losses for period 01/01/1994 through 12/31/1994

Description	Qty	Date Acq	Date Sold	Proceeds	Cost	Loss	Gain
Boeing	100	12/13/1993	04/18/1994	4,413	4,038		375
Collagen	200	12/18/1991	02/07/1994	5,158	3,775		1,383
Collagen	100	10/06/1992	02/07/1994	2,579	1,588		992
Collagen	300	04/26/1994	12/08/1994	5,900	6,175	−275	
Calgene	300	04/07/1994	04/19/1994	3,088	4,225	−1,138	
Calgene	300	05/23/1994	07/12/1994	3,013	4,113	−1,100	
Calgene	300	08/29/1994	09/12/1994	2,825	3,588	−763	
Chiron	100	04/19/1993	02/17/1994	7,963	4,700		3,263
Chiron	100	04/26/1994	06/30/1994	5,463	6,275	−813	
Chiron	100	08/08/1994	11/07/1994	5,788	5,938	−150	
Delta Air Lines	100	08/23/1993	01/25/1994	5,363	5,200		163
Electronics for IMA	300	05/23/1994	10/26/1994	6,950	4,975		1,975
		Total Gains and Losses				−4,239	8,151
		Net Gain/Loss					3,912

to-do lists, with time estimates shown for each based on a portfolio of 20 stocks. Exhibit 11.3 provides a handy checklist for the review.

These routines are discussed in this chapter as part of portfolio management, but they are also part of the sales process discussed in Chapter 12. Any of the routines could trigger a sales decision, for negative or positive reasons. *The importance of these routines cannot be overemphasized.* Without such a systematic review, we would never know early enough when a stock should be sold.

To Do—Daily

1. Check all news items on your stocks. With computerized tools, you may flag all the stocks in your portfolio; then, when you log on to the

Exhibit 11.3 A portfolio management checklist showing daily, weekly, monthly, and quarterly tasks.

Portfolio Management Checklist

Activity	Daily	Weekly	Monthly	Quarterly
Check any notices on flagged stocks.	X			
Run Price Alert Report and review targets and mental stops.	X			
Review all stock graphs with technical indicators.	X	X		
Run best searches to generate new prospects.		X		
Review asset allocation/market conditions.			X	
Review quarterly earnings reports.			X	
Review earnings estimates reports.			X	
Review S&P MarketScope reports.			X	
Review insider trading reports.			X	
Review industry group graphs.			X	
Run industry group search.			X	
Compare portfolio stocks with runner-up stocks.				X
Read quarterly and annual reports.				X
Evaluate portfolio performance against market index and/or mutual fund.				X

system, the computer will display a notice if there is any news for a flagged stock. These will trigger a notice: a news article, new insider trading report, new S&P Marketscope report, or revised earnings estimate report. You should check out all notices immediately and take action, if needed. This should take less than 5 minutes on most days.

2. Run a price alert report. Review the day's activity and note whether any targets or stops have been reached. Check out any alerts. A new product is under development by Telescan and McCaw Cellular that will alert your beeper or cellular phone when a stock reaches a target or a stop, or has "broken out" according to a selected technical indicator. If a stock is near its target, you might want to review "The Positive Sell" in Chapter 12; if it has reached a stop or is within 10 percent of a stop, review "The Negative Sell" in Chapter 12. About 5 minutes.

3. Review graphs for each stock using your favorite short-term technical indicator. (Graphs may be downloaded quickly with Telescan's "autorun" feature and then reviewed offline.) We use a 30-day moving average, trading bands, and Bollinger bands to determine if a stock is approaching a "sell status" (see "Warning Signs" in Chapter 12). This step takes about 10 minutes—2 minutes or so for online time; the rest for reviewing the graphs offline. This may be done weekly, rather than daily, for those who are more long-term oriented.

To Do—Weekly

1. Review graphs for each stock using *weekly* indicators, such as the weekly 8/17/9 MACD and the LSQ line. About 15 minutes.

2. Run searches to find new prospects. Even after your portfolio is completed, it is a good idea to keep an inventory of prospects (we call it a "watch list"). These are stocks that have gone through the two-stage analysis and can be considered for purchase when you sell one of your holdings or as an alternate to a current holding. About 30 minutes.

To Do—Monthly

1. Review the market index that best matches your portfolio—the Nasdaq index, New York Stock Exchange index, or S&P 500 index. If market is extended, consider your allocation of funds between stocks and cash (see the discussion of market analysis in Chapter 13). About 5 minutes.

2. Review the quarterly earnings report for each stock. This report compares the current quarter's earnings with last quarter's earnings. Check to see if the company made its estimates or not. If not, you may want to reevaluate the stock. At the end of a quarter, this monthly task may take considerable time because most companies file earnings reports on a calendar quarter basis; otherwise allow about 10 minutes.

3. Evaluate the earnings estimates report for each stock. Are the new estimates higher or lower than previous? If you have kept a purchase log, you'll be able to compare the new report to the previous report. Any revision downward is reason to sell. About 10 minutes.

4. Look at the S&P Marketscope report for each stock. If the STAR rating has been lowered or if there are sell recommendations, you may want to reevaluate the stock. About 5 minutes.

5. Check the insider trading report for each stock. If insiders are bailing out, it may be difficult to justify hanging in there. On the other hand, if insiders are buying heavily, you might want to increase your position. About 5 minutes.

6. Review the industry group graph for each industry represented in your portfolio, observing the current price trend of the group. You may also want to plot the weekly MACD to see if it may have broken down. If the industry group appears to be deteriorating, you may want to reevaluate the stock. About 20 minutes.

7. Run a new industry group search that ranks all industry groups (described in Chapter 14). Check the rankings of the industry groups in your portfolio to see if they have slipped. A possible reason to sell is that the industry group is breaking down. There may also be some new industries in the top 5 or 10 groups that you will want to consider for new purchases. About 20 minutes.

To Do—Quarterly

1. Once a quarter, compare the performance of your portfolio to that of "runner-up stocks," those stocks from searches that you rejected. Investing is a learning experience; this exercise allows you to see whether or not you made the right choice and, if not, to analyze why. About 30 minutes.

2. As a shareholder, you will receive quarterly and annual reports from your companies. Read them. It is unlikely that you'll learn anything totally new, since any newsworthy event will have already been announced, but it seems foolish to own a company and not read those few pages of information from the company's management. About 1 hour.

3. Run a Portfolio Summary Report to see the percentage return for your portfolio. (Always enter any dividends and interest income, if received, into your cash account.) Then evaluate your performance as described in the following section. About 20 minutes.

THE BOTTOM LINE

An important step in portfolio management is to monitor your performance and keep track of how well you are doing. If you're not keeping up with market averages or comparable mutual funds over a reasonable period of time, you would be better off by buying mutual funds instead of stocks. If you follow the investing process that we advocate in this book, this shouldn't happen. In any case, it is important to know how you're doing.

There are two ways to compare your performance: One is against the market index that most closely resembles your portfolio; the other is against a mutual fund that resembles your portfolio. If you're investing most heavily in smaller cap stocks, compare your performance against the Nasdaq index (NASD) or the Russell 2000 (IUX), which is an index composed almost entirely of small cap issues. If you have mostly larger cap stocks, use the New York Stock Exchange index (NYA) or the S&P 500 (SPX). If you have a mixture of both, try the Wilshire 5000 index (WIEIK). Compare the percentage return for your portfolio (including dividends or interest income from your cash account) with the appropriate index. The performance can be measured directly on the index graph.

Historically, the large cap indexes have gained about 10 percent a year and the Nasdaq, 12 to 14 percent per year. But that's not especially relevant on a quarter-by-quarter basis. If you have a quarter in which the average Nasdaq stock is down 7 percent and your portfolio is only down 3 percent, then you can assume that you did well. Even though you're down for that quarter, you did better than the market and you should give yourself a pat on the back.

It is not as easy to compare your performance against mutual funds as against market indexes. First, you need to find a fund that parallels your objectives and risk tolerance. The best way to do this is to use a mutual fund search product to identify a mutual fund that most closely resembles your risk and reward goals. Then you can check out the performance of the fund on a mutual fund graph. The important point is to be sure that

THE FOLLY OF DOWN-AVERAGING

The biggest mistake most investors make is to buy more of a stock that has dropped in price: They "down-average," hoping to lower their cost per share. But if a stock goes down after you buy it, there is at least one thought that should come to mind: *Maybe you made a mistake!* Maybe your analysis was faulty; maybe something negative happened to the company after you bought the stock. Whatever the reason, it went down and now is *not* a good time to buy more of the stock. You may or may not want to sell just because it went down a little, but the number one rule of investing is (or should be): Never, never, never buy *more* of a stock that has dropped in price. There are 9,000 other candidates to consider.

There *is,* of course, an exception to this rule. If you are intimately familiar with a company—for instance, if you work there or know someone who does—you may believe that the market is overreacting and any drop in price is temporary. If you're confident of your knowledge, act on it, assuming, of course, that your information is public and you are not violating insider trading rules.

the fund to which you're comparing your performance approximates the makeup of your portfolio.

If you're doing better than comparable indexes or mutual funds, keep up the good work! If you find yourself behind one quarter, don't rush to any conclusions. Give yourself another quarter or two before you conclude that you're wrong and they're right. If you are below their performance after two consecutive quarters, you might want to ask yourself a few questions. Have you missed a sell opportunity because you don't review your portfolio often enough? Are you ignoring group rotation? Are you unwilling to take your losses and move on to something else?

It is important to ask these kinds of questions, but don't take your pulse too often. You have to give your portfolio time to perform.

YOU MUST REMEMBER THIS . . .

Good portfolio management is an indispensable element in the investing process.

- Diversify by number of stocks, by market conditions (time), by type of search, and by industry group.

- Update your portfolio each day with current stock quotes and watch for "price alerts."

- Monitor each stock on a daily, weekly, monthly, and quarterly basis.

- Never buy more of a stock that has gone down.

- Compare your portfolio's quarterly performance with a comparable market index or mutual fund.

- Fine-tune your investing strategy as needed.

12

KNOW WHEN
TO FOLD 'EM

Until you sell a stock, your profits are only on paper (or bytes on your hard disk). Turning them into real profits is the reason you got into this game in the first place. The tricky part is in the timing. When do you let your profits run? When do you cut your losses and move on to something else? When do you trade a good stock for an even better one? The answers to these questions become clearer with computerized tools that let you see the changes in a stock's risk/reward relationship.

When we buy a stock, the potential reward is substantially greater than the potential risk, or we wouldn't buy it. Typically, we expect 50 to 100 percent on the upside and not more than 10 to 20 percent on the downside. When that relationship changes to a point where the potential risk is greater than (or even the same as) the potential reward, we start looking for a reason to sell. In fact, one of our most important trading rules is: *Never hold on to a stock when the downside potential is greater than the upside potential.* As a result, we sell a stock any time the risk/reward relationship that caused us to buy it in the first place becomes unfavorable. The actual events that trigger the sale may be positive or negative.

In the previous chapter, we provided a checklist for monitoring stocks so you will know when one of these events occur. In this chapter, we'll take a closer look at the positive and negative reasons to sell a stock. But first, we want to talk about technical analysis as it applies to the sale of a stock.

WARNING SIGNS

Our primary technical sell signals come from the MACD indicator, the stochastics index, trading bands, trendlines, and support levels. These are some of the same indicators that gave us our primary buy signals in Chapter 9. The indicators can be plotted on stock graphs and reviewed on a daily and weekly basis as part of the portfolio management routines. Whether or not we take one of these warning signs as a sell signal, depends on how close the stock is to its target and on our viewpoint at the time, as we'll talk about later.

- *MACD Breakout.* A negative breakout on the 8/17/9 daily MACD histogram (Exhibit 12.1).

Exhibit 12.1   Digital Equipment had a negative breakout on a daily 8/17/9 MACD.

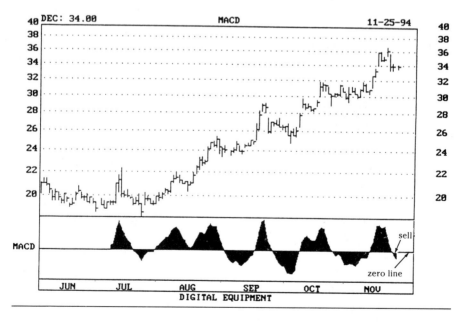

- *Stochastics.* A sell signal on a 14/5 daily stochastic (Exhibit 12.2).

- *Trading Bands.* A failure swing at the top of the band or failing to find support at the 30-day moving average is an early symptom of weakening momentum (Exhibit 12.3).

- *Trendline Break.* A trend break through a rising trendline is usually a signal that the trend is probably over and will soon reverse (Exhibit 12.4). Keep in mind that stocks exhibit a short-term trend and a long-term trend. Which trendline break you consider important depends on whether you are a short-term or long-term investor.

- *Trend Break with a Divergence between the Stock Price and the MACD.* Some traders consider trend breaks even more significant if there has been a divergence near the trend break between the stock price and a technical indicator, such as the MACD. For example, Placer Dome reached a new high in late September (Exhibit

Exhibit 12.2   Micron Technology had a negative breakout in early November on a 14/5 daily stochastic.

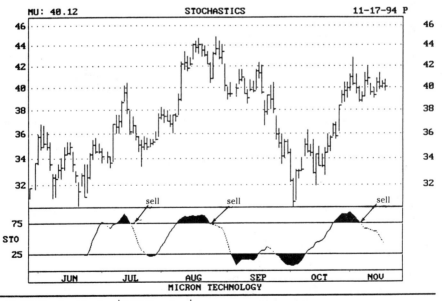

Exhibit 12.3 Herbalife International's trading bands show several signs of weakness throughout 1994.

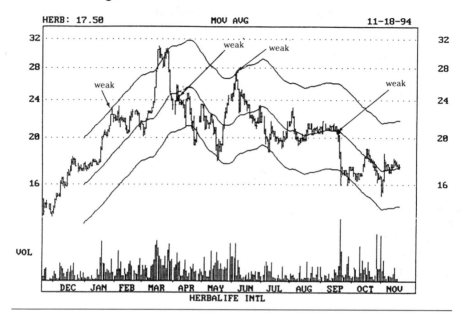

Exhibit 12.4 Adobe Systems had a short-term trend break in November 1994.

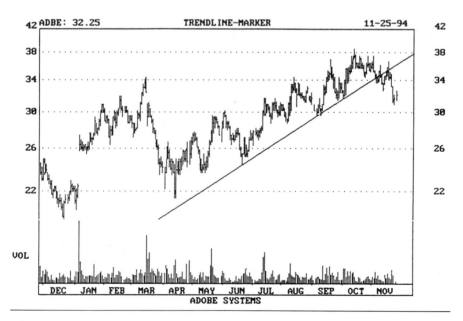

12.5) but the MACD histogram actually fell in value just before the trend break. That is considered a more ominous trend break than if the divergence had not occurred.

- *Resistance Level Reached.* When a stock hits a strong resistance level and fails, as BellSouth did in July 1994, it is time to reassess the situation (Exhibit 12.6).

- *Support Level Breach.* A support level that doesn't hold is a warning sign (Exhibit 12.7). As stated earlier, the number of times a stock has held at a support level determines how important or how strong that support is.

Any of these technical patterns should be taken as a message to reassess the stock. Where the stock is with regard to its target would dictate any action we take.

Exhibit 12.5   In mid-September Placer Dome showed a divergence between the rising stock price and the MACD graph. This is an example of an upward trendline being broken combined with a divergence in the MACD indicator as the stock reached a new high: A good time to sell.

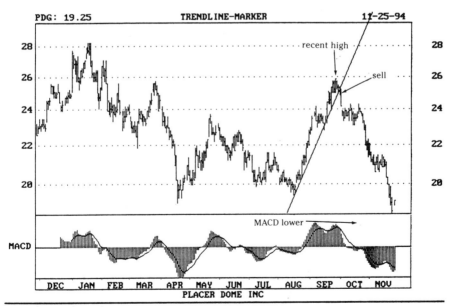

8 DY |17 DY |9 DY |

Exhibit 12.6 Bellsouth Corporation shows resistance just below $63.

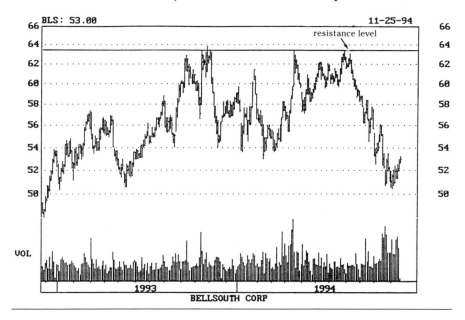

Exhibit 12.7 American Express broke through a strong support level in late November 1994.

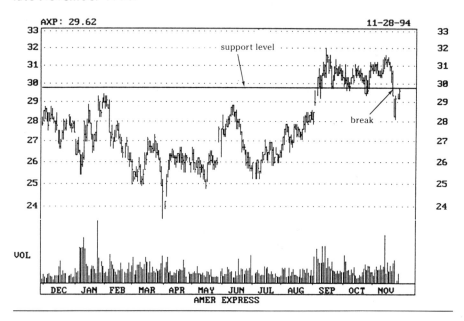

THE POSITIVE SELL

When a stock nears its target, we start looking for reasons to take our profits and move on to something else. We call this a "positive sell." The target, as discussed in Chapter 10, is usually the top of the long-term or short-term LSQ channel (or sometimes at the top of the trading bands or just below a strong resistance level). But we don't try to ride the stock all the way to the target. That could be flirting with danger. The closer a stock gets to the top of its long-term or short-term price trend, the more resistance it meets and the more likely the trend will reverse. In other words, the potential for risk increases while the potential for reward diminishes. So when the stock is about halfway between its LSQ line and the top of the channel, we will set a tight stop to protect our profits and start looking for a reason to sell. In effect, we become short-term traders at this point.

Any of these four events could signal a positive sell:

1. A technical indicator generates a short-term sell signal for the stock. If the stock is near its target, we'll pull out on any signal that reveals a weakness in the stock, such as approaching the top of the trading bands or a sell signal from the daily MACD or stochastics indicators.

2. The P/E ratio is nearing its all-time high or has exceeded the industry average. You can determine this by overlaying a P/E ratio channel on a stock graph to see the potential overvaluation (Exhibit 12.8). Also, Telescan's valuation report gives the stock's relative P/E ratio, and the Zacks report gives a comparison to the industry P/E.

3. The stock falls below the tight stop which we set to protect our profits.

4. Another stock with a better risk/reward relationship that is "waiting in the wings." (More about this later.)

The positive sell is important because we are *not* the only ones who are aware of the changing risk/reward relationship as a stock nears its target. Analysts who follow the company also use LSQ lines and other technical indicators. If they believe the stock is becoming overpriced, as it probably is near the top of its LSQ channel, one of them may say so publicly,

STOP! PROTECT YOUR PROFITS!

As a stock climbs toward its target, we adjust our protective mental stop so that it remains 20 percent below the current price. As the stock approaches the top of its LSQ channel, we tighten the stop to 10 percent below the current price, and as it moves even closer, we often switch to a 5 percent *hard* stop. This is one of the few times we use a hard stop. If the stock dips even a fraction, the hard stop will take us out, which, with our profits in hand, is desirable. It won't, however, protect us from a downward gap.

Exhibit 12.8   A P/E over/undervaluation channel is overlaid on a stock graph of Atmel Corporation with the P/E ratio plotted in the lower graph. Notice the points of relative overvaluation and relative undervaluation, according to the P/E ratio.

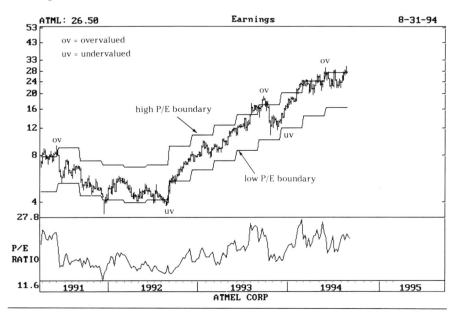

and when that happens the stock may gap down on the next day's opening. Then it will be too late to play sell-signal games with technical indicators.

So the closer the stock is to its target, the more we rely on a very short-term trigger to initiate the sell. It doesn't really matter which trigger you use; if you're looking for a reason to sell, one signal is as good as another. Nevertheless, if the stock doesn't generate any kind of sell signal, even if it is at the top of its LSQ channel, we would stay in and let our profits run. Unless we find a stock that we like better.

TRADING PLACES

With computerized search tools, you can always find more opportunities. In fact, we keep a watch list of stocks just for this purpose. These stocks have gone through our Stage One and Stage Two evaluation and are awaiting a technical buy signal. If we find one that is particularly attractive, we may consider selling a stock that is near its target and buying one on our watch list that has a better risk/reward potential.

A comparison of risk to reward is the key to trading one stock for another. Based on its long-term price trend, a stock at the top of its LSQ channel may have only a few points to gain—a small reward; but it may have many points to fall—a large risk. There is no reason to hang on for those last few points if a stock with a better risk/reward potential has just given a good technical buy signal. It that happens, we won't wait for a sell signal on the stock that is near its target. We will simply sell it and buy the new stock.

We used this risk/reward analysis on Computer Associates in 1993. Computer Associates, you may recall from Chapter 2, was one of our single highest-profit investments; we had bought it at $7⅝ in September 1991 and sold it at $26 in January 1993, for a 250 percent profit in less than two years. In late 1992, Computer Associates was about four points from the top of its LSQ channel (Exhibit 12.9). We could see another three or four points on the upside side, but the trading bands revealed the potential for a *seven-point drop* (Exhibit 12.10). We decided the risk was greater than the potential reward, especially since Intel, with an upside potential of about 20 and a downside of only 5 (Exhibit 12.11) had caught our eye. Shortly after we sold Computer Associates, it did, in fact, drop to $21, and even though it has since moved up to over $40, it was the right decision

Exhibit 12.9   In January 1993, Computer Associates was at the top of its short-term LSQ channel.

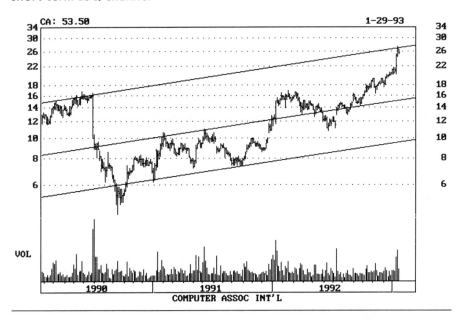

Exhibit 12.10   Computer Associates also had a potential for a 7-point drop in January 1993, based on its trading bands.

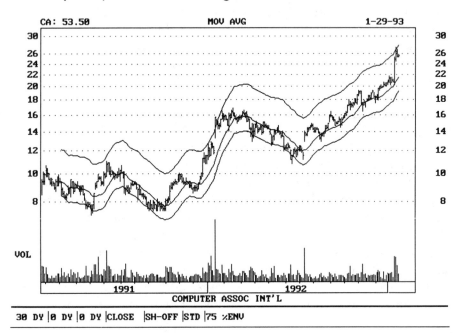

Exhibit 12.11 Intel Corporation's long-term LSQ channels demonstrate a superior risk/reward relationship in January 1993.

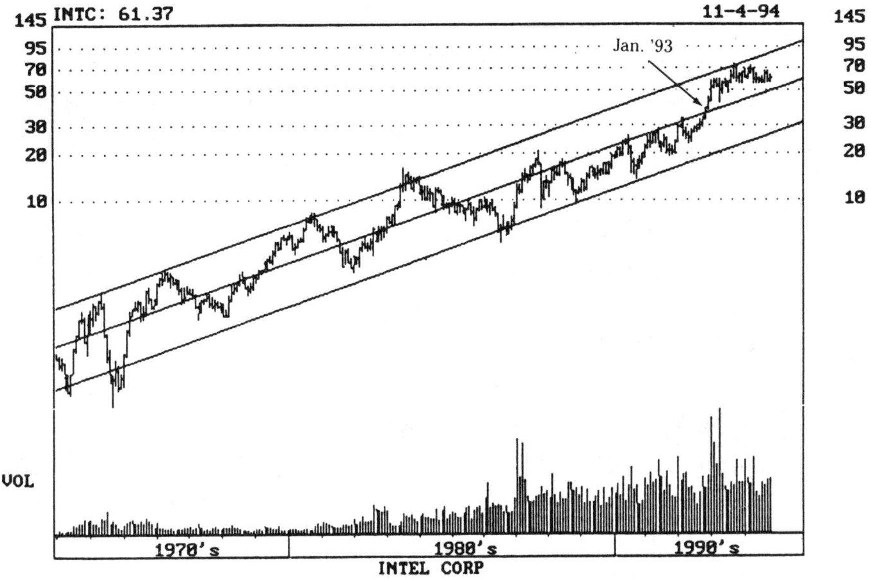

at the time. Meanwhile, Intel rose from $43¼ in January 1993 to $73½ on September 30, 1993.

Trading a good stock for a better one is a lot like trading an aging baseball player for a hot young rookie. The old veteran may still have a few hits left, but he could also retire next year and leave you holding the bat. Meanwhile, the rookie on the sidelines may have the makings of a super-star who could bat .300 for many, many years. Based on the risk/reward po-tential, we would not hesitate to trade the veteran for the rookie. The same goes for stocks.

THE NEGATIVE SELL

When we buy a stock, we base our decision on a number of specific rea-sons that are part of our two-stage evaluation process. If things don't work out as planned—if one or more of those reasons change for the worse—we will generally sell the stock. We call this a "negative sell."

Here are some negative events that might cause us to sell a stock:

- The stock falls and hits a stop. If you set a mental stop at 20 percent below the purchase price and the stock hits that stop, it is time to reassess the situation. That's the purpose of a stop.

- A significant downward revision is reported in earnings estimates. This is one of the surest predictors of a drop in stock price, and a strong signal to get out.

- The company announces disappointing earnings for a quarter. Ask yourself if you would have bought the stock had you been able to see that quarter. If not, either sell now or watch the stock closely and evaluate the next quarter's results.

- The company announces other bad news. For example, maybe it can't meet its earnings projections or a lawsuit has been filed with the potential of a material impact on the company. Bad news can take myriad forms, but you'll recognize it when you see it. Keep in mind, the market probably will have already taken the negative event into consideration by the time it becomes news, so if the consequences are short-term, the damage will already have been done. You will need to assess whether or not the consequences may have a long-term effect on the company.

- There is a large increase in insider selling. If the president sells 300,000 of his 500,000 shares, that is obviously a bad sign. So is four or five major officers selling large portions of their holdings. Such rampant insider selling is a sign that they perhaps know something you don't, which is a good reason to sell. However, a modest amount of insider selling is not a cause for alarm, particularly in technology stocks. These companies often use stock options to attract employees, and the options are viewed as part of their salary. Selling stock that has been acquired by exercising options is very common in the industry and shouldn't be taken too seriously.

- The industry group loses momentum. One of our requirements for buying a stock is that it must be in a high-ranking industry group; if the group loses momentum and starts looking like an "also-ran," it is time to consider selling.

- The stock generates a technical sell signal far from its target. Selling at this point depends on whether you are a short-term or long-term investor. A very long-term investor probably won't worry about technical signals when the stock is far from its target. They're in for the long haul. Short-term investors, however, may consider selling on any negative weekly (or even daily) technical breakout and then buying the stock back when it turns up, assuming the fundamentals have not changed. We have published a booklet on this subject,[1] and one of our conclusions was that selling on a weekly MACD breakout avoided most significant drops, except when a stock gapped down (which is difficult to protect against). When a trusted technical indicator produces a sell signal, it is certainly time to reassess the situation.

If you monitor your portfolio closely, as suggested in the previous chapter, you will be aware of these negative reasons to sell at the earliest possible time. Without the daily monitoring, however, a negative event might sneak up and zap one of your stocks before you have time to act.

YOU MUST REMEMBER THIS . . .

There are positive reasons and negative reasons to sell a stock.

- When a stock nears its target, consider selling on any short-term technical sell signal or an extended P/E ratio.
- Set stops to protect your profits as a stock moves toward its target.
- Keep a watch list of stocks that have been through the evaluation process. Use this inventory to replace stocks that you sell.
- Consider trading a stock near its target for one with a better risk/reward relationship.
- Monitor your stocks regularly so you will be aware of any negative reason to sell.
- Don't let your emotions control your decision to sell.

---

[1] Kassandra Bentley, *MACD: An Indicator for All Seasons* (Houston: Telescan, Inc., 1988).

Nothing is more detrimental to your bottom line than being in love with the companies you own, unless it is being afraid to take a loss. The question you must continually ask yourself is, "Would I buy this stock with what I know about it today?" The minute the facts don't support your original decision, it is time reassess the situation. Loyalty is great in romance, but it can be deadly in the stock market.

13

WHAT BIG BAD MARKET?

"The market goes up, the market goes down." That was the wry response of Robert Rubin, Secretary of the Treasury in the Clinton administration and former chairman of Goldman Sachs, when asked about the latest gyrations on Wall Street. And that pretty well sums it up. If you're going to invest in the stock market, you will have to get used to market fluctuations and not panic every time the Dow wiggles.

This is not to say you should ignore the market. When the market is extremely high, you may want to take a few chips off the table, convert some stocks to cash. When the market is extremely low, you may want to increase your rate of investment to take advantage of buying opportunities. In this chapter, we are going to show you tools that can be used to identify market extremes. Nevertheless, in our opinion, too much emphasis is placed on market analysis. For one thing, no one really knows where the market is going, not even the experts. Tune in to *Wall Street Week* or CNBC. For every guru proclaiming disaster, there are two touting buying opportunities. In fact, the smart money says that when the great majority thinks the market is going up, it will go down, and vice versa. Even that rule is difficult to follow. It is very difficult to tell up from down when the market going sideways—which is most of the time.

There is another reason why we think market analysis is overemphasized. If your investing strategy is built on value investing and if you are watching your technical indicators and industry group rotation, the dilemma of "How high is the market?" needn't worry you. The investing process itself should protect you, adjusting your stocks-to-cash ratio at market extremes and keeping you in positive industry groups.

In this chapter, we'll show you how to recognize a market extreme and what to do when it happens. We will discuss three technical lenses through which to view the market: the LSQ line and the MACD indicator, both of which we've used before, and a special indicator designed for group indexes, called the "overbought/oversold indicator." We'll also include a short section on fundamental evaluation of the market, because the market doesn't operate in a vacuum. It is affected by interest rates, corporate earnings, corporate dividends, and other fundamental imponderables.

Again, we want to point out that we are concerned in general with market extremes. It does not take an economic expert to judge market extremes. The tools and techniques we are going to show you are simple to use and need be done only on a weekly basis.

TECHNICAL LENSES

Technical analysis is one way to determine market extremes. Certain technical indicators, such as long-term moving averages and LSQ lines, are just as appropriate for market indexes as for stocks. In addition, specialized indicators have been developed for analyzing market indexes. In essence, they are like X rays that let you see through the current confusion of the market to its bare-bones reality.

Which Market Is the Market?

Before you analyze a market, you have to decide which market is the market. When the media report "The market is up" or "The market is down," they're almost always talking about the Dow Jones Industrial Averages (the "Dow"). But the Dow with its 30 blue chip stocks is much too narrow for market evaluation. The New York Stock Exchange, the S&P 500, or the Nasdaq market offer much broader indexes. The New York Stock Exchange index represents about 2,500 of the large capitalized stocks; the Nasdaq index represents about 4,000 companies, most of them smaller than the ones on the New York index; and the S&P 500 almost always parrots the

New York index, which is weighted for capitalization. Use the one that most closely represents your portfolio, or use both the New York Stock Exchange index and Nasdaq, as we do, for a broader view.

The LSQ Lens

Market extremes become very clear when viewed through the lens of our old friend, the LSQ line. A market index, like a stock, moves in a predictable range around its long-term and short-term LSQ lines. Most of the time it stays somewhere in the middle. In November 1994, neither the Nasdaq index nor the New York Stock Exchange index was extended. They were both hovering just below their long-term LSQ lines (Exhibits 13.1 and 13.2). Their short-term LSQ shows both indexes lower in the bottom channel (Exhibits 13.3 and 13.4).

The time to be concerned is when an index is at or very near the top of its LSQ channel, as occurred for both the Nasdaq and the New York Stock Exchange indexes in October 1987. That becomes the "dangerous extreme" that we mentioned, signaling that the market is likely to turn

Exhibit 13.1   In November 1994 the Nasdaq market was just below its long-term LSQ line.

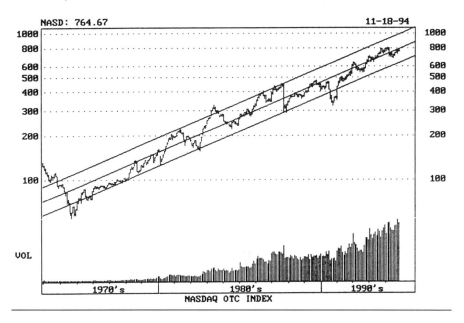

Exhibit 13.2 In April 1991, the New York Stock Exchange index reached a new high, but it was still well below the top of its LSQ channel.

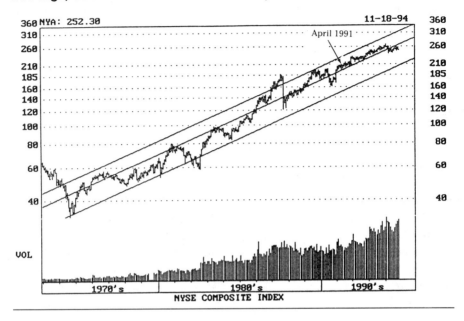

Exhibit 13.3 The Nasdaq market was well below its short-term LSQ line in November 1994, and the weekly MACD shows an overbought condition.

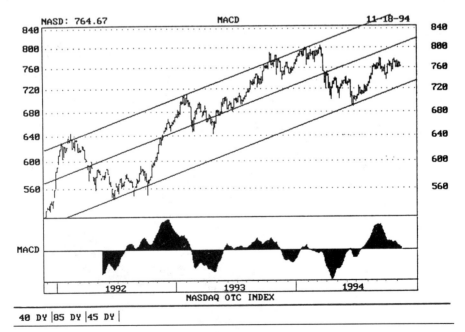

40 DY | 85 DY | 45 DY |

Exhibit 13.4   In November 1994, the New York Stock Exchange index is barely above the bottom of its LSQ channel, and the weekly MACD shows an oversold condition.

down, which, as we all remember, it did. In fact, a market index at the top of its LSQ channel is more dangerous than a stock at the top of its channel. Why? Because it is much more difficult for an entire market to break out of a long-term trading channel, so the odds of a reversal are greater than a stock in a similar position.

What should you do when the market is near the top of its LSQ channel? First, look at another market index to see if its LSQ position is any better. If you usually evaluate the New York Stock Exchange index, look at the Nasdaq. Or vice versa. They do not always move together. There have been times when the New York Stock Exchange and the S&P 500 (both large cap stocks) were very extended according to their LSQ lines, while the Nasdaq market was lingering near the bottom of its channel (see early 1991 in Exhibits 13.1 and 13.2). A smart investor would have switched to Nasdaq stocks at that time; by late 1993, the Nasdaq market had almost doubled while the New York index increased just 30 percent. Once you have assessed the market according to its LSQ line, look at the other technical indicators, such as the MACD and overbought/oversold indicator, as well as market fundamentals described later in this chapter.

The MACD Lens

The weekly MACD indicator provides an insight into market momentum. It does this in two ways. One is by showing the deterioration of market momentum, which tells you that an index (or stock) is topping. The other is the classic sell signal, when the MACD histogram crosses the zero line, which is a sign of a forthcoming correction.

In mid-November 1994, the Nasdaq (Exhibit 13.3) was still positive on the MACD, although nearing the zero line; momentum had stopped and the market was essentially basing in the 760 range. The New York Stock Exchange index (Exhibit 13.4) had crossed the MACD zero line into the negative zone and dropped from a high of about 260 to around 252, or about 3 percent. Neither was very bullish.

The Overbought/Oversold Lens

An indicator designed for group indexes is the overbought/oversold (OB/OS) indicator, which is based on the net of advancing and declining issues. Exhibit 13.5 shows the OB/OS for a 10-year chart of the New York Stock Exchange index. As you can see, the OB/OS gave very clear signals for two previous great buying opportunities—after the October 1987 crash and in late 1990. Another signal given in early 1994 produced only a modest gain.

Overbought signals are not nearly as reliable as oversold signals. We would rely more upon the LSQ line and a more fundamental evaluation of the market (described later) to assess overbought conditions.

Other Technical Lens

There are other technical indicators that can help you determine market extremes. Stochastics, trading bands, and trendlines can be used with market indexes just as they are with stocks (see Chapters 9 and 12). Or you might use other indicators, such as on-balance volume, rate of change, and the newly popular candlestick charts. We don't think these are necessary, but if you care to use them they are adequately defined in the user's manuals of the programs that produce them or in various books on technical analysis.

Exhibit 13.5   The overbought/oversold indicator is shown on a 10-year graph of the New York Stock Exchange index. Note the three "buy" signals in late 1987, late 1990, and early 1994.

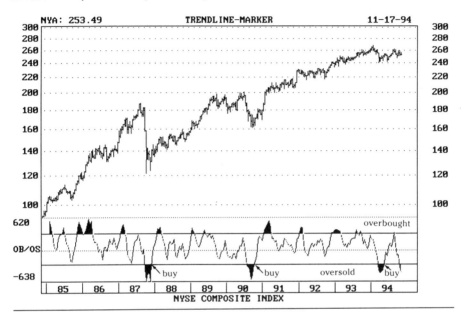

MARKET COMMENTARY FROM THE PROS

Newsletters that offer market commentary by experts are an excellent way supplement your own evaluation of the market. In general, these experts comment on near-term market direction based on their interpretation of government economic indicators, sentiment data, and market technical indicators. You might want to evaluate a few of the experts during your free look at various online newsletters (which is part of your Cyber-Investing Kit). We will caution you, however, that the experts don't always agree on the direction of the market. Often, for every three experts who are bullish there will usually be two to four who are bearish. Choose the ones whose analyses and techniques are comfortable to you.

Technical analysis is much less precise when applied to the market than when applied to an individual stock. The bottom line is the "preponderance of evidence" rule: go with the direction of the majority of the signals.

Breaking Barriers

A common mistake by investors (even some experienced ones) is to assume that when a new high is reached in a widely reported index such as the Dow, that the market is likely to fall. When this happens, they often rush to convert their stocks to cash, which is one of the surest ways *not* to participate in great market rallies. (We recall when even market gurus were predicting that the Dow would never break 1000!) When the market broke 4000 in February 1995, the Dow was still well

---

THE BROWN BREAKOUT RATIO

Another interesting gauge of *short-term* market direction is the Brown Breakout Ratio (BBR). The BBR uses ProSearch to find the ratio between positive and negative breakouts based on the Wilder Relative Strength Index (RSI).* Briefly stated, breakout searches are run on three market surrogates (optionable stocks, the New York Stock Exchange stocks, and Nasdaq stocks); then a calculation is made of the total number of positive breakouts (previously oversold stocks) and the total number of negative breakouts (previously overbought stocks) in each market. The ratio of the positive breakouts to negative breakouts is the BBR.

A divergence between the BBR and the direction of the market is the key. On a day when the market goes up but the BBR is negative (more negative breakouts than positive breakouts), that's a sign the market is topping and a downturn is imminent. In other words, even though the market is going up, there are more people taking profits than there are bargain hunters, so the market is likely to turn down.

Conversely, if the market has been going down for some time and suddenly the BBR turns positive (more positive breakouts than negative), that's a sign that the decline is over. The profit-takers have

---

below its upper long-term LSQ band (Exhibit 13.6). Since the market is expected to grow at 10 percent per year, the Dow would have to reach about 4400 before it would be considered extended from a technical viewpoint.

The same holds for other market indexes. In early 1991, the New York Stock Exchange index reached a new high of 210 (Exhibit 13.2). It was slightly above its long-term LSQ line, but far enough down in the channel that it had a lot of room to grow. And, in fact it did go 30 percent higher within a few months.

The market obviously cannot reach new highs without going through old highs. The key is to consider the current position in relation to the long-term trend. Otherwise, you could end up sitting on the sidelines when the Dow breaks the 10,000 barrier in the new millennium.

(Continued)

wound down, and the bargain hunters are out in full force, so an upturn is likely.

The BBR provides a much clearer short-term signal than LSQ channels or other technical indicators plotted on a stock graph. It has given us some of the most consistent and important indications of significant turnarounds after a sharp rise or fall in the market. It has not, however, been particularly effective in sideways markets; for this we have adapted an "alternative indicator."

The alternative indicator compares the ratio of stocks moving into overbought territory (as defined by the Wilder RSI) to the number of stocks moving into oversold territory. Instead of measuring breakouts, we measure the traffic "across the border," so to speak. If there is more traffic moving into the 30 percent territory than into the 70 percent territory, that's a sign of continuing bearishness. And vice versa: if more traffic is moving into the 70 percent area than into the 30 percent area, that's a sign of retreating bears. Again, a divergence is the important sign. We are continuing our research to fully evaluate the effectiveness of this indicator.

---

* David L. Brown and Mark Draud, *The Brown Breakout Ratio: Market Timing Indicator* (Houston: Telescan, 1992).

Exhibit 13.6 In late February 1995 the Dow broke the 4,000 barrier, but it was still well below the top of its long-term LSQ channel.

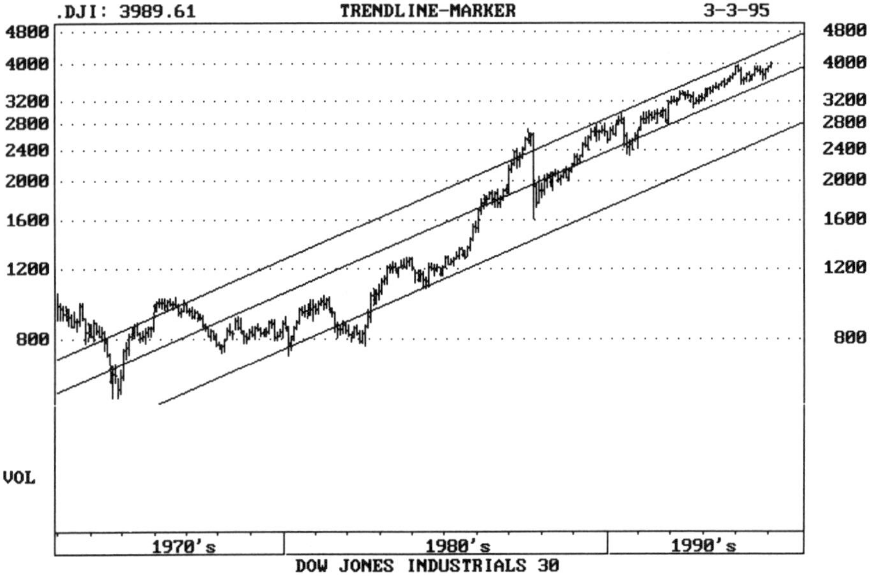
.DJI: 3989.61
TRENDLINE-MARKER
3-3-95
4800
4000
3200
2800
2400
2000
1600
1200
800
VOL
1970's
1980's
1990's
DOW JONES INDUSTRIALS 30

BACK TO BASICS

As the market moves above its LSQ line, it is wise to consider market fundamentals: specifically, market P/E ratio, market price-to-book value, and market dividend yield.[1] How high are the market P/E and the price-to-book—and how low is dividend yield—compared with historical figures? Then you need to take into account competing rates from fixed income investments, such as bonds. If bond yields are low, the market can absorb higher than normal P/E ratios and price-to-book values and lower than normal dividend yield. Why? Because low bond yields aren't as likely to lure investors away from the market. Conversely, if bond yields are high, the market can take a beating despite reasonable fundamentals, due to money exiting stocks for attractive bond yields—a sort of "flight to safety."

Essentially, in a fundamental evaluation of the market, we compare the effective yield on stocks to the yield on bonds. We're not talking about

[1] These figures can be found in major financial publications, such as *The Wall Street Journal, Investor's Business Daily,* or *Barron's.*

dividend yield now, but about earnings yield, which is the inverse of the P/E ratio: A 20 P/E would equal a 5 percent yield; a 24 P/E would equal an approximate 4 percent yield. Earnings yields usually bear some relationship to the yield available on bond rates.

Take the market environment in early 1994. The average market P/E ratio was 24 (an all-time high for the S&P 500), or an effective earnings yield of 4.2 percent. This would normally have been a danger signal for the market. But interest rates had been steadily declining throughout 1993, and by January 1994, the long bond rate was below 5¾ percent (near an all-time low) and represented only a 1.5 percent premium to market earnings yield. Certificates of deposits (CDs) were much lower, so people were looking for some place other than cash or bonds to put their money. Therefore, in early 1994, the market continued to make some headway despite the high P/E's. By November, long bond yield had risen to 8.2 percent, but market earnings yield had kept pace at 6.7 percent (market P/E had fallen to about 15 due to rising corporate earnings).

To put it into perspective, stocks and bonds are involved in a tug of war. During the past 20 years, bond yields have ranged from a high of 4 percent to a low of 0.5 percent above market earnings yield. At the higher end of the range, money flows out of the riskier stocks into bonds; at the lower end of the range, money flows out of bonds and into stocks. Obviously, then, stocks are relatively undervalued when the bond yield approaches the market earnings yield; they're relatively overvalued when the bond yield exceeds market earnings yield by 3 to 4 percent.

Two other examples might help to clarify this issue. In late 1982, the market was at a low, with market yield at 12.5 percent versus a Treasury bond yield of 12.9 percent. With almost no premium involved, stocks staged a great rally with the Dow gaining some 400 points over the next several months. On the other hand, at a market high in October 1987, market yield was 5.3 percent while Treasury bond yield was 9.1 percent, very close to its all-time high premium. We all know what happened soon thereafter—the Crash of '87!

The point is, the effective yield on stocks must be close enough to the effective yield on bonds to justify taking the extra risk in stocks to obtain the rewards of potential growth.

This type of market analysis is often confusing to a beginning investor or even to some seasoned investors. Just keep in mind that there are significant tradeoffs between market P/E and market interest rates—and the time to beware is when these figures are bumping into historical highs and lows.

WHEN TO CONVERT STOCKS TO CASH . . .

When the market is extended, based on the conditions we've just discussed, it is prudent to consider the composition of your portfolio. Should you convert any stocks to cash? If so, how much? And when? This is particularly important if you are a momentum player. Momentum stocks tend to have very high P/E ratios which can get corrected in a hurry if the market peaks, so the momentum investor should be particularly cautious at market highs.

If you are using the cyber-investing process described in this book—buying fundamentally attractive stocks and monitoring them closely for technical signals—the process should take care of itself during normal market conditions. As the market becomes extended, the process itself should move you more heavily into cash. However, this process will not work as well for long-term investors since, by definition, they do not use technical signals as aggressively as do short-term investors. Technical indicators trigger buy and sell signals for short-term investors, and absent these signals, there is little to prompt long-term investors to move into cash at market highs—unless most of their stocks happen to be reaching their targets at the same time, which is not very likely.

We have prepared a somewhat simplistic grid (Exhibit 13.7) as a guideline for stock-versus-cash allocation during market extremes. The grid is based on a long-term and short-term LSQ lines and a weekly 8/17/9 MACD. As the market's LSQ lines become more and more extended, the chart indicates a bias toward cash, especially when the MACD is negative. The percentages are general goals, of course, not hard-and-fast rules. Long-term investors may wish to utilize asset allocation programs to accomplish this function.

In the end, your ratio of stocks to cash must be based on your own risk tolerance, on whether you're a short-term or long-term player, on how closely you're watching your industry group rotation, and, as always, on common sense.

YOU MUST REMEMBER THIS . . .

The market is difficult to predict. None of the technical indicators is foolproof; no market theory is infallible. Our advice is to go with the preponderance of the evidence, tempered by a little common sense.

Exhibit 13.7 This grid shows the approximate levels of investment when the market is in various positions in its short-term and long-term LSQ channels. For example, if the market index is above its long-term LSQ line but below its short-term LSQ line, you would be between 20 and 60 percent invested. Where exactly you fall in this range will depend on whether you are a short-term or long-term investor and whether the weekly MACD is negative or positive. Short-term investors will gravitate toward the lower end of the range when the MACD is negative; long-term investors will gravitate toward the higher end of the ranges when the MACD is positive.

Percentage Invested

Market Position in Long-Term LSQ Channel	Near Bottom	Below LSQ	Above LSQ	Near Top
Near Top	20–60%	15–50%	15–40%	10–30%
Above LSQ	25–70	20–60	20–60	15–50
Below LSQ	30–90	25–80	25–70	20–60
Near Bottom	50–100	35–90	30–80	25–70

Market Position in Short-Term LSQ Channel

- About once a month, review a market index that mimics your portfolio.

- Review the short- and long-term LSQ channels, along with a technical indicator or two. Consider the market P/E in light of bond yields. If all these are average, don't worry.

- The time to worry is *if* the market should move to the high side of the LSQ channel or *if* bond yields should move toward 10 percent or *if* market P/E should return to the 16, 17, 18 range or higher.

- The effective yield on bonds has to be enough greater than the effective yield on stocks to justify giving up the potential growth in the stock.

- Don't panic when the Dow goes through 5,000, 6,000, or any other century mark. It is just a number.

- Keep an eye on your emotions, especially when you're listening to the market gurus.

We're all human, and it is human nature to get carried away when everything you hear and read is positive—and to think the sky is falling when the general attitude is negative. Remember that the smart money does just the opposite. And with cyber-investing tools, there is no reason why you can't be among the ranks of the smart investors. Moreover, if you watch your industry groups closely (as described in the next chapter), you can afford to be wrong about the market.

14

THE "IN" CROWD

Industry groups were created for the purpose of tracking and analyzing groups of stocks.[1] When viewed as a group, stocks in a common industry behave like a miniature market index and can be analyzed in much the same way. The most important thing about industry groups is the way they rotate into and out of favor with institutional investors. This rotation, which we have mentioned in previous chapters, can be very beneficial to the small investor, because when an institutional investor moves into a group the P/E ratios and stock prices in that group inevitably rise. The astute small investor can piggyback a group that is rotating upward and reap the benefits of rising stock prices and rising P/E's.

There is nothing magic about industry group rotation. It happens because institutional investors—mutual funds, pension funds, and large brokerage houses—control the great bulk of money in today's market (70 percent of all trading). Competition among them for investment dollars is fierce, which creates a demand for short-term (quarterly) performance. As a result, institutions track industry groups with the tenacity of Scotland

---

[1] Industry groups were created by companies that serve the investing public, such as Standard & Poor's, *Investor's Business Daily,* Telescan, MarketGuide Investment Service, and others. They arbitrarily classify the approximately 9,000 listed stocks into 75 to 200 industry groups. A service that uses only 75 groups might lump pharmaceuticals, medical supply companies, and medical equipment manufacturers into one group, whereas another service might make each of these a separate industry group. Telescan has approximately 200 groups.

ROUND AND ROUND THEY GO . . .

Investor's Business Daily has published a chart showing "35 Years of Best Industry Groups." This chart is a fascinating study of industry group rotation. Some groups stay in favor over several years, which is partially because economic trends that drive a rotation can last a very long time, but it also has to do with the slowness with which institutional investors move. A sampling from the chart on page 219 can give you an idea of how and why industry groups rotate. As you can see, there are bullish groups even in bear markets.

Yard. They employ analysts who study demographic trends, economic cycles, and other factors, and try to predict which industry groups have the brightest prospects for growth over the next year or two. Once an opportunity is clearly identified, one institution after another begins to accumulate shares in the top companies of the industry. This creates something like a tidal wave that drives up stock prices and P/E ratios within the group. Such a group is said to be rotating upward or "into favor."

Some months or years later, the industry's earnings potential will peak or become diminished or the shares of the group will be considered fully priced or overpriced. When that happens, institutional money will flow out of that group and related stock prices and P/E's will fall. Such a group is said to be rotating downward or out of favor.

And so it goes. The rotation is not an orderly one, with one group after another rotating upward single file. Instead, there may be 10 to 20 groups or more in favor during a bull market, and maybe four or five groups during a bearish period. Over time, most industry groups will have their day in the sun.

WHO'S IN? WHO'S OUT?

With computerized search tools, we can find positively rotating industry groups early in their rotation. We can see how each group is ranked against all other groups, which direction it is rotating, and how rapidly it is moving. One search we use frequently is shown in Exhibit 14.1. All the indicators were used for the stock searches in Chapter 5; the only

A sampling of top performing industry groups over history as published by *Investor's Business Daily*.

Bull Markets	Industry Group	Reason for Ascendancy According to *Investor's Business Daily*	% Increase over Period of 2 to 4 Top Stocks
10/93–present	Cable TV	Proposed 500 channels; interactive/multi-media systems; convergence with entertainment & telecommunications.	300–380
4/88–10/89	Cable TV	Deregulation.	164–300
8/84–10/87	Cable TV	New programming and strong subscriber gains.	210–314
10/91–10/93	Oil and Gas Products	More favorable supply/demand relationship for natural gas.	143–433
5/90–1/92	Biotech industries	Actual and anticipated development and approval of new drugs.	473–782
2/88–7/90	Telecommunications	Modernization of networks and increased competition caused by the breakup of AT&T.	203–500
Bear Markets or Sideways Markets			
1/78–11/80	Electronics	Increased demand from computer, tele-communications, aerospace, and automation industries.	500–904
8/76–9/78	Hospitals and Nursing Homes	Medicare payments; increased efficiency of investor-owned facilities.	210–309
2/73–8/74	Gold	Increased inflation, monetary turmoil, political unrest.	285–331
4/71–5/72	Mobile Homes	Increased development of mobile home parks; increased availability of financing.	143–433

Source: Courtesy of *Investor's Business Daily* Library, P. O. Box 661780, Los Angeles, CA 90066.

219

Exhibit 14.1   An industry group search for industries with positive momentum.

Indicator	Action	
Group Rank (GrpRk)	Eliminate all groups under a rank of 40	
Group Rank (GrpRk)	The higher, the better	60%
Group Rank Change—1-Week (cGRP1)	The higher, the better	100%
Group Rank Change—3-Week (cGRP3)	The higher, the better	80%
Group Rank Change—6-Week (cGRP6)	The higher, the better	60%
Group Rank Change—13-Week (cGP13)	The higher, the better	40%
LSQ Deviation—3-Yr (3LDv)	List only	
LSQ Deviation—5-Yr (5LDv)	List only	
LSQ Deviation—10-Yr (10LDv)	List only	
LSQ Deviation—15-Yr (15LDv)	List only	
LSQ Deviation—Maximum (MaxDv)	List only	
Relative Performance—1-Day (1-Dy)	List only	
Relative Performance—1-Week (1-Wk)	List only	
Relative Performance—3-Week (3-Wk)	List only	
Relative Performance—6-Week (6-Wk)	List only	
Relative Performance—18-Week (18-Wk)	List only	

difference is that we must select industry groups as the search universe before we submit the search.

- The group rank indicator is used to eliminate all groups that are not ranked among the top 60 percent of all groups; then it will rank the groups in descending order.

- Four group rank change indicators will favor those industry groups that are moving up the fastest over the past 1 to 13 weeks; these indicators are weighted to favor groups with a recent move.

- Five LSQ deviation indicators and five relative performance indicators (used to list information) will reveal where a group is within its trading channel.

- The search report will rank all industry groups, but we will ask only for the top 20 groups here.

It is important to use both the *group rank* indicator and the various *group rank change* indicators. The group rank indicator tells how the group compares with other groups; a rank of 70 is obviously higher than a rank of 60. But that doesn't tell us whether the group is on the way up or on the way down. The group rank change indicators tell us this.

Search Results: The Innies

Exhibit 14.2 shows the top 20 industry groups with positive momentum on the date of the report. These results are based on the relative movement of an industry with respect to the other industries. You have to examine the rankings to determine whether a group is rotating upward or downward. Computer-Local Networks has the best group momentum (i.e., greatest change in group rank) over the past four periods and is now ranked in the top 1 percent in overall group rank. It is still 34 percent below its 5-year LSQ line and 5 percent below its 10-year LSQ line. All of which indicates that it was rotating into favor on the date of the report.

Another interesting group in this search is Retail/Wholesale Jewelry. While it is ranked only in the 80th percentile at this time, the group rank change indicators show that it is clearly rotating favorably. For the past three weeks, it has been moving up faster than even the number 1 group—and it is below its LSQ line in all time periods.

The Outies

Watch out for groups that are rotating the wrong way. The Electrical Parts Distributors group is in the 85th percentile group overall, but it is rotating negatively. How do we know? Its rank change has decreased each of the past four periods. It was doing fine over the past 13 weeks, but less so over the past 6 weeks, even less so for the past 3 weeks, and in the past week it has actually declined. Obviously, we would eliminate that group from the list, as well as Soap and Cleaning Preparations and Tobacco for the same reason.

This list can be narrowed somewhat further by eliminating some of the groups that are high on their LSQ historical charts, such as Electrical Components or those that have had the least impressive recent performance. The goal is to end up with at least 10 groups that seem to be rotating the most positively at this time, and that have the most room to grow. After eliminating the preceding four groups, we would end up with

Exhibit 14.2   The top 20 industry groups with positive momentum on November 17, 1994, based on the search criteria in Exhibit 14.1.

Prosearch 4.0 Top Industry Group Report
11/17/94

1> .TNT—COMPUTER-LOCAL NETWORKS WID   .TNT

GrpRk = 118.5	(99)	3LDv = 1.2	(78)	1-Dy = 99.7	(50)
cGRP1 = 3.7	(99)	5LDv = −34.0	(9)	1-Wk = 104.7	(90)
cGRP3 = 6.7	(99)	10LDv = −5.0	(48)	3-Wk = 108.2	(91)
cGRP6 = 20.6	(99)	15LDv = 7.4	(72)	6-Wk = 122.6	(95)
cGP13 = 31.8	(99)	MaxDv = N/A	( )	18-Wk = 133.4	(92)
GrpRk = 118.5	(99)				

2> .TJS—RETAIL/WHOLESALE-JEWELRY WI   .TJS

GrpRk = 105.4	(80)	3LDv = −2.2	(72)	1-Dy = 98.4	(17)
cGRP1 = 3.9	(99)	5LDv = −11.8	(43)	1-Wk = 106.7	(93)
cGRP3 = 8.6	(99)	10LDv = −21.5	(17)	3-Wk = 109.5	(93)
cGRP6 = 11.2	(98)	15LDv = −33.0	(20)	6-Wk = 108.6	(87)
cGP13 = 12.7	(98)	MaxDv = −43.5	(17)	18-Wk = 105.1	(71)
GrpRk = 105.4	(80)				

3> .TSM—ELEC-SEMICONDUCTORS WIDX   .TSM

GrpRk = 105.6	(82)	3LDv = −16.5	(22)	1-Dy = 100.7	(82)
cGRP1 = 2.8	(99)	5LDv = −1.0	(69)	1-Wk = 103.3	(86)
cGRP3 = 2.4	(94)	10LDv = 28.2	(80)	3-Wk = 104.4	(84)
cGRP6 = 12.5	(99)	15LDv = 46.0	(88)	6-Wk = 116.0	(93)
cGP13 = 4.8	(82)	MaxDv = 53.9	(94)	18-Wk = 109.1	(77)
GrpRk = 105.6	(82)				

4> .TEI—ELEC MEASRNG INSTRUMNTS WIDX   .TEI

GrpRk = 110.8	(95)	3LDv = 5.7	(83)	1-Dy = 100.3	(79)
cGRP1 = 2.0	(97)	5LDv = 9.6	(81)	1-Wk = 101.3	(77)
cGRP3 = 0.8	(83)	10LDv = 71.8	(91)	3-Wk = 99.6	(61)
cGRP6 = 7.7	(92)	15LDv = 58.6	(91)	6-Wk = 108.4	(86)
cGP13 = 9.2	(96)	MaxDv = 8.4	(82)	18-Wk = 115.1	(82)
GrpRk = 110.8	(95)				

5> .TSO—COMPUTER-SOFTWARE WIDX   .TSO

GrpRk = 112.8	(98)	3LDv = 15.4	(90)	1-Dy = 99.1	(25)
cGRP1 = 1.4	(91)	5LDv = −5.2	(62)	1-Wk = 101.1	(76)
cGRP3 = 1.2	(86)	10LDv = −15.3	(26)	3-Wk = 101.8	(77)
cGRP6 = 7.9	(94)	15LDv = −17.0	(43)	6-Wk = 112.7	(91)
cGP13 = 8.4	(95)	MaxDv = −19.0	(48)	18-Wk = 116.5	(83)
GrpRk = 112.8	(98)				

Exhibit 14.2   (continued)

6> .TCX—TELECOMMUNICATION EQUIP WIDX   .TCX

GrpRk = 110.5	(95)	3LDv = −6.4	(57)	1-Dy = 99.1	(25)
cGRP1 = 1.5	(94)	5LDv = 19.0	(87)	1-Wk = 102.1	(81)
cGRP3 = 0.6	(82)	10LDv = 68.4	(91)	3-Wk = 101.5	(76)
cGRP6 = 8.7	(96)	15LDv = 99.8	(95)	6-Wk = 114.0	(92)
cGP13 = 7.7	(91)	MaxDv = 46.6	(94)	18-Wk = 115.8	(82)
GrpRk = 110.5	(95)				

7> .TGR—COMPUTER-GRAPHICS WIDX   .TGR

GrpRk = 118.3	(99)	3LDv = 19.2	(91)	1-Dy = 99.0	(23)
cGRP1 = 1.7	(96)	5LDv = 30.1	(91)	1-Wk = 103.5	(86)
cGRP3 = 0.3	(74)	10LDv = 24.1	(78)	3-Wk = 103.6	(83)
cGRP6 = 11.2	(98)	15LDv = 19.2	(79)	6-Wk = 118.2	(94)
cGP13 = 19.7	(99)	MaxDv = N/A	( )	18-Wk = 130.2	(91)
GrpRk = 118.3	(99)				

8> .TMI—MEDICAL INSTRUMENTS WIDX   .TMI

GrpRk = 109.7	(92)	3LDv = 26.9	(94)	1-Dy = 101.4	(87)
cGRP1 = 1.7	(96)	5LDv = −8.3	(54)	1-Wk = 102.6	(83)
cGRP3 = 1.5	(90)	10LDv = −15.6	(26)	3-Wk = 102.5	(80)
cGRP6 = 3.5	(82)	15LDv = 2.1	(67)	6-Wk = 105.9	(82)
cGP13 = 7.3	(89)	MaxDv = −7.9	(65)	18-Wk = 113.3	(80)
GrpRk = 109.7	(92)				

9> .THF—RETAIL-HOME FURNISHINGS WIDX   .THF

GrpRk = 102.1	(65)	3LDv = −32.2	(7)	1-Dy = 99.5	(40)
cGRP1 = 1.2	(89)	5LDv = −34.1	(9)	1-Wk = 99.8	(56)
cGRP3 = 3.2	(97)	10LDv = 25.6	(79)	3-Wk = 99.7	(62)
cGRP6 = 9.8	(97)	15LDv = 15.0	(77)	6-Wk = 104.1	(78)
cGP13 = 20.6	(99)	MaxDv = 2.5	(77)	18-Wk = 104.6	(70)
GrpRk = 102.1	(65)				

10> .TCT—MEDIA-CABLE TV WIDX   .TCT

GrpRk = 102.4	(67)	3LDv = −15.4	(24)	1-Dy = 101.6	(88)
cGRP1 = 2.0	(97)	5LDv = −10.0	(49)	1-Wk = 104.5	(89)
cGRP3 = 4.2	(98)	10LDv = −9.1	(40)	3-Wk = 106.7	(89)
cGRP6 = 8.0	(94)	15LDv = −27.3	(27)	6-Wk = 111.2	(90)
cGP13 = 4.0	(77)	MaxDv = −59.2	(5)	18-Wk = 105.3	(71)
GrpRk = 102.4	(67)				

Exhibit 14.2   (continued)

11>   .TEZ—ELEC-MISC COMPONENTS WIDX   .TEZ

GrpRk = 105.9	(85)	3LDv = −7.1	(54)	1-Dy = 99.9	(54)
cGRP1 = 1.5	(94)	5LDv = −6.0	(60)	1-Wk = 101.8	(80)
cGRP3 = 0.6	(82)	10LDv = 48.7	(86)	3-Wk = 101.4	(76)
cGRP6 = 2.5	(78)	15LDv = 52.3	(90)	6-Wk = 103.8	(77)
cGP13 = 4.6	(80)	MaxDv = 16.0	(86)	18-Wk = 110.1	(78)
GrpRk = 105.9	(85)				

12>   .TAA—AEROSPACE/DEFENSE WIDX   .TAA

GrpRk = 103.0	(70)	3LDv = −3.8	(67)	1-Dy = 99.9	(54)
cGRP1 = 0.8	(86)	5LDv = 2.8	(74)	1-Wk = 101.4	(78)
cGRP3 = 3.3	(97)	10LDv = 8.9	(68)	3-Wk = 104.1	(84)
cGRP6 = 4.7	(87)	15LDv = −4.3	(60)	6-Wk = 103.9	(77)
cGP13 = 4.7	(80)	MaxDv = −22.0	(44)	18-Wk = 101.7	(63)
GrpRk = 103.0	(70)				

13>   .TCA—FOOD-CANNED WIDX   .TCA

GrpRk = 105.2	(80)	3LDv = 6.9	(84)	1-Dy = 101.4	(87)
cGRP1 = 0.9	(87)	5LDv = −3.0	(66)	1-Wk = 102.7	(83)
cGRP3 = 1.5	(90)	10LDv = −21.4	(18)	3-Wk = 106.0	(88)
cGRP6 = 4.1	(86)	15LDv = −34.3	(18)	6-Wk = 110.0	(89)
cGP13 = 3.4	(73)	MaxDv = −20.1	(46)	18-Wk = 114.7	(81)
GrpRk = 105.2	(80)				

14>   .TSC—SCHOOLS WIDX   .TSC

GrpRk = 105.5	(81)	3LDv = 3.4	(81)	1-Dy = 99.6	(45)
cGRP1 = 1.1	(89)	5LDv = 10.9	(83)	1-Wk = 102.1	(81)
cGRP3 = 0.3	(74)	10LDv = −1.0	(56)	3-Wk = 102.2	(79)
cGRP6 = 5.2	(88)	15LDv = −28.2	(26)	6-Wk = 106.5	(83)
cGP13 = 5.3	(85)	MaxDv = −60.3	(5)	18-Wk = 105.2	(71)
GrpRk = 105.5	(81)				

15>   .TRT—RETAIL-RESTAURANTS WIDX   .TRT

GrpRk = 103.7	(75)	3LDv = −3.2	(69)	1-Dy = 99.9	(54)
cGRP1 = 0.6	(85)	5LDv = −6.7	(59)	1-Wk = 101.2	(76)
cGRP3 = 1.4	(88)	10LDv = 5.8	(64)	3-Wk = 102.0	(78)
cGRP6 = 3.7	(84)	15LDv = 6.4	(71)	6-Wk = 106.1	(82)
cGP13 = 3.5	(76)	MaxDv = 21.7	(88)	18-Wk = 107.0	(74)
GrpRk = 103.7	(75)				

Exhitib 14.2   (continued)

16> .TSP—SOAP & CLNG PREPARATNS WIDX   .TSP

GrpRk = 107.2	(88)	3LDv = 4.5	(82)	1-Dy = 99.5	(40)
cGRP1 = −0.5	(66)	5LDv = −0.4	(71)	1-Wk = 101.9	(80)
cGRP3 = 1.6	(92)	10LDv = −7.7	(43)	3-Wk = 101.5	(76)
cGRP6 = 4.0	(85)	15LDv = −4.4	(60)	6-Wk = 106.1	(82)
cGP13 = 11.3	(97)	MaxDv = 23.5	(88)	18-Wk = 110.4	(78)
GrpRk = 107.2	(88)				

17> .TTT—COSMETICS/PERSONAL CARE WID   .TTT

GrpRk = 102.5	(68)	3LDv = 0.2	(76)	1-Dy = 99.6	(45)
cGRP1 = 0.6	(85)	5LDv = −15.0	(31)	1-Wk = 100.9	(75)
cGRP3 = 1.3	(87)	10LDv = −14.7	(28)	3-Wk = 100.8	(73)
cGRP6 = 4.1	(86)	15LDv = −3.0	(62)	6-Wk = 105.2	(81)
cGP13 = 4.1	(78)	MaxDv = 27.3	(89)	18-Wk = 105.0	(71)
GrpRk = 102.5	(68)				

18> .TTO—TOBACCO WIDX   .TTO

GrpRk = 109.6	(91)	3LDv = 24.5	(93)	1-Dy = 100.6	(81)
cGRP1 = 1.8	(96)	5LDv = −2.5	(67)	1-Wk = 103.1	(85)
cGRP3 = −0.4	(65)	10LDv = −32.5	(8)	3-Wk = 98.5	(44)
cGRP6 = 0.6	(64)	15LDv = −34.4	(18)	6-Wk = 104.3	(78)
cGP13 = 7.7	(91)	MaxDv = −25.2	(39)	18-Wk = 114.9	(82)
GrpRk = 109.6	(91)				

19> .TAP—RETAIL/WHLSLE-AUTO PARTS WIDX   .TAP

GrpRk = 102.5	(68)	3LDv = −5.9	(59)	1-Dy = 100.7	(82)
cGRP1 = 1.1	(89)	5LDv = −10.2	(48)	1-Wk = 101.4	(78)
cGRP3 = 0.0	(69)	10LDv = 6.8	(65)	3-Wk = 100.7	(73)
cGRP6 = 6.6	(90)	15LDv = −1.3	(63)	6-Wk = 107.6	(86)
cGP13 = 4.1	(78)	MaxDv = 6.5	(80)	18-Wk = 102.0	(64)
GrpRk = 102.5	(68)				

20> .TED—ELEC-PARTS DISTRIBUTORS WID   .TED

GrpRk = 106.0	(85)	3LDv = −8.5	(47)	1-Dy = 98.8	(20)
cGRP1 = −0.5	(66)	5LDv = −11.5	(44)	1-Wk = 98.8	(33)
cGRP3 = 0.0	(69)	10LDv = 8.1	(67)	3-Wk = 101.1	(75)
cGRP6 = 6.0	(89)	15LDv = 13.4	(76)	6-Wk = 106.5	(83)
cGP13 = 12.3	(98)	MaxDv = −20.5	(46)	18-Wk = 113.4	(80)
GrpRk = 106.0	(85)				

a list of 16 groups. The next step would be to search for stocks in those groups, as we will talk about in a moment.

The Industry Group Graph

Another way to judge the direction of an industry group is to look at a price-and-volume graph. Industry groups cycle between high valuation and low valuation, much like stocks, so some of the same technical analysis tools can be used, such as LSQ lines, the MACD, and the overbought/oversold indicator which was used with market indexes in the previous chapter. Exhibit 14.3 shows a short-term LSQ channel for the Computer-Local Network group with a weekly MACD plotted in the lower graph. You can see that the group began an upward move in late 1990 that lasted over a year. Then it went through a flat period until mid-1992 when it started another positive move. It took a steep dive in early 1994 but started recovering in late summer, and by November it had enough momentum to appear as the top stock on our industry group search. At that time, the weekly MACD was positive, as shown in Exhibit 14.3.

Exhibit 14.3   The Computer-Local Networks industry group has a very positive weekly MACD reading and a favorable position on the LSQ channel.

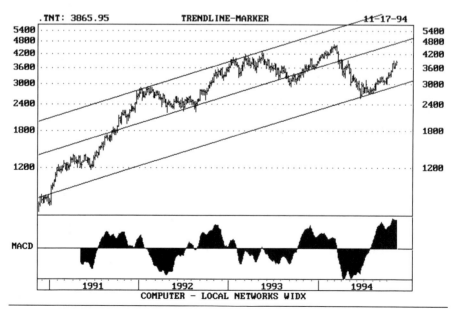

RISING STARS

Once you have a list of top industry groups, the next step is to search for stocks that are rotating upward within the selected industries. This rotation of stocks within a rotating industry group is also a function of institutional favor.

When an institution decides to move into a group, it typically starts to accumulate shares of the top company in the group. (Deciding which is the "top" company is a very subjective judgment.) As more institutions move in, the price and the P/E ratio of the number one stock rise, and as it moves toward being overpriced, the money starts to flow into the number two stock, and so on down the line.

For example, if the semiconductor industry should rotate into favor, the first institutions to make a move might buy Intel (generally recognized as the leader). If the trend toward that industry should gain momentum, other institutions might also buy Intel, which would clearly cause an upward trend in Intel's stock. At some point, however, Intel might seem overpriced, compared with other stocks in the industry; then perhaps National Semiconductor or Advanced Micro Devices might begin to look like bargains and might attract the institutional money.

This is an oversimplification, of course. In reality, the rotation is much less precise. Some stock is going to be the favorite, but in many groups the second favorite stock will rotate closely behind the number one stock. In other groups, there might be one outstanding performer that rotates far ahead of a cluster of runners-up that rotate together.

The objective, once you have a list of positively rotating industries, is to find a stock that has just begun its upward rotation in a rotating industry group. You may use any search to do this (such as any of the three in Chapter 5), but be sure to limit the search to the industries that have been identified as rotating upward. This will allow only stocks in the top industry groups to be returned.[2]

Incidentally, there is another way to find superior companies in an industry and that is to compare the fundamental performance of all companies within a group. Specifically, with Telescan's ProSearch, you may rank companies by their ability to generate a return on sales (ROS), return on assets (ROA), and return on equity (ROE), as well as a host of other

---

[2] Limiting stocks to particular industries is a simple procedure in ProSearch. First, specify the industries that you want to use. Then, before submitting the stock search, select the search universe as "stocks in specified industries."

Exhibit 14.4   The top 25 stocks in the Local Computer Networks group on November 18, 1994, ranked by return on sales, assets, and equity.

ProSearch 4.0 Top Stock Report
Stocks in Specified Industries
11/18/94

1> CYE—CHEYENNE SOFTWARE   .TNT
ROS 5 40.1   (98)   ROA = 41.9   (99)   ROE = 46.3   (98)

2> BNET—BAY NETWORKS   .TNT
ROS = 16.2   (95)   ROA = 34.0   (99)   ROE = 44.7   (98)

3> CS—CABLETRON SYSTEMS   .TNT
ROS = 19.9   (96)   ROA = 28.3   (99)   ROE = 33.0   (97)

4> CSCO—CISCO SYSTEMS   .TNT
ROS = 18.8   (96)   ROA = 29.8   (99)   ROE = 37.3   (97)

5> XIRC—XIRCOM INC   .TNT
ROS = 12.3   (92)   ROA = 19.3   (98)   ROE = 23.3   (93)

6> NOVL—NOVELL INC   .TNT
ROS = 13.1   (93)   ROA = 14.9   (96)   ROE = 19.1   (90)

7> ODSI—OPTICAL DATA SYSTEMS   .TNT
ROS = 9.5   (89)   ROA = 18.4   (97)   ROE = 21.7   (92)

8> LNOPF—LANOPTICS LTD   .TNT
ROS = 28.6   (97)   ROA = 13.7   (95)   ROE = 14.7   (84)

9> ASFT—ARTISOFT INC   .TNT
ROS = 10.4   (90)   ROA = 14.8   (96)   ROE = 18.3   (89)

10> OLCMF—OLICOM A/S   .TNT
ROS = 11.6   (91)   ROA = 12.8   (94)   ROE = 15.6   (85)

11> DLNK—DIGITAL LINK   .TNT
ROS = 10.9   (91)   ROA = 10.8   (92)   ROE = 12.7   (80)

12> NETF—NETFRAME SYSTEMS   .TNT
ROS = 8.9   (88)   ROA = 11.1   (93)   ROE = 13.2   (81)

13> ASPX—AUSPEX SYSTEMS   .TNT
ROS = 9.9   (89)   ROA = 10.4   (92)   ROE = 12.8   (80)

Exhibit 14.4   (continued)

14>   SMSC—STANDARD MICROSYSTEMS   .TNT
  ROS = 6.2   (82)   ROA = 11.0   (92)   ROE = 15.5   (85)

15>   MTST—MICROTEST INC   .TNT
  ROS = 11.0   (91)   ROA = 9.8   (91)   ROE = 10.9   (76)

16>   XLGX—XYLOGICS, INC   .TNT
  ROS = 6.2   (82)   ROA = 10.3   (91)   ROE = 14.1   (82)

17>   ALTC—ALANTEC CORP   .TNT
  ROS = 13.4   (93)   ROA = 9.0   (89)   ROE = 10.2   (74)

18>   CHPM—CHIPCOM CORP   .TNT
  ROS = 6.4   (82)   ROA = 9.1   (90)   ROE = 11.8   (78)

19>   CITA—CITATION COMPUTER SYS   .TNT
  ROS = 6.3   (82)   ROA = 7.9   (88)   ROE = 12.3   (79)

20>   TRCD—TRICORD SYSTEMS   .TNT
  ROS = 6.4   (82)   ROA = 7.1   (86)   ROE = 8.7   (72)

21>   LANTF—LANNET DATA COMMUN   .TNT
  ROS = 8.9   (88)   ROA = 5.8   (82)   ROE = 6.0   (67)

22>   NWTH—NETWORTH INC   .TNT
  ROS = 4.6   (77)   ROA = 5.8   (82)   ROE = 9.1   (72)

23>   ASNT—ASANTE TECHNOLOGIES   .TNT
  ROS = 1.4   (66)   ROA = 2.8   (72)   ROE = 5.0   (65)

24>   NWK—NETWORK EQUIP TECH   .TNT
  ROS = 0.2   (62)   ROA = 0.3   (61)   ROE = 0.9   (61)

25>   XCOM—CROSSCOMM CORP   .TNT
  ROS = 0.5   (63)   ROA = 0.3   (61)   ROE = 0.3   (61)

fundamental criteria. Exhibit 14.4 shows such a ranking for the Computer-Local Networks group. Much can be gained by studying one of these reports and comparing companies in the same industry.

WHAT GOES UP . . .

Industry groups rotate downward as well. If you monitor your portfolio closely, you shouldn't get caught in a group that is going the wrong way. It is instructive, however, to see what can happen to a perfectly sound stock if its industry group falls out of favor. The medical industry is a good example of the rise and fall of an industry group.

The Health Care Scare

During the late 1980s and early 1990s, medical stocks were growing at 15 to 30 percent or more a year (Exhibit 14.5), and P/E ratios ranged from 20 to 100 or more (recall U.S. Surgical). But by early 1994, these same stocks were selling for P/E's of 10 to 12. Why? Because the specter of

---

Exhibit 14.5   In mid-November 1994, the Medical Instruments group was below its long-term LSQ line.

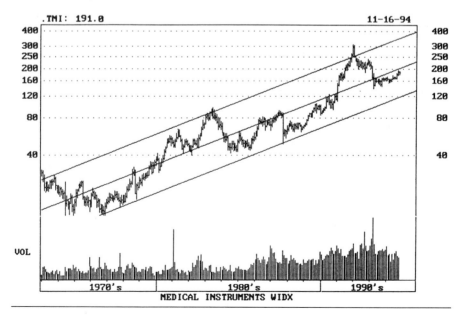

health care reform unnerved investors who feared the high growth rates couldn't continue.

The rotation away from medical stocks started even before the 1992 Presidential election. Widespread concern about spiraling medical costs had created a general feeling that there would be margin pressure in medical products companies. So investors began to pull out. P/E's for the entire industry fell from an average of 30 to below 15, and stock prices tumbled 30 to 80 percent—*even though many of the stocks' earnings were increasing at 10 to 15 percent or more.*

A classic example of a solid performer that got caught in a downward spiraling group is St. Jude Medical Corporation. Before 1992, St. Jude had a P/E ratio of 25 to 30, which it deserved, based on the previous seven years' earnings growth. Its earnings increased from 30 cents in 1989 to $2.32 in 1993, more than 60 percent per year compounded. But when the rotation away from medical stocks began, St. Jude's stock price fell from the mid-$50's to the mid-$20's, and its P/E fell from 28 to 13 (Exhibit 14.6). The irony is, St. Jude's earnings have never gone down. Granted, earnings flattened out because government posturing put margin pressure on the company, but St. Jude remains the dominant player in its industry with

---

Exhibit 14.6   This graph shows that St. Jude's earnings increased dramatically throughout the early 1990's and flattened out in mid-1993.

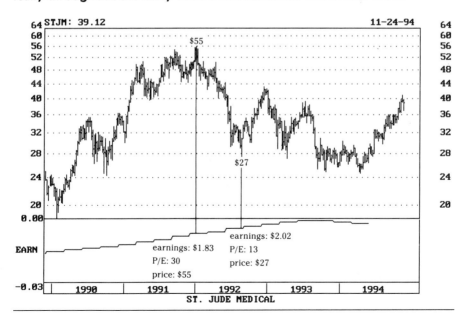

projected earnings of $2.63 for 1995 and a respectable projected five-year growth rate of 13 percent.

Medical stocks were down but not out. They began a recovery in the summer 1994. They were so undervalued, with P/E's at historically low levels, that investors began to move back in. At that time, the Clinton health care reform act was in deep trouble and there were rumblings of more moderate solutions, so investors began to focus on the higher quality issues within the medical group, including St. Jude. By late fall 1994, the medical industry was the Comeback Kid, with St. Jude leading the way. Even though earnings were flat, St. Jude rose from $27 in July 1994 to about $40 in mid-November.

The health care scare should be a lesson to us all. Facts don't count for much when rumors and fears take hold; it is the market's *perception* that counts. When institutions flee an industry because of fears, real or imaginary, about its future, stocks in that group may take a beating even while earnings continue to rise. Eventually, if the industry doesn't go into a secular decline, the industry group will start rotating upward again.

YOU MUST REMEMBER THIS . . .

Industry group rotation is a way to benefit from the activity of institutional investors. With computerized tools, you can see the upward rotation of a group begin and you can see it weaken as it starts to go the other way. With these tools, you should be able to find the best stock in a group, ride its upward surge, and then clear out as the downward rotation begins.

- Pay attention to group rotation. It's a lot easier to swim with the tide than against it.

- Stocks themselves rotate within an industry group; the goal is to find ones that are rotating upward.

- Find the leaders within a group by ranking stocks on their fundamental performance (such as return on sales, return on equity, and return on assets).

- After you've found the best stocks within a favorable industry group, be sure to evaluate them as described in earlier chapters.

- What goes up must come down. Stay abreast of what's happening to the industry groups of stocks that you own.

15

OPPORTUNITIES IN OPTIONS

Options. You either love 'em or you hate 'em. They start the adrenalin flowing for some investors and send others scurrying for the hills. If you're one of the former, you'll be pleased to know there are computerized tools to help you tame those puts and calls. If you're one of the latter, we'll show you a way to do a little low-risk speculation that could result in some spectacular profits.

Options, as you probably know, are derivative securities, which means they track the performance of the underlying stock. The advantage of trading options is the higher reward potential for fewer dollars risked. The disadvantage is the higher risk that comes with the limited duration of the option (if the underlying stock does not move before the expiration date of the option, the entire "premium" will be lost). There are far too many variations on options to go into here. Volumes have been written on the subject, and we won't attempt even a cursory treatment. We'll just preach to the choir by mentioning a couple of computerized tools that make option trading a whole lot easier.

The first is an options search tool designed specifically for options. It allows you to specify requirements for price, performance, volume, and volatility; it lets you stipulate the technical patterns of both the option and the underlying stock; and it helps you find the optimum spread and straddle opportunities for a given stock. Like stocks, the options will be ranked on the search report in order of how well they fit your search strategy. (Take a look at Telescan's Options Search™, which is part of the Cyber-Investing Kit.)

Other option tools include valuation programs which use complex mathematical formulas, such as the Black-Scholes formula,[1] to measure an option's inherent overvaluation or undervaluation. (All formulas are transparent to the user, which means the programs are not difficult to use.) Option valuation programs can also be used to estimate decay rates of premiums, evaluate spreads, and perform other sophisticated option analyses, such as determining the ideal option position for taking advantage of a projected stock move.

A more thorough discussion is beyond the scope of this book. But we'll will show you how to dabble in options with a bit of low-risk speculation.

LOW-RISK OPTIONS: AN OXYMORON?

Recall in Chapter 5 how we extolled the virtues of following the insiders' lead? Another way to do this is with options. Insiders often purchase speculative options in anticipation of an event that might cause a sharp rise in the price of the underlying stock.[2] Such an event might be a merger or acquisition that is under negotiation; it might be the release of a new product which has been under development; or it could be anything that might positively affect earnings, which insiders know about long before the investing public. When insiders learn of such an event, they often purchase large quantities of speculative *options,* rather than the stock itself. Why? Because one option contract is a fraction of the cost of the actual 100 shares of stock. (One contract is an option to purchase 100 shares of stock.) That means investors can acquire more shares with options than they could buy directly. So, if the speculative event falls through, the option holder stands to lose relatively little.

We have observed that many major corporate events over the past several years have been preceded by unusual option activity. With com-

---

[1] The Black-Scholes formula is a method for arriving at the theoretical value of an option, based on the underlying stock price, volatility, and the number of days left until option expiration.

[2] Insiders, in this case, may simply be individuals, such as employees of investment bankers, accounting firms, or law firms, who are aware of an emerging event in the company and not necessarily officers or directors.

puterized option search and analysis tools, we can discover this kind of insider speculation and join in the fun for very little money. The rewards, as you will see, can be substantial.

Is this illegal? Not for the outsider. If those purchasing the options are trying to profit from information that has not yet been made public, their actions may be considered illegal. But the information we use to find *their* speculative option activity is certainly not illegal. It is public information, and we are not insiders!

Before we go further, let's look at a couple of option graphs so you can see the possibilities.

- Exhibit 15.1 shows a September 17.5 call for Syntex Corporation. From February through mid-April, the volume fluctuated between zero and 400 contracts a day. Then, it shot up to over 1,000 contracts in one day. If you had observed this activity the next day and purchased just 10 contracts for about $900, you would have owned a position that was worth over $5,800 about a week later, an increase of over 600 percent.

Exhibit 15.1   A graph of a Syntex call showing the emergence of unusual volume and the subsequent speculated-upon "event."

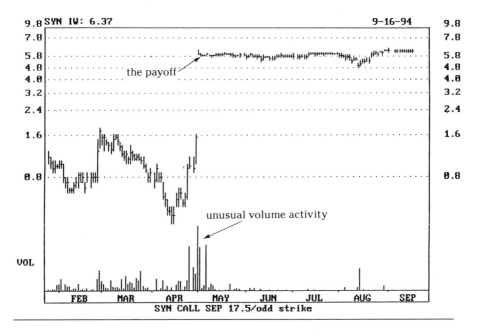

- Exhibit 15.2 shows a September 35 call for H. J. Heinz . In late July, the volume jumped from virtually zero to over 500 contracts in one day and to over 1,000 contracts two days later. Within the next three days, you could have bought 10 contracts for less than $400. In less than three weeks, ten contracts were worth about $3,500, an increase of almost 1000 percent.

- Exhibit 15.3 shows an October 65 call for American Cyanamid. In early July, the volume steadily increased from very low levels to more than 150 contracts, dropped off, and then repeated the same pattern. Any time during the first half of July, you could have bought ten contracts for between $2,500 and $3,000. By the third week of July, ten contracts were worth more than $25,000 and by mid-August, almost $35,000.

As you can see, these are very exciting investments. Even if you had bought only one contract—which you could do in most cases for a couple of hundred dollars—you could have had outstanding gains. There are

---

Exhibit 15.2   A graph of an H. J. Heinz call showing the emergence of unusual volume and the subsequent sharp rise.

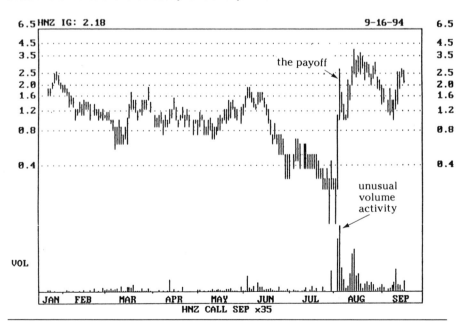

Exhibit 15.3   A graph of an American Cyanamid call showing the emergence of unusual volume and the subsequent speculated-upon "event."

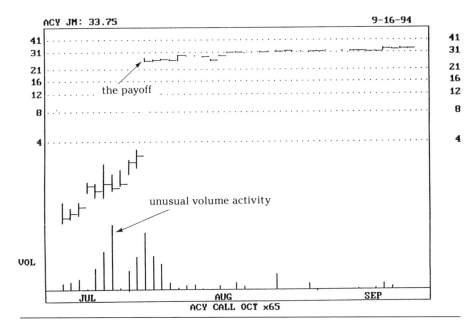

ACY JM: 33.75   9-16-94

the payoff

unusual volume activity

VOL

JUL   AUG   SEP
ACY CALL OCT x65

pitfalls, as we'll talk about later, but the potential reward of this kind of low-cost speculation makes it fun, if nothing else. The best news is that there is a computerized search that will identify these opportunities for you as they occur.

THE OPTION SEARCH

To find speculative situations like those described, we designed a search to look for options with unusual volume activity. We want a very high ratio of current 1-day volume to 14-day average volume, together with a fairly high volume of current contracts. Here's how we structured the search. (You may wish to create this search with Telescan's Options Search, which is part of the Cyber-Investing Kit.)

Narrow the Universe

We want only options that have a volume today of at least 50 contracts and have been averaging at least 10 contracts per day over the past 14 days. If a stock has been averaging 10 or so contracts a day, and suddenly trades 100 contracts in one day, there may be something up. So we'll use the following:

- *Today's volume indicator* to eliminate all options that didn't trade at least 50 contracts on the day of the search.

- *14-day average volume indicator* to eliminate all options that have not averaged at least 10 contracts per day over the past 14 days.

- *Put or call indicator* to eliminate puts. We are looking for positive speculation here.

Score and Rank the Options

The preceding indicators are *minimum* requirements. We are actually looking for much larger numbers. We want to see options previously averaging 20 or 30 contracts that suddenly trade 400, 500, or even 1,000 contracts in one day. This would be a clear sign of speculative activity and would bear careful scrutiny. So we'll have the program rank the options from high to

---

AT THE MONEY, IN THE MONEY, OUT OF THE MONEY . . .

These terms have to do with how close the strike price of the option is to the current price of the underlying stock. "At the money" refers to an option (put or call) whose strike price is about the same as the current stock price.

An "in-the-money" option is either (1) a put whose underlying stock price is below the strike price or (2) a call whose underlying stock price is above the strike price. These are obviously higher priced than at-the-money or out-of-the-money options.

An "out-of-the-money" option is either (1) a put whose underlying stock price is above the strike price or (2) a call whose underlying stock price is below the strike price. Out-of-the-money options are the least expensive, and the further out of the money they are, the less expensive they are. So, you don't necessarily have to buy an option where all the activity is; you could buy one further out of the money. You would not make as much money, but you wouldn't be risking as much, either.

low according to the ratio of the 1-day to 14-day average volume and the amount that the option is out of the money. We'll use:

- *1/14-Day Average Volume Ratio.* The higher, the better.
- *Dollar out-of-the-Money Indicator.* The higher, the better.

Out-of-the-money calls are a better indication of speculative activity, particularly if they are well out of the money. In-the-money calls, on the other hand, are frequently used by regular purchasers to accumulate the shares for nonspeculative purposes, which wouldn't necessarily indicate unusual activity in the stock price.

List Information

We will use the list-only indicators shown in Exhibit 15.4, to retrieve information needed to make the final selection. We don't think it is necessary to give a detailed explanation of these indicators, as we did with the stock searches, because this is a highly speculative search and out of the mainstream of a long-term, prudent investing process. If you use Telescan's Options Search, the indicators are adequately defined in the user's manual.

CHECK IT OUT

After you find a list of options, pick out the ones with the highest one-day volume and the largest ratio of 1-to-14-day average volume. Then look at their price-and-volume graphs for a graphic representation of the speculative activity.

Next, print a list of the option quotes for the stocks that look good (Exhibit 15.5). This list is helpful in two ways. First, it lists the option symbols so you can look up other options near the same time frame and strike price to see if they reflect anomalous activity as well. Second, if you decide to speculate, you can use the list to select an option that is further out of the money (at a lower cost).

Finally, try to determine the reasons for the speculative activity. Check the news and other reports on the underlying stock. Rumors of a merger or acquisition may or may not have reached the news media, or there could be something going on besides a pending takeover. If an in-the-money call exhibits unusual activity, it may mean nothing at all. Some

Exhibit 15.4   This is the search strategy for speculative calls.

Indicator	Action
Today's Volume (Vol)	Eliminate all options with less than 50 contracts
14-day Average Volume (AvgVl)	Eliminate all options that have not averaged at least 10 contracts perday for 14 days
Put or Call (P/C)	Eliminate all puts
1-Day-to-14-Day Average Volume Ratio (1/14V)	The higher, the better 100%
Dollar Out of Money ($/Mon)	The higher, the better 80%
Bid (Bid)	List only
Asked (Asked)	List only
Last Trade (LTrade)	List only
Stock Close (StkCl)	List only
Black-Scholes Value (BSVal)	List Only
Delta (Delta)	List Only
Gamma (Gamma)	List Only
Theta (Theta)	List Only
Vega (Vega)	List Only
Implied Volatility/Statistical Volatility— 20-Day (IV-20)	List Only
Percent Over/Undervalued (%O/U)	List Only
Relative Performance-Stock/1-Dy (1-Dy)	List Only
Relative Performance-Stock/1-Wk (1-Wk)	List Only
Relative Performance-Stock/3-Wk (3-Wk)	List Only
Relative Performance-Option/1-Dy (1DyOp)	List Only
Relative Performance-Option/1-Wk (1WkOp)	List Only
Relative Performance-Option/3-Wk (3WkOp)	List Only
Open Interest (OpInt)	List Only
Total Volume/Total Open Interest (TVTOI)	List Only
Put/Call Open Interest (P/COI)	List Only

Exhibit 15.5   Option quotes for H. J. Heinz Corporation on November 18, 1994.

11/18/94—HEINZ (H.J.)—37.000

Symbol	Issue	Bid	Asked
HNZ AF	HNZ CALL JAN x30	7.000	7.500
ZHN AF	HNZ CALL JAN x30	9.375	9.875
HNZ AG	HNZ CALL JAN x35	2.562	2.937
ZHN AG	HNZ CALL JAN x35	6.375	6.875
HNZ AH	HNZ CALL JAN x40	0.437	0.625
ZHN AH	HNZ CALL JAN x40	3.875	4.250
HNZ AI	HNZ CALL JAN x45	0.000	0.000
HNZ AJ	HNZ CALL JAN x50	0.000	0.000
ZHN AJ	HNZ CALL JAN x50	1.000	1.250
HNZ CF	HNZ CALL MAR x30	7.250	7.750
HNZ CG	HNZ CALL MAR x35	3.125	3.500
HNZ CH	HNZ CALL MAR x40	0.875	1.125
HNZ CI	HNZ CALL MAR x45	0.187	0.437
HNZ FG	HNZ CALL JUN x35	3.750	4.125
HNZ FH	HNZ CALL JUN x40	1.312	1.562
HNZ KG	HNZ CALL NOV x35	0.000	0.000
HNZ KH	HNZ CALL NOV x40	0.000	0.000
HNZ KI	HNZ CALL NOV x45	0.000	0.000
HNZ LF	HNZ CALL DEC x30	7.000	7.500
HNZ LG	HNZ CALL DEC x35	2.125	2.500
HNZ LH	HNZ CALL DEC x40	0.187	0.250
HNZ LI	HNZ CALL DEC x45	0.000	0.000
HNZ MF	HNZ PUT JAN x30	0.000	0.000
ZHN MF	HNZ PUT JAN x30	0.687	0.937
HNZ MG	HNZ PUT JAN x35	0.562	0.812
ZHN MG	HNZ PUT JAN x35	2.062	2.437
HNZ MH	HNZ PUT JAN x40	3.375	3.750
ZHN MH	HNZ PUT JAN x40	4.500	4.875
HNZ MI	HNZ PUT JAN x45	7.875	8.375
HNZ MJ	HNZ PUT JAN x50	12.625	13.375
ZHN MJ	HNZ PUT JAN x50	12.625	13.375
HNZ OF	HNZ PUT MAR x30	0.000	0.000
HNZ OG	HNZ PUT MAR x35	0.875	1.125
HNZ OH	HNZ PUT MAR x40	3.625	4.000
HNZ OI	HNZ PUT MAR x45	7.875	8.375
HNZ RG	HNZ PUT JUN x35	1.250	1.500
HNZ RH	HNZ PUT JUN x40	3.750	4.125
HNZ WG	HNZ PUT NOV x35	0.000	0.000
HNZ WH	HNZ PUT NOV x40	0.000	0.000
HNZ WI	HNZ PUT NOV x45	0.000	0.000
HNZ XF	HNZ PUT DEC x30	0.000	0.000
HNZ XG	HNZ PUT DEC x35	0.000	0.312
HNZ XH	HNZ PUT DEC x40	3.000	3.125
HNZ XI	HNZ PUT DEC x45	7.750	8.250

investors, when routinely acquiring a position in a stock, add to their positions by purchasing in-the-money calls, instead of buying the stock outright (which may protect them if the stock goes down). The high volume could also be merely the "unwinding" of previous option positions. You'll need to do a little detective work to track this down. Here's how.

Inspect a six- or nine-month option graph and pay attention to the price of the transactions on the day in question. If the volume reflects buying, the option price would be going up; if it reflects selling, the option price would be going down. If the volume seems to be reflecting selling, look back over earlier periods and see if the volume-spread over a day or two equals the volume in question. If so, it probably is the unwinding of a previous position and therefore nothing to get excited about. Usually, these are fairly obvious.

YOU MUST REMEMBER THIS . . .

Keep in mind this sort of option trading is a *speculative* activity, and there are several places where you could go wrong.

- There may be no speculation at all. The unusual volume could be the unwinding of an earlier purchase, or it could be part of an acquisition program. Buying out-of-the-money options protects against the latter.

- Your option could expire before any increase in price occurs. Speculative option activity sometimes occurs a long time before any corresponding activity in the stock.

- The anticipated event may fail to take place. Mergers and acquisitions often fall through; product releases may be delayed; expected earnings often don't materialize. Any number of factors could prevent the underlying stock from rising to speculated heights in the time frame allowed by your particular options.

- Even if the event should occur, it may not be greeted with the enthusiasm hoped for by the original speculators. Both you and they could lose.

Nonetheless, opportunities exist for low-cost option speculation. Just use reasonable care, and treat this activity like a hobby—one with some very serious money attached when you happen to be right.

16

THE FUTURE
OF CYBER-INVESTING

As we move into the 21st century, we will surely encounter new cyber-investing tools and techniques. It is certain that we will have better information and more of it. That the tools will become more sophisticated and at the same time, more user-friendly. That interfaces between programs will become more seamless. The rest of this chapter will give you a preview of the tools of the future. But they will begin where today's tools leave off, and the basics of the cyber-investing process will remain the same. You will still need to find the stocks that have the best chance for growth and evaluate them thoroughly; you will still need to consider the risk/reward relationship when buying and selling stocks; you will still need to manage your portfolio carefully to ensure the greatest possible return on your investments. So the time to start is now.

If you have never before invested in stocks, start with paper-trades and a dummy portfolio until you learn the programs and gain confidence in your decisions. Once you start investing for real, remember this: What distinguishes successful traders from the rest of the crowd is finding a methodology that works and having the discipline to stick with it. Remember, too, that you have the nimbleness of the individual investor and the computerized tools of the professional. If you use your advantages properly, you *can* make spectacular returns on Wall Street.

PREVIEW: GLOBAL INVESTING

It becomes clearer every day that we live in a global economy. Communication with other countries becomes more streamlined every day. Information on foreign companies becomes more accessible. Currency transactions between nations become more seamless. With every passing day it becomes easier to invest in securities outside the United States and to diversify away from a specific economy. By the end of this century, we predict that the individual investor will be trading stocks in foreign markets as effortlessly as the professionals do.

Global investing is already an arena for sophisticated investors. Foreign stocks simply represent more companies in which to invest, companies which can be evaluated on exactly the same basis as domestic stocks, by looking at earnings, stock graphs, technical analysis, and so forth. As this information becomes more readily available, global investing tools will catch up and amateur investors will also be able to play. Many sources, such as CompuServe®, Prodigy® and America Online®, already offer information on foreign stocks. Standard & Poor's recently announced a service called European MarketScope®, which provides a company profile on European companies. Daily price and volume information in the form of stock graphs has been hard to come by, but that too is changing. Nearly 50 foreign exchanges will be added to the Telescan to its database by mid-1995, which means you'll be able to download stock graphs and obtain company information on foreign stocks. Canadian stocks are already online.

The major difference, of course, between trading American stocks and foreign stocks is currency risk. Because most stocks are traded in the local currency, fluctuations of that currency can be a problem (witness the devaluation of the Mexican peso in early 1995). Analyzing foreign currencies is part of global investing and can be done through various online services, but that subject is well beyond the scope of this book. The good news is, you don't have to know anything about foreign currencies in order to invest in some foreign companies. Many are traded in U.S. dollars on domestic exchanges as American Depository Receipts (ADRs). A complete list of ADRs, as of early 1994, can be found in Robert Schwabach's book *Global Investments Using Electronic Tools,* which, by the way, is a good general guide to global investing for beginners and experts alike.

Global investing is the wave of the future. If you learn the tools and techniques for investing in the domestic markets, you'll be ready to join the global game when the time comes.

PREVIEW: THE INTERNET

The Internet has been much ballyhooed in the recent press, but until the last year or so, it has been pretty much a playground for accomplished computer hackers. It was difficult to use and, as far as usable information for investors, a virtual desert. It simply wasn't worth the trouble.

All that is changing rapidly.

Three improvements have begun to make the Internet a more hospitable place for ordinary users: advances in graphical interfaces, new World Wide Web site servers, and—more relevant to investors—a gradual increase in investing-related content (see "Hot Spots for Investors on the Internet" in the sidebar). Undoubtedly, this content will be enriched significantly over the next few years.

There are many ways to gain access to the Internet. The new Windows® 95 plans to offer access, as do most major online services. (Delphi offers a particularly robust Internet access.) We cannot go into the complex peculiarities of navigating the Internet, but we have listed a few site addresses that you might find useful as an investor. At any rate, it is probably a good idea to acquaint yourself with the Net, since it threatens to enmesh us all in the near future.

PREVIEW: TOOLS OF TOMORROW

Telecommunications and the personal computer have forever changed the world of the individual investor. But that world will continue to expand and evolve. Here are a few of the cyber-investing tools and services that we see on the horizon.

- Stock search programs will become more efficient and user-friendly. Search optimizers will create searches that have been previously backtested to produce the biggest winners in past markets. Search builders will create searches in response to user's questions about their investment goals. Information such as news, earnings estimates, and company profiles will be retrieved based on search results.

- Superior asset allocation programs will use dynamic models. As more and different financial instruments become available through the true globalization of the investing process, dynamic asset allocation will become more important.

- Improved portfolio management programs will offer electronic "file drawers" which can be used as purchase logs.

- Improved chart pattern recognition through expansion of artificial intelligence help identify patterns that have proven successful in the past.

- 3-D graphics and other advanced tools will improve visual appeal of stock graphs *and* increase the amount of information that can be communicated by the graph.

- Increased electronic trading should further lower commissions and open up more proprietary research from the brokerage firms. These programs may allow for much more complex buy and sell instructions than could be accommodated comfortably by a human broker. For example, one might enter a sell order such as: "Sell IBM or Compaq or Apple, whichever hits its target first, and then cancel the sell order on the remaining two." Or an even more complex buy order such as: "Buy Microsoft when it breaks out of a basing pattern."

- Wireless products will interact with pagers or cellular telephones to alert you to intra-day changes in individual stocks or the market.

- EDGAR, which is the government's name of the electronic filing of S.E.C. documents, such as 10K's and 10Q's, is scheduled for completion by the end of 1998. This will provide quicker access to more in-depth information on public companies.

- Specialized information, such as government statistics for economic or industry analysis, will be more easily accessed.

HOT SPOTS FOR INVESTORS ON THE INTERNET

Here are a few Internet addresses that may be of interest to the investor. New investing-related sites are being added regularly (and some occasionally withdrawn). Drop by the Telescan Investment Center on the Net (address below) for an updated list and a direct launch to the investing "hot spot" of your choice.

Brokerage Information
http://www.cs.cmu.edu:8001/afs/cs.cmu.edu/user/jdg/www/
   invest_brokers.html
Identifies brokerage services that would be most helpful to investors.

Commerce Business Daily
gopher://usic.savvy.com
Current and historical business articles.

Currency Exchanges
gopher://una.hh.lib.umich.edu00/ebb/monetary/tenfx.frb
Current and historical exchange rates for more than 100 different monetary types.

DTN Wall Street
http://www.secapl.com/dtn/info/top.html
Details on subscriptions to DTN real-time quote service.

Edgar: Filing Retrieval
http://edgar.stern.nyu.edu/tools.shtml
SEC filings on more than 8,000 issues, including 10Ks, 10Qs, and other detailed reports.

Edgar: Mutual Funds Reporting
http://edgar.stern.nyu.edu/mutual.html
SEC filings on more than 2,000 mutual fund groups.

GNN Personal Finance Center
http://www.digital.com/gnn/meta/finance/index.html
Broad spectrum of money management, investment, and financial planning resources.

Internet's Link to Managing Money
http://riskweb.bus.utexas.edu/articles/post.html
Help articles on the financial sources provided by the Internet.

LawTalk: Business Law & Personal Finance

http://www.law.indiana.edu/law/bizlaw.html

Articles written by attorneys on legal issues and personal finance.

Morningstar Spotlight

http://networth.galt.com/www/home/mutual/morning/mspot.htm

Reports on selected and unique mutual funds sponsored by Morningstar analyst.

NETworth

http://networth.galt.com

A collection of free services about investing information on the Internet (directed to the individual investor).

QuoteCom Home Page

http://www.quote.com

Provides five free quotes per day on any issue. Subscriptions available for additional quotes.

Telescan Investment Center

http://www.telescan.com/tscn.html

Provides free updates on market averages, articles on technical and fundamental analysis, dictionary of technical and fundamental terms, and a "launch pad" for investing hot spots on the Net. Subscriptions available for financial market information.

Zacks Investment Research

http://aw.zacks.com

Free current consensus estimates and stock quotes for up to 5 stocks. By subscription: earnings estimates reports, screening capability with 86 investment ratios, E-mail and model portfolio alerts for changes in estimates, broker recommendations, earnings surprises and Zacks rank.

- Interactive communication with companies, brokers, and Wall Street analysts will be offered through advanced E-mail, forums, and roundtables.
- Educational opportunities in the investment field will become interactive.
- Mutual fund analysis programs will become more sophisticated, more specialized, and more global.
- Bond analysis programs will be created for the individual investor.
- Financial services will continue to expand on the Internet.
- Global investing tools will proliferate as global investing expands.

YOU MUST REMEMBER THIS . . .

Tomorrow's cyber-investing will make today's tools look like tinker toys. They will be more powerful and more sophisticated—not less so. But they will begin where today's tools leave off. That makes it important to get started now. Pick a program and start using it. Practice with paper trades to build your skill and confidence. You may feel a bit overwhelmed at first, but cyber-investing is a lot like swimming. You simply have to jump in and start paddling. In cyberspace, it doesn't matter how deep the water is, once you know how to swim.

THE CYBER-INVESTING KIT

The publisher of *Cyber-Investing* has arranged for you to have free access to a wide variety of tools to introduce you to the world of cyber-investing. These tools will assist you in implementing the investing techniques described in this book and may well whet your appetite for more. A complete description of each tool and how to access it follow this list.

CONTENTS OF YOUR CYBER-INVESTING KIT

- TELESCAN 3.0 SYSTEM. The powerful investment research and analysis software used in the searches and analyses in this book. Software included; 30-day free online access.

- PROSEARCH. Stock search tool. Free searches for 30 days.

- ZACKS ESTIMATE SERVICE. 30-day free online access to earnings estimates.

- STANDARD & POOR'S MARKETSCOPE® DATABASE. 30-day free online access.

- MUTUAL FUND SEARCH. Mutual fund search tool. Free searches for 30 days.

- OPTIONS SEARCH. Options search tool. Free searches for 30 days.

250

- METASTOCK™.   One of the world's best-selling technical analysis programs. Software included.

- INVESTMENT NEWSLETTERS ONLINE.   Free access for 30 days to more than 20 online investment newsletters, including David Brown's *Cyber-Investing* newsletter which uses the investing strategies described in this book.

- INVESTMENT NEWSLETTERS BY MAIL.   Free trial copies to three popular print newsletters: *The Big Picture, The Dick Davis Digest,* Stan Weinstein's *The Professional Tape Reader,* and *The Zweig Forecast.*

- CYBER-INVESTING SEMINARS.   Free or discounted admission to cyber-investing seminars held in various locations throughout the country.

- CHARLES SCHWAB & CO.   Discounts on electronic trades, plus special offer on the StreetSmart® software.

DETAILS OF YOUR CYBER-INVESTING KIT

TELESCAN 3.0 SYSTEM

Free Software with This Book, Plus Free Online Time

Telescan 3.0 is a complete system of information, including news and reports, charts, estimates, and search tools that form the basis of a computerized investor's toolkit.

Your 30-day Free Trial Includes:

- Non-prime-time access for 30 days to the Telescan database dating back to 1973. Non-prime-time hours are 6:00 P.M. to 7:00 A.M. your local time, plus weekends and some holidays. Note: A long distance call is required to access the Telescan database outside the continental United States.

- Toll-free Customer Service is available 7 days a week to activate your software and answer any questions:

Monday–Friday: 7:00 a.m. to Midnight, Central Time
Saturday and Sunday: 9:00 a.m. to 6:00 p.m., Central Time

- The Telescan 3.0 System is user-friendly and easy to operate. A Quick Start guide appears in Appendix B. If you wish, you may order a complete set of documentation for a shipping and handling charge of $12.75.

- You may pay to upgrade to Telescan Analyzer for Windows®. (For more information on the windows upgrade, call Telescan's toll-free number below.)

- System requirements for the Telescan 3.0 System are:

    An IBM-PC (286 or faster) or 100% compatible computer
    MS DOS 2.1 or higher
    640K Memory
    3MB Hard disk space; CGA, EGA, or VGA board
    EGA or VGA color monitor
    Hayes Smartmodem (1200, 2400, or 9600 baud) or 100% compatible
    Mouse (contains optional mouse interface)
    Printer

To activate your software, call 1-800-780-2332 or 713-952-1060, and identify yourself as a *Cyber-Investing* customer.

When you call, a Telescan Customer Service representative will give you:

- The local telephone number for accessing the database.

- Your user ID number.

- Your password.

Install the program and complete the log-on setup screen according to the instructions in Appendix B.

Telescan Analyzer

Telescan Analyzer was used for the Stage Two evaluation in this book, as well as for the industry group analysis and market analysis. With Telescan Analyzer you can:

◆ Access charts that include current price and volume information and as far back as 1973 on more than 77,000 securities which include stocks, bonds, mutual funds, options, futures, industry groups, and market indexes.

◆ Retrieve online stock quotes for the NYSE, AMEX, NASDAQ and Canadian exchanges, updated on a 15-minute delay.

◆ Perform technical and fundamental analysis.

◆ Retrieve news and a variety of textual reports.

How to access Telescan Analyzer: This application will be available automatically after you install the Telescan 3.0 System. To use the program, select Analyzer from the Program Menu. Refer to the Quick Start guide in Appendix B for assistance.

ProSearch

ProSearch is the stock search program used in the searches described in Chapters 4, 5, and 14 of this book. ProSearch offers:

◆ Over 200 fundamental and technical indicators for defining a search request; up to 40 may be used in a single search.

◆ Three search methods: (1) Eliminate stocks from the search universe, (2) score and rank stocks, and (3) list useful information.

◆ Previously defined search requests.

◆ The ProSearch online database is updated each day.

How to access ProSearch: ProSearch will be available automatically after you install the Telescan 3.0 System and log on to the database to activate the program. To use it, select ProSearch from the Program Menu or press Ctrl-S. Refer to the Quick Start guide in Appendix B for assistance.

Zacks Estimate Service

Zacks Estimate Service compiles earnings estimates from thousands of research analysts for approximately 5,000 companies. A sample report appears in Chapter 8 (Exhibit 8.6).

How to access Zacks: Zacks Estimate Service will be available automatically after you install the Telescan 3.0 System. To access Zacks, select Earnings Estimates from the Special Reports Menu, which appears on the Text Services Menu or, with a stock graph displayed, on the Indicator Menu.

S&P MarketScope®

S&P MarketScope is an investment database from Standard & Poor's. It contains a wealth of investment information on over 5,000 companies, including company references like the one in Chapter 8 (Exhibit 8.7). In addition, the S&P database offers market commentary based on worldwide research and comments on economic indicators; interest rates, exchange rates and bond yields; a wide variety of investment ideas and stock picks; plus its Stock Appreciation Ranking System (STARS).

How to access S&P MarketScope: The S&P MarketScope database will be available automatically after you install the Telescan 3.0 system.

- To use the S&P database, select S&P MarketScope from the Program Menu; then select the desired service.

- To view a MarketScope report for a particular stock, select MarketScope Report from the Special Reports Menu, which appears on the Text Services Menu or, with a stock graph displayed, on the Indicator Menu.

Mutual Fund Search

Mutual Fund Search is a search program designed exclusively for mutual funds. It operates like ProSearch, with the following differences:

- The 82 search criteria are designed exclusively for mutual funds; up to 30 may be used in a single search.

- Funds are classified by investment objective and by type of fund (equity, fixed income, municipal bond, and money market funds).

How to access Mutual Fund Search: Mutual Fund Search will be available automatically after you install the Telescan 3.0 System and log on to the database to activate the program. To use the program, select Mutual Fund Search from the Program Menu.

Options Search

Options Search was used to find the speculative calls in Chapter 15. It uses Telescan's online database of more than 35,000 options on stocks and indexes, and more than 300,000 option combinations (spreads and saddles). The program operates like ProSearch, except it has 120 search criteria designed exclusively for options, and up to 30 criteria may be used in a single search.

How to access Options Search: Options Search will be available automatically after you install the Telescan 3.0 System and log on to the database to activate the program. To use the program, select Options Search from the Program Menu.

Investment Newsletters Online

Investment newsletters can assist you in market analysis, as well as point you toward specific securities and emerging industry groups. You may access more than 20 online investment newsletters from the world's leading investment advisors without charge during your 30-day free trial. The following list may change, as new newsletters are added frequently and occasionally deleted.

- *Cyrus J. Barton's 52-Week Review.* Mr. Barton offers weekly commentary and stock picks based on the 52-week-high investment technique.

- *John Bollinger's Capital Growth Newsletter.* Mr. Bollinger, one of the best-known investment professionals in the country, offers an analysis of the market, along with his investment recommendations.

- *Cyber-Investing.* Published weekly by David Brown and Mark Draud, this newsletter offers market commentary and stock recommendations using the undervalued growth investing principles outlined in this book.

- *Daily Market Reports.* Four daily reports, published by Market Consensus, offer a sampling of the day's commentary on the financial markets and the economy.

- *The Delta Speculator.* Published monthly. Uses a proprietary "parabolic correlator" to forecast potentially profitable opportunities.

- *Downing & Associates Technical Analysis.* A technician's letter with strong emphasis on very short-term analysis. Markets, industry groups and stocks are covered.

- *Financial World Portfolio.* Specific buy and sell recommendations for currency and commodity futures, stocks, options, and mutual funds.

- *Futures Choice.* Edited by Greg Reagan, this daily newsletter makes specific futures recommendations.

- *High Tech Watch.* Published monthly by Henry Bannoch. Specializes in long-term investment opportunities in small, undervalued, technology-oriented companies.

- *The IPO Insider.* Marc Clark provides detailed evaluation of selected new offerings.

- *Macro*World Stock Market Advisory.* Dr. Douglas Graham offers weekly market commentary and specific stock recommendations based on his unique econometric analysis.

- *Man-Edge.* Edited by Don Fishback, this newsletter offers market analysis based on popular sentiment, monetary, and technical readings.

- *Marketline Letter.* Published daily by Steve Naremore. Includes market commentary and the latest "rumors" on Wall Street.

- *The Mutual Fund Advisor.* Don Rowe makes monthly recommendations on all types of mutual funds.

- *Price-Trax.* A weekly newsletter based on technical timing. Tracks stock trends and trend reversals.

- *The Princeton Portfolio.* Michael Gianturco provides weekly buy/sell recommendations on science and technology stocks.

- *Stock of the Week Report.* Published monthly by Harry Plate. Makes stock recommendations based on value, timing, and growth.

- *Top-Performing Initial Public Offerings.* A survey by Larry A. Stockett and Peter Stansill of the top performing IPO's between January 1993 and June 1994.

- *Trendmaster.* Published daily by Jim Doty, this technically-oriented letter focuses on commodity options, metal futures, and stocks.

- *The Wall Street Digest.* Published monthly by Don Rowe. Contains market commentary and investment recommendations.

▶ *Woodward Investment Newsletter.* Ian Woodward offers monthly advice on momentum investing, particularly in high growth stocks. This letter has significant educational value.

▶ *Jim Yates' Dyr Report.* Published daily. Mr. Yates blends market analysis with an understanding of the mechanics of option pricing.

How to access online market letters: All online newsletters will be available automatically after you install the Telescan 3.0 System. To access a newsletter, log on to the database, then select Newsletters from the Text Services Menu. Select the desired newsletter from the list.

METASTOCK™

Free Special Edition Software Included with this Book

MetaStock™ is one of the world's best-selling technical analysis software programs. With MetaStock, you can analyze stocks, bonds, commodities, options, mutual funds, and more. MetaStock SE gives you a sample of one of the most comprehensive investment analysis tools available: drag-and-drop charting, detailed system testing with optimization and comparison testing, ranking and filtering on any criteria, built-in indicators and line studies, an Indicator Builder to design your own market indicators, OptionScope™ to do "what-if" analysis on equity and future-based options, and built-in data downloading capabilities. (The requirements are the same as for Telescan as noted on p. 252.)

The all new MetaStock for Windows® is Certified Microsoft Office™ Compatible, which means that it looks and feels like Microsoft Word™, Excel™, and other Office compatible products. You'll spend less time figuring out how to run the software and more time figuring out how to make more profits. MetaStock gives you Visual Control™ over your investments by letting you run the program with just two commands: "Click and Pick," and "Drag and Drop." Thanks to the modern object-oriented interface, you can change anything in MetaStock just by clicking on it and choosing how you want to modify it. And it's easy to set up your charts just the way you want by dragging and dropping any number of price bars or indicators together until they make sense to you. MetaStock is produced by Equis International, a leader in investment software for the past eleven years.

For more information on the complete version of MetaStock, call toll-free:

1-800-882-3040, ext. 82a, or (801) 265-8888, ext. 82a.

How to access MetaStock: Appendix B contains installation and operating instructions for MetaStock.

INVESTMENT NEWSLETTERS BY MAIL

Trial issues of following investment newsletters are available by mail:

- *The Dick Davis Digest.* Mr. Davis publishes this 12-page digest every two weeks. Covers the top stock picks from over 450 advisors and analysts, plus forecasts of broad market direction by the top market timers and mutual fund recommendations. Three free issues.

- *The Professional Tape Reader.* Edited by Stan Weinstein and published every two weeks (supplemented with a bi-weekly telephone hotline). Mr. Weinstein offers a technical approach to investing with specific advice for model stock and mutual fund portfolios. Three free issues.

- *The Zweig Forecast.* Edited by Dr. Martin Zweig and published every three weeks with a telephone hotline update, often daily. Dr. Zweig concentrates on risk-averse, short-term investments using stock index futures contracts and options as hedges. One free sample copy of the latest Zweig Forecast.

See Appendix C for information on how to receive your free trial issues.

CYBER-INVESTING SEMINARS

Telescan routinely offers various levels of investment seminars throughout the country. As a *Cyber-Investing* book purchaser, you will receive free or discounted admission to all seminars.

How to get more information on cyber-investing seminars: Call Telescan at 1-800-324-8246 or 713-952-1060 for a schedule of seminars and registration procedures.

CHARLES SCHWAB & CO.

Charles Schwab & Co. is one of country's the leading discount brokers. It offers to *Cyber-Investing* book purchasers special discounts on electronic trades through Schwab. See Appendix C for details.

Appendix A

SOURCE LISTS

There are many, many products and services that can be used for cyber-investing, and more are being introduced every day. What follows is a partial listing, by category, of those that were available in late 1994. An exhaustive list, with full descriptions, may be found in *The Individual Investor's Guide to Computerized Investing* (Chicago: American Association of Individual Investors, 1995).

ASSET ALLOCATION PROGRAMS

Macro*World™ Investment Plan
Macro*World Research Corporation
4265 Brownsboro Road, Suite 170
Winston Salem, NC 27106-3429
(800) 841-5398

WealthBuilder™
Reality Technologies, Inc.
2200 Renaissance Boulevard
King of Prussia, PA 19406
(800) 521-2475 or 610-277-7600

Thinkware™
Fidelity Brokerage Services, Inc.
161 Devonshire Street
Boston, MA 02110
(800) 544-9375

ELECTRONIC TRADING SERVICES

The following offer online and automated telephone trading, as well as regular discount brokerage services.

AccuTrade®
4211 South 102nd Street
Omaha, NE 68127-1031
(800) 535-4444 or 402-331-2526

E*Trade™
E*Trade Securities, Inc.
480 California Avenue
Palo Alto, CA 94306
(800) 786-2575

Fidelity On-line Xpress™
Fidelity Brokerage Services, Inc.
161 Devonshire Street
Boston, MA 02110
(800) 544-9375

Investex Securities Group, Inc.
50 Broad Street
New York, NY 10004
(800) 392-7192

PC Financial Network
One Pershing Place
Jersey City, NJ 07339
(800) 825-5723

QuickWay™
Quick & Reilly
26 Broadway
New York, NY 10275
(800) 252-9909

StreetSmart™
Charles Schwab & Co.
101 Montgomery Street
San Francisco, CA 94104
(800) 334-4455

ONLINE STOCK QUOTES AND FINANCIAL SERVICES

The following online services supply quotes and some financial services, some more extensive than others. A more complete, annotated list may be found in Robert Schwabach's *Global Investments Using Electronic Tools,* along with a list of overseas data providers. Also see the Internet listings in Chapter 16.

America Online®
8619 Westwood Center Drive
Vienna, VA 22182
(800) 827-6364

BMI
3 Triad Center, Suite 100
Salt Lake City, UT 84180
(800) 255-7374 or 801-532-3400

CompuServe®
P.O. Box 20961
5000 Arlington Center Boulevard
Columbus, OH 43220
(800) 848-8199

Dial Data®
Global Market Information, Inc.
56 Pine Street
New York, NY 10005
(800) 367-5968

Dow Jones News/Retrieval®
Dow Jones & Company
P.O. Box 300
Princeton, NJ 08543
(800) 522-3567 or 609-520-8349

GEnie™
GE Information Services
401 N. Washington Street
Rockville, MD 20850
(800) 638-9636 or 301-340-4442

Prodigy® Services Company
22 North Plains Industrial Highway
Wallingford, CT 06492
(800) 776-3449

Reuters® Money Network
Reality Technologies, Inc.
2200 Renaissance Boulevard
King of Prussia, PA 19406
(800) 346-2024 or 215-277-7600

Signal®
Data Broadcasting Corporation
1900 South Norfolk Street
San Mateo, CA 94403
(800) 551-1322 or 415-571-1800

Telemet America, Inc.
325 First Street
Alexandria, VA 22314
(800) 368-2078 or 703-548-2042

Telescan, Inc.
10550 Richmond, #250
Houston, TX 77057
(800) 324-8246 or 713-952-1060

Track Online®
Global Market Information, Inc.
56 Pine Street
New York, NY 10005
(800) 367-5968

Zacks Investment Research
155 North Wacker Drive
Chicago, IL 60606
(800) 767-3771 or 312-630-9880

PORTFOLIO MANAGEMENT PROGRAMS

CapTool™
TechServe, Inc.
P.O. Box 9
Issaquah, WA 98027
206-747-5598

Kiplinger's Simply Money™
Computer Associates International, Inc.
One Computer Associates Plaza
Islandia, NY 11788
(800) 225-5224

Market Manager PLUS®
Dow Jones & Company
P.O. Box 300
Princeton, NJ 08543
(800) 522-3567 or 609-520-8349

Portfolio Analyzer™
Hamilton Software, Inc.
6432 East Mineral Place
Englewood, CO 80112
(800) 733-9607 or 303-795-5572

Quicken™
Intuit, Inc.
66 Willow Place
P.O. Box 3014
Menlo Park, CA 94026

Telescan Portfolio Manager™
Telescan, Inc.
10550 Richmond, #250
Houston, TX 77057
(800) 324-8246 or 713-952-1060

STOCK SEARCH PROGRAMS

CompuServe®
P.O. Box 20961
5000 Arlington Center Boulevard
Columbus, OH 43220
(800) 522-4477

Dial Data® Retriever Program
Global Market Information, Inc.
56 Pine Street
New York, NY 10005
(800) 367-5968

Dow Jones News/Retrieval®
Dow Jones & Company
P.O. Box 300
Princeton, NJ 08543
(800) 522-3567 or 609-520-8349

ProSearch™
Telescan, Inc.
10550 Richmond, #250
Houston, TX 77042
(800) 324-8246 or 713-952-1060

U.S. Equities OnFloppy
Morningstar, Inc.
225 West Wacker Drive
Chicago, IL 60606
(800) 876-5005 or 312-427-1985

Value/Screen III®
Value Line, Inc.
220 East 42nd Street
New York, NY 10017-5891
(800) 654-0508

TECHNICAL ANALYSIS PROGRAMS

AIQ TradingExpert™
AIQ Incorporated
916 Southwood Boulevard
P.O. Box 7530
Incline Village, NV 89452
(800) 332-2999 or 702-831-2999

Market Analyzer PLUS®
Dow Jones & Company
P.O. Box 300
Princeton, NJ 08543
(800) 522-3567 or 609-520-8349

MetaStock™
Equis International
3950 South 700 East, Suite 100
Salt Lake City, UT 84107
(800) 882-3040

NavaPatterns™
Nava Development Corporation
251-A Portage Road
Lewiston, NY 14092-1710
(800) 532-0041

SuperCharts™
Omega Research
9200 Sunset Drive
Miami, FL 33173
(800) 556-2022 or 305-270-1095

TeleChart 2000™
Worden Brothers, Inc.
4905 Pine Cone Drive, Suite 12
Durham, NC 27707
(800) 776-4940

Telescan Analyzer™
Telescan, Inc.
10550 Richmond, #250
Houston, TX 77057
(800) 324-8246 or 713-952-1060

TickerWatcher™
Linn Software, Inc.
8641 Pleasant Hill Road
Lithonia, GA 30058
404-929-8802

Windows on Wall Street™
MarketArts, Inc.
1810 N. Glenville Drive, Suite 124
Richardson, TX 75081
(800) 998-8439

MUTUAL FUND SEARCH PROGRAMS

Fund Master TC™
Time Trend Software
337 Boston Road
Billerica, MA 01821
508-250-3866

Mutual Fund Search™
Telescan, Inc.
10550 Richmond, #250
Houston, TX 77057
(800) 324-8246 or 713-952-1060

Morningstar Mutual Funds
Morningstar, Inc.
225 West Wacker Drive
Chicago, IL 60606
(800) 876-5005 or 312-427-1985

OPTIONS PROGRAMS

Option Pricing Analysis™
OPA Software
P.O. Box 90658
Los Angeles, CA 90009
310-545-3716

Options Master™
Institute for Options Research, Inc.
P.O. Box 6586
Lake Tahoe, NV 89449
(800) 334-0854 or 702-588-3590

Options Analyzer™
Options Search™
Telescan, Inc.
10550 Richmond, #250
Houston, TX 77057
(800) 324-8246 or 713-952-1060

OVM/Focus
Radix Research Limited
P.O. Box 91181
West Vancouver, BC V7V 3N6 Canada
604-926-5308

Appendix B

A QUICK START GUIDE TO YOUR CYBER-INVESTING SOFTWARE

GETTING STARTED WITH TELESCAN

The Telescan 3.0 software comes with 30 days of free *non-prime-time* access to the Telescan database. Your 30 days begins with your first log-on.

NON-PRIME-TIME HOURS:
6:00 P.M.–7:00 A.M.
your local time
(Prime time rate is $0.94 per minute.)

- The first time you log on to the database, you will be asked to enter some general information to ensure that your account is set up properly for your free trial.
- If you log on to the Telescan database during prime time hours or if you request a report or service that carries a surcharge, you will be asked for credit card information for billing purposes.

To Continue Using Telescan after the 30-Day Free Trial

At the end of your free 30 days, you will see a list of Telescan's monthly billing options when you log on:

- To activate your account at that time, choose a billing plan at the online prompt and enter the requested credit card information.

Customer Service

Telescan's Customer service hours are *toll-free seven days a week:*

1-800-780-2332

Monday-Friday: 7 a.m. to Midnight

Saturday & Sunday: 9:00 a.m. to 6:00 p.m.

Outside the continental U.S:
Telephone: (713) 952-1060 or
Fax: (713) 952-0236

PC Requirements

The Telescan 3.0 System requires the following hardware and peripheral equipment:

- IBM PC (286 or faster) or 100% compatible computer
- MS DOS 2.1 or higher
- 640K Memory
- Hard disk; CGA, EGA, or VGA board
- Hayes Smartmodem (1200, 2400, or 9600 baud) or 100% compatible
- Mouse (optional)

The Telescan Database

Telescan offers a wealth of statistical and textual information on more than 77,000 securities, including stocks, bonds, mutual funds, industry groups, market indexes, futures, and options. The database contains the latest online quotes, with a 15-minute delay; historical price and volume data (dating back to 1973); fundamental information on securities listed on the New York Stock Exchange, the American Stock Exchange, and Nasdaq; and information on Canadian stocks. Other information includes news from Reuters and Comtex news services, insider trading information, company profiles, earnings estimates, stock forecasts, and other special reports on listed securities.

GENERAL KEYSTROKE AND MOUSE COMMANDS

The following general keystrokes and mouse commands are used in the Telescan program:

Action	Keystroke	Mouse
Open a menu:	Press the Right Arrow or Left Arrow key to highlight the menu. Then press the Down Arrow key to open it.	Click the menu with the left mouse button.
Select a menu item:	Press the Down Arrow key or Up Arrow key to highlight the item; then press Enter.	Double-click the menu item with the left mouse button.
Select a data field:	Press the Tab key or Enter to move the yellow cursor *down* one field. Press Shift and Tab simultaneously to move the yellow cursor *up* one field.	Click a field to activate it.
Choose an option button:	Press the Spacebar to toggle the option on and off.	Click on an option button to select it.

Note: Option buttons are highlighted in red when selected.

Hot Keys

Hot keys initiate actions without opening a menu. Press and hold the (Ctrl) key while pressing the letter or F-key.

Ctrl-A	Opens QuoteLink.
Ctrl-E	Opens the AutoRun window.
Ctrl-F	Opens the File Manager window.
Ctrl-G	Opens graph window with stock prompt.
Ctrl-L	Opens the Log-on Setup window.
Ctrl-O	Log on or log off the database.
Ctrl-P	Deletes graphs marked for deletion, offline.
Ctrl-Q	Exits the Telescan program, online or offline.
Ctrl-R	Opens the Telescan Mail window, online.

Ctrl-S	Opens ProSearch.
Ctrl-V	Starts AutoRun online or AutoPrint offline.
Ctrl-F1	Opens one graph window.
Ctrl-F2	Opens two graph windows.
Ctrl-F4	Opens four graph windows.

NOTE: The above hot keys do not work if the "Menu On/Off" sign on the menu bar is OFF. Press Escape to turn the sign to "Menu On."

INSTALLING TELESCAN

Before attempting to install the Telescan software, be sure that your computer meets the minimum system requirements listed previously. If you need assistance installing the program, please call Telescan's Customer Service.

To install Telescan:

1. Insert the Telescan 3.0 diskette in the a: or b: drive.
2. If using the a: drive, type **a:/install** and press Enter.

   If using the b: drive, type **b:/install** and press Enter.
3. The Telescan System will be located in a newly created directory on your hard drive called tele30.
4. After the program is installed, you will see the following graphics card selections:

1	EGA Color
2	VGA Color
3	Exit to DOS

   Select the number for your type of graphics card. You will advance to the offline Telescan screen.
5. You must complete the log-on setup screen, described below, before going online.

NOTE: To access the program in the future, type **cd\tele30** to change to the Telescan directory; then type **t**.

LOG-ON SETUP

1. Call Telescan Customer Service at 1-800-780-2332 and identify yourself as a *Cyber-Investing* customer. You will be given:

   ♦ The local telephone number of your communications carrier. Be sure to specify your baud rate.

   ♦ Your password.

   ♦ Your user ID number.

2. Select Log-on Setup from the System Menu on the menu bar.

3. Complete the Log-on Setup screen as follows:

Baud Rate: Select the baud rate of your modem.
Access: Specify the communications carrier for your area.

 ‣ SprintNet serves most U.S. metropolitan areas.

 ‣ Datapac serves Canadian residents only.

Com Port: Select the com port to which your modem is connected. If you select COM-X, you must specify the Interrupt number and HEX address.

ID# and Password: Enter your user ID number and password as obtained from Telescan. *NOTE:* Enter your password in all capital letters.

Phone Number: Enter your local access telephone number as obtained from Telescan. *NOTE:* Do not use hyphens, dashes or spaces. Keep in mind the following when entering a phone number:

- Enter T for Touchtone dialing or P for Pulse.
- If 9 or any other access code is required for an outside line, be sure to enter it, followed by a comma.
- Enter the area code if the local access number is in a city different from your area code; precede the area code with a 1.

 Example of the above: T9,5551234 or T17135551234

Modem Program: Reserved for networked computers. Call Tele-scan Customer Service for assistance.

4. Click Save (Alt-S) to save the log-on parameters or press Esc.
5. Perform a modem test by choosing Modem Test from the System Menu. If the modem is properly connected, you will see a confirmation.

You are now ready to use the program.

USING TELESCAN ANALYZER

Telescan Analyzer offers stock quotes, price-and-volume graphs on all securities, complete technical and fundamental analysis, and a variety of text services.
 NOTE: Each time you log on you will see a "What's New" screen, with information about Telescan's products and services. To escape this screen, make a menu selection.   .

To Retrieve a Graph

Online, choose New Graph from the Analyzer Menu, or press Ctrl-G. At the Stock prompt, type the symbol for the security and press Enter. *NOTE:* Security symbols must be entered in CAPITAL LETTERS.

- To plot technical or fundamental indicators, make a selection from the Indicators Menu.

- To save the graph, press S.
- To print the graph, press P.
- To plot a different time span for the displayed graph, use the button bar at the top of the graph or press the following keys:

Alt-F1 through Alt-F10:	1 day through 10 days
F1 through F12:	1 month through 12 months
1 through 9:	1 year through 9 years
0:	10 years
= (the equal key):	maximum time span for the stock.

- To retrieve a new graph, press G and enter the symbol.

To Access Zacks Estimate Service

Zacks earnings estimates are free for 30 days to book purchasers.

- *With a graph displayed:* Select Special Reports from the Indicator Menu; then select the desired report.
- *Without a graph displayed:* Open the Text Services Menu and select Special Reports; then select the desired report and enter the security symbol when prompted.

To Access the S&P MarketScope Database

The full S&P MarketScope database is free for 30 days to book purchasers.

- Select S&P MarketScope from the Text Services Menu; then select the desired information.
- To access the S&P MarketScope report:

  With a graph displayed: Select Special Reports from the Indicator Menu; then select MarketScope Report.

  Without a graph displayed: Open the Text Services Menu and select Special Reports; then select the MarketScope Report and enter the security symbol when prompted.

To Access News

Business news relating to a stock may be obtained directly with the stock graph displayed.

- *With a graph displayed:* Select Special Reports from the Indicator Menu; then select Comtex Newswire or Reuters Newswire. A list of headlines will be displayed for that stock. Select the article you wish to see.
- *Without a graph displayed:* Open the Text Services Menu and select Special Reports; then select the desired report and enter the security symbol when prompted.

To access General News: Select Main News from the Text Services Menu; then select the type of news you would like to see.

To Access Newsletters

Select Newsletters from the Text Services Menu *online*. A list of currently available newsletters will be displayed. Double-click the letter preceding the desired newsletter or press the corresponding letter key and Enter. The ten most recent issues may be listed by date. If so, double-click the letter preceding the desired date, or press the corresponding letter key and Enter.

To Print or Save Articles or Reports

- To print an article or report, click Print or press Alt-P.
- To save an article or report, click Save or press Alt-S; enter a file name when prompted.

Saved articles are stored in the File Manager as a text file. (See "To Use the File Manager" to review or print the article offline.)

To Create an AutoRun File

AutoRun files are used to retrieve multiple graphs quickly for viewing offline. First, create a file of security symbols with desired technical or fundamental indicators (called an Autorun file) and then perform an Autorun. To create an Autorun file:

1. Offline, select Edit AutoRun from the Analyzer Menu. You will see a blank Edit AutoRun screen.
2. Click on the Add button or press Alt-A. A window will open which contains text boxes for the security symbol, name, and time span, plus a list of indicators. A yellow arrow will point to the active box. Use the mouse or the Tab key to move the arrow between the different boxes.

   - You must enter the ticker symbol; the name is optional. If you do not know the symbol, use the online Symbol LookUp described on the next page.

3. Be sure to save your selections.
4. Repeat these steps for the next security you wish to include.

To Perform an AutoRun

1. Select Log On from the System Menu or press Ctrl-O.
2. Select Start AutoRun from the Analyzer Menu. After AutoRun is complete, you may view or print the graphs *offline*.
3. Select Log-off from the System Menu or press Ctrl-O.

4. Open the graph file by pressing Ctrl-G or selecting One Graph from the Analyzer Menu, offline; then use the PgDn or PgUp keys (or left and right mouse buttons) to view the graphs in the file.

5. To print graphs retrieved by the Autorun and other saved graphs, open the graph file, *offline,* then:

   - Select Tag All Graphs from the Analyzer Menu or press Ctrl-T; then select Start AutoPrint from the Analyzer Menu or press Ctrl-V to print the tagged graphs.

   - To print selected graphs, display the graph and press Alt-T; then start the AutoPrint.

   - To print the displayed graph only, press P.

To Use the File Manager

Saved files may be found in the File Manager under the appropriate File Type. To retrieve or view a saved file:

1. Select File Manager from the System Menu.

2. Click the File Type button or press the Tab key to move the yellow cursor to the desired file type. A list of files for that category will be displayed in the window.

3. To open a file, highlight it and click Open or press Alt-O or Enter.

When a saved file is opened, it will be displayed in the appropriate window.

To Look Up a Stock Symbol

1. Online, select Symbols Menu from the Text Services Menu.

2. Select Symbol LookUp.

3. Type in the partial or full name of the security and click Send or press Alt-S. The security symbol will appear on the screen.

To Use Telescan Mail

You may use Telescan Mail to communicate with other Telescan users or with Customer Service.

Sending a Message:

1. Select Log On from the System Menu.

2. Select Telescan Mail from the Program Menu.

3. Using the mouse, click on the department to which you want to send the message, or use the Tab key to toggle between the departments.

4. Type the message, then click on the Mail-Send box.

5. The system will tell you if the mail was delivered successfully. To continue, click OK or press Alt-O.

NOTE: If you are sending a message to another Telescan user, you must know his or her Telescan user ID number.

Receiving a Message:

When you log on, if you have any Telescan mail messages, you will see a prompt that you have unread mail.

1. Select Telescan Mail from the Program Menu.

2. Click Receive or press Alt-R to display the message.

USING PROSEARCH

NOTE: If you have not already logged on to the database, you must do so in order to activate Prosearch. Choose Log On from the System Menu. When you see the "Telescan What's New" screen, press Escape. Select Log Off from the System Menu. ProSearch will be highlighted in white on the Program Menu if it has been activated.

• You may use up to 40 criteria in a single search.

• Searches may be created offline or online but must be submitted online.

To Create a Search

1. Select ProSearch from the Program Menu or press Ctrl-S.
   The ProSearch screen will appear, with a list of indicators to be used as search criteria in the left window.

2. Scroll through the indicators to find the one you wish to use. The definition of the highlighted indicator will appear in the upper right window.

3. Press Enter to selected the highlighted criteria.

4. A window will open, allowing you to specify the search mode for the indicator.

   • "Absolute" allows you to eliminate stocks from the search universe based on the raw score for the indicator.

   • "Rank" allows you to eliminate stocks from the search based on their percentile rank.

   If you select Absolute or Rank enter the minimum and maximum ranges. All stocks outside those ranges will be eliminated from the search.

   • "Relative" is the "score-and-rank" mode of operation. It enables you to search the universe of stocks to find the optimal issues that best fit your criteria, and rank them in the order of how well they fit. The weighting percentages let you tell the program how important an indicator is to your strategy.

- "List Only" lets you retrieve information without affecting the search.

NOTE: You may use the Absolute and Relative modes *or* the Absolute and Rank modes for the same indicator.

5. After you select a search mode, click Save or press Alt-S, and you will return to the initial ProSearch window.

6. Repeat the above steps for each indicator you wish to use.

To Save a Search

To save a search, select Save from the System Menu and enter a filename when requested.

To Submit a Search

To submit a search you must log on to the Telescan database.

1. Select Log On from the System Menu or press Ctrl-O.

2. Online, select File Manager from the System Menu.

3. Click the ProSearch File Type button or press Alt-P. The saved ProSearch files will appear in the window.

4. Highlight the saved file and click Open or press Alt-O. The search will appear in a ProSearch window.

5. Click Submit or press Alt-S to open the Submit Search screen. Complete the information on this screen as follows:

- Title: Enter a title if you wish one to appear on your search report.

- # Securities: Enter the number of stocks you wish to see on the search report. 10 is the default; the maximum is 200 or fewer, depending on the number of indicators used in the search.

- Search: These buttons allow you to specify the search universe: Stocks, Optionable Stocks, Mutual Funds, Industry Groups, or Stocks in Specified Industries. The latter should be used only if you first select industry groups, as described later.

- Back Test: Select Yes if you wish to backtest a search; then enter the test parameters. Months Back refers to when the backtest shall start; Days for Return refers to the time period over which you wish to test the results.

- Report Format and Report Data: These refer to various formats for the printed report. The default is Standard with both Absolute and Rank data.

6. Click Submit or press Alt-S to submit the search. In a few seconds you will the search report in a text window. Use the Down Arrow key to scroll through the stocks.

7. The buttons at the bottom of the report window perform various functions for the search report. Click the button or press the Alt key and letter key that corresponds to the first letter of the function word.

- Save: This saves the report in the File Manager under the ProSearch File Type. Enter a filename when prompted.

- Print: This prints the search report.

- Text Save: Use this function to save the report as a text file for importing into a word processing or other program.

- IndFlag: Use this function only with an industry group search. It automatically flags the industry groups found by the search.

- AutoRun: This automatically transfers the stock symbols to an AutoRun file, for the retrieval of stock graphs.

- Quote>Link: This automatically transfers the stock symbols to a QuoteLink file for the retrieval of stock quotes.

To Select Industry Groups

At the ProSearch main screen, click the IndGrp button or press Alt-I. Telescan's industry groups will be listed in a window. You may scroll through the window using the mouse, Arrow keys, or PgUp and PgDn keys. An asterisk (*) denotes a selected group. Use the option buttons on the right of the screen as follows:

All On/Off (Alt-A) flags all groups or removes all flags.

Reverse On/Off (Alt-R) reverses the current selections.

Find (Alt-F) opens a Find window to allow you to search for a group by name or partial name.

Next/Find (Alt-N) is used after the Find command to find the next group with the same word in the name.

Save (Alt-S) saves the group selections and returns to the main screen. *Be sure to save your selections.*

Cancel cancels the selections and returns to the main screen.

USING MUTUAL FUND SEARCH OR OPTIONS SEARCH

Both programs operate similarly to ProSearch. Mutual Fund Search uses Telescan's database of some 2,000 mutual funds; Options Search uses Telescan's database of some 35,000 options on stocks and indexes and more than 300,000 option combinations. The main differences in the program structure are these:

- The 82 search criteria in Mutual Fund Search are designed expressly for mutual funds; the 122 criteria in Options Search are designed expressly for options.
- 30 criteria may be used in a single search, rather than 40.
- The percentile rank is not shown on the mutual fund or options search report.
- The Objectives button at the bottom of the Mutual Fund Search corresponds to ProSearch's Industry Group button, allowing you to limit a search to funds with specific investment objectives.
- The search universes are program-specific.
- Backtesting does not work with mutual funds or options.

METASTOCK SE

Getting Started with MetaStock SE

The next three pages explain the steps necessary to install and run MetaStock SE.

Installing MetaStock SE

MetaStock SE comes on one 1.44 megabyte floppy disk. The program includes a variety of data files you can experiment with until you set up your own data files.

> Insert *Disk 1* in drive *A*.
>
> At the DOS prompt, type **A:INSTALL** and press **ENTER.**

The installation program will ask you several questions. Instructions regarding the installation process will be displayed on your screen. When the installation is complete, we recommend that you go through the self-running guided tour that follows.

A Short Lesson

MetaStock SE should now be installed. You are now ready to put MetaStock SE to work.

A Self-Running Guided Tour

If you are new to MetaStock, you should run the special lesson. This lesson provides an on-screen guided tour of many of MetaStock SE's features. After installing MetaStock SE, you can run the lesson by doing the following:

> At the DOS prompt, type *C:* and press **ENTER.**
>
> Type **CD\MSSE** and press **ENTER.**
>
> Type **AUTORUN** and press **ENTER.**

Load and Display a Chart

Run MetaStock SE using the following commands:

At the **C>** prompt, type **CD\MSSE** and press **ENTER** to make sure you are in the **\MSSE** subdirectory.

Type **MS** and press **ENTER.**

If this is the first time you have run MetaStock SE, you may be prompted to enter the drive and path to your MetaStock SE data files (e.g., C:\msse\data).

The Load Security menu will appear. From this menu, do the following:

Select any security to load with your mouse by pointing to a security and double-clicking. (Keyboard users can use the UP/DOWN arrow keys to highlight the security and then press ENTER).

The Data Range window will be displayed. When prompted for the "First Record," type **-150** and click **OK.** (This loads the most recent 150 periods of data). A bar chart of the security should now be displayed. You can also type in a specific data range (i.e., 1/1/94 in First Record and 7/1/94 in Last Record) rather than typing in -150.

Display an Indicator

On the Menu Bar, click the option name **Indicators,** then on the pull-down menu, click on **Indicators.**

Double-click **MACD** to plot the MACD indicator. (Keyboard users can use the DOWN arrow key to highlight MACD and press ENTER).

A bar chart of the security will now be displayed in the security inner window (bottom half) and the MACD indicator in the indicator inner window (top half). (The MACD will not plot if less than 26 periods of data are loaded).

Display a Moving Average

On the Menu Bar, click the option name **Indicators,** then on the pull-down menu, click on **Moving Averages.**

Complete the dialog by clicking **Moving Average, Simple, Close, Periods** and typing **10.** Click **OK** to plot the moving average.

A 10-day simple moving average of the closing price will be displayed in the security inner window.

Pointer Mode

A whole new set of analysis tools can be accessed while in the "Pointer mode." The pointer mode can be accessed by clicking within the chart's inner window (i.e., anywhere within the inside borders of the chart). Note that the upper right corner of the Menu Bar displays the word "POINTER" to remind you that you are now in the pointer mode. The Menu Bar and Toolbar will change and a set of cross-hairs will appear on the chart.

Drawing a Trendline

You can draw a trendline while in pointer mode by clicking on the spot you want the trendline to start, holding down the mouse button, and moving the mouse across the chart to where you want the trendline to end.

Click anywhere outside of the chart to exit the pointer mode.

The Help Index

Pressing F1 displays the Help Index. The Help Index lists all of MetaStock SE's commands and the keystrokes used to select the commands. Use the Find command to find commands in the Help Index.

MetaStock SE also provides "alternate help" (ALT + F1). Pressing ALT + F1 when a chart is displayed provides interpretational information on the currently displayed indicator.

Quit MetaStock SE

On the Menu Bar, click the option named **Other.** Click **Quit to DOS** from the pull-down menu. Click **Yes** to exit MetaStock SE.

Navigating in MetaStock SE

This section explains how to get around in MetaStock SE using MetaStock SE's menus and toolbars. It also explains how to use the menus and toolbars with a mouse and/or keyboard.

Mouse versus Keyboard

MetaStock SE can be operated using a mouse or keyboard. The use of a mouse is completely optional.

Commands versus Menus and Toolbar

You can operate MetaStock SE by selecting from a series of pull-down menus, a toolbar, or by typing commands. This approach combines the ease-of-use of a toolbar- and menu-driven program with the speed and power of a command-driven program.

For example, the Moving Average dialog can be displayed by selecting Moving Averages from the Indicators pull-down menu (using the mouse or keyboard), by clicking on the Moving Average tool in the Toolbar, or by pressing the hot key M (for Moving Average) while a chart is displayed.

The advantage of the toolbar/menu method is that it is much easier to find commands. You simply select them from the Toolbar or pull-down menus. However, the command method is faster. MetaStock SE lists the hot-key commands to the right of the pull-down menu options—making it easy to learn frequently used commands.

Appendix C

SPECIAL OFFERS FOR CYBER-INVESTORS

The following section provides practical details on some of the special telephone and mail-in offers made available only to you, the Cyber-Investor. You can write or phone for the free trial options described, to request a full subscription or just call for more information. Don't forget to mention that each special offer has been made available through purchase of this book!

CHARLES SCHWAB & CO.

Charles Schwab & Co. is one of America's leading discount brokers.

Charles Schwab TeleBroker

By trading with Charles Schwab's TeleBroker, the touch-tone telephone trading system, you will receive a 10% discount on all trades placed through TeleBroker. Placing trades is as simple as picking up any phone. Sign-up is free.

Charles Schwab StreetSmart

StreetSmart is Charles Schwab's securities trading, research and portfolio management software. With StreetSmart you can check your portfolio, review market information, research companies, and place trading orders 24 hours a day. For only $49, you'll receive the StreetSmart software which includes:

- One hour free access time on Dow Jones News/Retrieval®
- 100 free real-time quotes[1]
- $25 off commission on first trade placed through StreetSmart[2]
- 10% discount on commissions for trades entered online[3]
- One free Company Report
- One hour free access time on Standard & Poor's Marketscope

To take advantage of this offer and learn more about Charles Schwab's services, please call: 1-800-334-4455.

THE DICK DAVIS DIGEST

The Dick Davis Digest ranks at the top among financial newsletters. For almost 15 years the financial community has relied on The Digest for winning stocks culled from over 450 analysts and advisors. Survey insights. Astute analysis. Market intelligence. Delivery every two weeks at an affordable price. What do the experts say about The Digest?

"I read a lot of advisor letters, but if I was forced to survive on one alone, this would be the one."—James Russell, Financial Editor, *The Miami Herald*

Brokers insist on it. Investors swear by it. See for yourself.

Call now for your free trial subscription to The Dick Davis Digest: Toll free: 1-800-654-1514, ext. 1247, or fax to (305) 467-6444.

Or, write to: The Dick Davis Digest, P.O. Box 350630, Ft. Lauderdale, FL 33335-0630.

---

[1] Schwab guidelines allow each user 100 free quotes plus an additional 100 quotes for each executed trade.

[2] Trade must occur within six months of purchase and applies to stock and option trades only. Offer applies only to full-price purchases of StreetSmart.

[3] Discount is based on Schwab's current commission schedule, available upon request. Discount may be used in conjunction with other promotional offers, at Schwab's discretion, with the 10% StreetSmart discount applied first. May not apply to securities sold by Prospectus.

THE ZWEIG FORECAST

The Zweig Forecast is rated #1 by Hulburt Financial Digest among all investment services for risk-adjusted return over the last 15 years (as of 12/94). Dr. Martin E. Zweig, bestselling author of *Winning on Wall Street* has an investment philosophy he calls "Never Get Badly Hurt." Safety first can mean greater long-term wealth.

Let The Zweig Forecast tell you how to invest the smart way.

**Call now to receive your free issue of *The Zweig Forecast*.
Toll free: 1-800-538-9649.**

Or, write to: The Zweig Forecast, Post Office Box 360, Bellmore, New York 11 710-0751.

THE PROFESSIONAL TAPE READER

The Professional Tape Reader is a highly rated stock market advisory published twice monthly. It gives readers 8 full pages of charts, advice, and up-to-the-minute information presenting objective forecasts for long and short term trends. Features include advice about the markets most promising stocks, an Option Fund Scan, a No-Load Mutual Fund Section, a Sector Fund Section with advice on which funds are buys, holds, and sells, as well as an Indicator Scan. The service also includes a twice weekly telephone Hotline Update.

**Call now to receive your free issue of *The Professional Tape Reader*.
Toll free: 1-800-222-7857 or (305) 963-8188.**

INDEX